TRAJECTORY OF DEMOCRACY *in* NEPAL

Krishna Hachhethu

Adroit Publishers
New Delhi

Published by

ADROIT PUBLISHERS

4675/21, Ganpati Bhawan, Ansari Road,
Daryaganj, New Delhi-110 002

Phone : 011-23266030

Distributors

AKHIL BOOK DISTRIBUTORS

email: akhilbooks@yahoo.com
akhilbks@gmail.com

ISBN : 978-81-87393-11-5

Printed in India on behalf of M/s Adroit Publishers by
Akhil Sharma, E-mail: adroitpublishers@gmail.com

CONTENTS

FOREWORD

Krishna Hachhethu is well known as one of the best-informed, most acute, and least partisan observers of Nepali politics. His prime interest is and has always been in the formal institutions of political life – political parties, elections, governments, and how these have changed. But unlike many political scientists, he is not content with observing politics from the coffee shops, bookshops, seminar rooms, and conference halls of Kathmandu, though he is no stranger to those milieux. He is in fact never happier than when in the field interacting with the politically aware and politically active outside the capital. As part of his research into the radical changes that have occurred over the last twenty-five years he has visited most of Nepal's 75 districts and conducted focus groups or interviews wherever he has gone.

Professor Hachhethu is no mere academic observer, however. He is personally acquainted with all the major figures of Nepali politics (note the extraordinary admission from Girija Prasad Koirala that neither he nor King Birendra had any idea what the role of the Prime Minister was). Furthermore, Krishna Hachhethu has himself been an advisor and player in some of the key events of Nepal's recent political history. Most crucially, he was on the High-Level State Restructuring Recommendation Commission that came up with a proposal for a federal structure in the last days of the first Constituent Assembly in 2012. He has been an advocate of moderate federal proposal and a mediator between the conflicting demands of those who seek some measure of constitutional recognition for marginalized groups and those who oppose any such formal structure. The two main traditional political parties, Nepali

Congress (NC) and the UML (or Communist Party of Nepal Unified Marxist-Leninist, to give its full and formal title), woke up only, very late in the day to the strength of feelings on the part of Janajati and Madheshi activists and politicians, and even now are frequently in denial about the need to provide some recognition of the historic wrongs and injustices which have been suffered by marginalized groups. Krishna Hachhethu has had to plough a lonely furrow as someone who both recognizes these claims and at the same time is highly conscious of politics as 'the art of the possible', of the many and necessary compromises that must be part of any actual solution. It is Nepal's misfortune that its political actors do not seem to possess the necessary statesmanship to see beyond their own immediate advantage (defined in terms of achieving high ministerial berths) to permitting a compromise constitutional settlement that would enable the country as a whole to move forward under a new dispensation.

To have collected in one place Krishna Hachhethu's various analyses of Nepali politics, both inside and outside Parliament, over the last 25 years is very valuable. No one knows more about the inner workings of Nepal's major parties and how these have evolved since the early 1990s. At the time of writing it is unclear whether a new constitution will be agreed by the deadline of 22 January, 2015. Whether a constitution is finally agreed or not, this volume will be an indispensable source for any serious student seeking to understand Nepal's tumultuous recent history.

David N. Gellner
University of Oxford

PREFACE

The ten papers included in this volume were written different times between 1990 and 2005 and also published in different journals and edited books. These scattered pieces are now put into a single volume so that readers will have a survey of the whole gamut of Nepali politics of the 1990s and the first half of 2000s. I would like to thank Prof. David N. Gellner of Oxford University (UK) and Dr. Pratyoush Onta of Martin Chautari (Nepal) for sensitizing me to the academic value of putting dispersed stories into one box.

This book covers political development in Nepal from the inception of a system of constitutional monarchy and parliamentary democracy in 1990 to its demise in 2005. The second experiment with democracy (1990-2005) eventually faced the same fate as the first experiment (1951-1960). But the course of political events in the aftermath of these experiments was very different: the first experiment with democracy was replaced by an authoritarian monarchical regime known as the partyless panchayat system,which lasted for three decades (1960-1990), whereas the second experiment with a system of constitutional monarchy was formally replaced by a republican system in May 2008. Hence the third experiment with democracy begins with radically new attributes: republicanism, secularism, federalism, and inclusivity. These new features are not the focus of this book,which rather attempts to explain the background and context of Nepal's third experiment with democracy.

The book begins with a brief overview of the third wave of democracy, i.e. the fall of communism in the former Soviet Union and Eastern Europe and the overthrow of military and civilian dictatorial regimes in Asia,

Africa and Latin America. The multiparty system was restored in Nepal in 1990 through a mass movement which was part of this third wave of democracy. Accordingly, Chapter One (Mass Movement 1990) analyses the beginning of the second experiment with democracy in Nepal in this international context. Two factors provided a favourable external environment: the fact that human rights were an important element in the foreign policy of Western countries in the post-Cold War period and the detente in relations between Nepal's two giant neighbours, India and China, following the past record of the India-China war of 1962. This Chapter also analyses the multiple dynamics of internal politics, i.e. the internal contradictions of the establishment that intensified after the victory of the partyless panchayat system over the multiparty system in the 1980 referendum, unity among the opposition despite being ideologically polarized between democratic and communist parties, and the rise of the critical middle class, which all together eventually contributed to the 1990 mass movement being able to achieve its goal, namely,the end of the partyless panchayat system and the restoration of the multiparty system.

The transition to democracy in its initial phase was relatively smooth in translating the achievement of the mass movement into the provisions of the constitution. Though the stated goal of the 1990 mass movement was limited – to lift the ban on political parties and hold elections under an interim government –the environment that emerged after the success of the popular movement was conducive to reducing the position of the king from absolute ruler to constitutional monarch. Chapter 2 (Negotiation Behind Constitution Making, 1990) depicts the most critical time of constitution making, April-November 1990, marred by conflict, complexity and compromise among three contending parties (palace, democrats and communists) involved in negotiations. The very tricky game of negotiation ended with the promulgation of the constitution in November 1990. It established a system of constitutional monarchy and parliamentary democracy but also vested power in the king in critical situations.

Obviously political parties played a key catalytic role in the introduction of democracy in Nepal in 1951 and also in its restoration in 1990. They are indeed the main architects of the 1990 Constitution. Chapter 3 (Political Parties) focuses on the two major political parties, Nepali Congress (NC) and the Communist Party of Nepal, Unified Marxist-Leninist (UML), and investigates their origin and evolution as 'change agents', their ideological position (NC as democrat and UML as Left), and their policy commitments. Besides, this Chapter critically examines the performance of the NC and UML governments in the 1990s and the early 2000s. The transformation of the NC and the UML from movements into mere power-seeking organizations brought them much closer to the state but introduced a certain distance from society. This had a cost in terms of the de-legitimation of the political system introduced by the 1990 Constitution.

Speaking of a democratic transition begs the question of the impact of elections in expanding and deepening democracy at the grassroots level. Chapter 4 (Elections) discusses the three general elections held in 1991, 1994, and 1999 and also the local elections of 1992 and 1997. It covers two broad areas: the internal dynamics of the way the parties managed elections (in particular, the selection of candidates) and their strategies for vote mobilization (i.e. election campaigns at national and local level). There was a wide gap between parties' promises made during elections and their performance in post-election time, suggesting a gap between plebiscite and performance legitimacy.

The lack of performance legitimacy in the system of constitutional monarchy and parliamentary democracy is critically examined in Chapters 5 and 6 (Parliament and Prime Minister, and Problem of Governance respectively). The lack of coherent actions of the party in government under the prevailing system of fragmented collective leadership of the party and domination of hostility rather constructive competition in treasury-opposition relations brought democracy into disorder. Consequently, politics degenerated into a power game as described in Chapter 6. None of the governments, whether it was NC-majority governments or coalition governments of different political parties, managed to endure for its full tenure. So democracy in its functional attribute was overwhelmed by power-centric intra-party conflicts, unhealthy inter-party competition, frequent changes of the government (17 times in the 15 years between 1990 and 2005), erosion in leadership quality, pervasive corruption, and political instability, crises and chaos. Dysfunctional democracy was the order of the day during the second experiment.

As much as democracy eroded, the extra-systemic forces expanded their space in politics. Chapter 7 (Maoist Insurgency) gives an account of how a small radical Maoist party eventually emerged as a dominant political force. Within a short span of time from the beginning of the Maoist armed insurgency in 1996, the CPN (Maoist) expanded its influence through making a fusion of class ideology and ethnic concerns, and also through cultivating internal conflicts and contradictions between the mainstream political parties and the palace.

The palace itself behaved like an extra-systemic force to the political set up of the second experiment of democracy, despite its being one of the prominent actors in bringing out the 1990 Constitution which placed the king in a position of constitutional monarchy. Chapter 8 (Monarchy and its Legitimacy Crisis) discusses the decline of Hindu-based traditional legitimacy of the Nepali monarchy that heightened after the royal massacre of June 2001 (in which the incumbent King Birendra and all his immediate family members were murdered). Furthermore, its political legitimacy had been weakened as the palace manipulated the ambiguous provisions of the 1990 Constitution – taking advantage of the role of the king in crisis situations, e.g. dissolution of the House of Representatives, declaration of emergency and mobilization of army – to revive the power of the king. Parliamentary democracy was glaringly derailed when King Gyanendra resumed executive power in October 2002. His ambition drove him to the extent of taking all power back by a coup in February 2005. Consequently, the international community challenged his legitimacy and the internal political equation changed from palace-mainstream parties coalition vis-à-vis the Maoists in the 1990s to an alliance between mainstream parties and the Maoists against the future of the institution of monarchy. In this way King Gyanendra's ambition and his political miscalculations were largely responsible for the introduction of a republic in Nepal in May 2008.

It would be a mistake to assume that everything about Nepal's second experiment with democracy was bad. Local government in Bhakapur Municipality, as examined in Chapter 9, can be taken as an example of how local elections and accountability introduced considerable dynamism across the country. There may be different stories of local government in different places, but the case study of Bhaktapur Municipality shows how democracy can contribute to the inclusion of hitherto excluded groups in political processes. This chapter draws the lesson that the smaller the political/administrative unit, the better the governance.

The rise of civil society, discussed in Chapter 10, could also be taken as a positive development that occurred as a part of the second experiment with democracy in Nepal. Apart from its involvement in a series of democracy movements as far back as the 1930s, its role in the 1990s and the early 2000s was remarkable for raising its voice against corruption and the abuse of power and also for its contribution to awareness-building on the issues of marginalized and excluded groups, i.e. women, Dalits, and Janajatis.

All ten papers included in this volume, though published earlier, are slightly revised to avoid repetition (for instance, the table of elections results appeared in each of Chapters 3, 4 and 5, when these were produced as separate pieces; it now occurs only once, in the chapter on elections); to make citation uniform (now in APA format); and to make the presentation more coherent both chronologically and thematically.

For granting permission to reproduce the papers in revised form, I gratefully acknowledge the Centre for Nepal and Asian Studies (CNAS), Tribhuvan University (Chapters 1, 2 and 6), Nepal Centre for Contemporary Studies (NCCS), Kathmandu (Chapters 4, 5, 7, 8, 9 and 10) and David Gellner [editor of *Resistance and the State: Nepalese Experiences*, 2002] (Chapter 3). I am also grateful to Prof. Gellner for his contribution in writing the foreword to this book.

Krishna Hachhethu

LIST OF TABLES

ABBREVIATIONS

BASE	Backward Society
BDP	Bhaktapur Development Project
BJP	Bharatiya Janata Party
BM	Bhaktapur Municipality
BYVY	Build Your Village Yourself
CBO	Community Based Organization
CC	Central Committee
CDO	Chief District Officer
CPI	Communist Party of India
CPM	Communist Party, Marxist (India)
CPN	Communist Party of Nepal
CRC	Constitution Reform Commission
CRRC	Constitution Reform Recommendation Committee
DC	District Committee
DDC	District Development Committee
FPTP	First-Past-The-Post
HOR	House of Representatives
INC	Indian National Congress
INGO	International Non-Governmental Organization
JSP	Jana Shakti Party

ML	Marxist-Leninist
MP	Member of Parliament
MRD	Movement for Restoration of Democracy
NC	Nepali Congress
NC-PP	Nepali Congress Parliamentary Party
NGO	Non-Governmental Organization
NP	National Panchayat
NSP	Nepal Sadbhawana Party
NWPP	Nepal Workers and Peasant Party
PM	Prime Minister
POLSAN	Political Science Association of Nepal
PLA	People's Liberation Army
PP	Parliamentary Party
RPP	Rashtriya Prajatantra Party
RPP-PP	Rashtriya Prajatantra Party's Parliamentary Party
RNA	Royal Nepal Army
ULF	United Left Front
UML	Unified Marxist-Leninist
UML-PP	Unified Marxist-Leninist Parliamentary Party
UNF	United National Front
UNPM	United National People's Movement
UPF	United People's Front
VDC	Village Development Committee

Chapter I

MASS MOVEMENT 1990

The late 1980s and the early 1990s will long be remembered as "the time of great upheavals" in the history of democracy and human rights. Mikhail Gorbachev's "New Thinking" *Perestroika* (restructuring) and *Glasnost* (openness) has changed Soviet life and has also worked as a catalyst in transforming the communist world. In Eastern Europe, i.e. Hungary, Poland, Czechoslovakia, East Germany, Bulgaria, and Yugoslavia, decades-old orthodox communist regimes were replaced by multiparty system after the "velvet Revolution" – a remarkably gentle overthrow of communism. Similarly, the Soviet Union, the fatherland of communism, and Mongolia, the first Asian communist country, have changed their political system from the totalitarian rule of the communist party to multiparty democracy. Only Ceausescu in Romania was toppled by a bloody revolution.

In the broad sweep of the revolution for democracy all over the world, not only were the so-called dictatorships of the proletariat defeated, many dictators, the high profile generals or civilians or monarchs were also eliminated from Asia, Africa and Latin America. Latin America – the

* This paper is largely based on personal observation. It also includes information obtained through interview – conducted mainly during the time of movements (February-April 1990) – with some activists of the movement, i.e. Shyam Kuju (representative of the NWPP to the ULF), Bal Krishna Khan (President of the NC's student wing) Ghanashyam Bhusal (leader of the ML's student wing), and also with some figures of the panchayat establishment, i.e. D.P. Adhikari (member of the NP) and Hemanta Rana (historian). Besides, it uses materials like media reporting and literature review.

erstwhile paradise of dictators – has been greatly affected by the global wave of democratic movement. But for Noriega of Panama who was toppled by the US army, the rule of the generals in Colombia, Chile, Brazil and Nicaragua was peacefully replaced by civilian governments. The fall of "Green" dictators from Latin America and "Red" from Eastern Europe encouraged the struggle for democracy in Black Africa. Consequently, multiparty democracy made inroads into Algeria, Benin, Gabon, Ivory-Coast, Zaire, etc. In the mid-1980s, movements for the restoration of democracy in Asia gathered strong momentum. Through popular movements, two civilian dictators, Marcos of the Philippines and Chun Doe Hwan of South Korea were ousted from power in 1986 and 1988 respectively. Though the military holds democracy in Burma, a popular uprising in mid-1988 led to the end of the 26-year-old absolute rule of Ne Win. And the death of Zia-ul-Haq in a mysterious air-crash on 17 August 1988 resulted in the revival of the multiparty system in Pakistan. The "winds of change" sweeping the world also touched the Himalayan Kingdom of Nepal where the politicized section of society, at large, had been long discontented with the authoritarian partyless panchayat system.

With two explicit demands: establishment of the multiparty system and formation of an interim government, the banned Nepali Congress (NC) party and the United Left Front (ULF)[1] launched a joint mass movement from 18 February 1990. Within days the popular agitation gathered pace turning the Kingdom into "the land of turbulence". The panchas were obviously determined to face this challenge to the system. But there was a lack of coherent approach among them in tackling the problem. One section favoured the government's stand that the movement should be forcibly suppressed while others urged the search for a "political solution". The palace was in a dilemma over which approach to adopt but it avoided the latter option as long as possible. In its effort to diffuse the crisis, the panchayat regime came up with a three-pronged strategy that at times seemed self-contradictory. First, it tried to delegitimize the movement by invoking nationalism in the usual way of India bashing. Second, officially the government tried its best to give the impression of an increasing rapprochement with Delhi, and at the same time, it was equally careful to seek ways of reducing external support for the movement. Third, coercive measures were taken to counter the opposition campaign.

Since the NC had sounded the battle call at its January conference, the panchas also mounted a counter-propaganda war, organizing pancha rallies in different parts of the country. They reiterated the viability of the "active leadership" of the King and "partyless" character of the system equating them with the notions of nation and nationalism. The multiparty system was defamed as an "alien idea". The call for the restoration of democracy and the subsequent popular demonstrations were labelled as anti-social, anti-national, anti-constitutional and destructive/subversive/hooliganism. The propaganda machinery largely succeeded in gathering paid yokels to demonstrate public support for the panchayat system. But observers regarded such frantic and loud posturing of the panchas as ridiculous.

Another dimension of panchayat nationalism was buttressed by anti-Indianism. Though the panchas were conspicuously divided on the means to be adopted to resolve the country's political crisis, all of them suspected India's hand, seen or unseen, in the internal developments in Nepalese politics. As it was said by Ganesh Raj Sharma, a member of the establishment think-tank, "This movement is inspired and encouraged by India with the aim of creating a chaotic and anarchic situation in Nepal to make it soften its stand" (*Samikshya Weekly*, 9 March 1990). In the hope of diverting the people's attention or alienating the masses from the opposition movement the establishment sought to weaken and defuse the crisis by playing on anti-Indian sentiments arising from the prevailing prolonged deadlock in the trade relations with India. The panchayat propaganda described the opposition movement as the handiwork of a handful of ill-advised elements with foreign backing that harmed independence, sovereignty, nationalism and national unity. But the earlier exposure of the secret 1965 agreement between the then panchayat government and India was adequate enough to show the hollowness of the panchayat nationalism.

Examining the manoeuvres of the panchayat government, it should be pointed out that till the first few days of the movement, the panchas openly charged that the movement was launched by a handful of illegal NC "riding on the back of foreigners". The intention behind this ploy was obvious. The panchayat regime still hoped to manipulate the line of convergence between the panchas and communists in regard to India with the aim of disrupting the remarkable unity between the NC and the ULF. There was, in the background, a common tendency between the panchayat and the left parties to regard anti-Indianism as a part of Nepalese nationalism. The regime, therefore, forcefully tried to make a major issue of the address by Indian leaders at the NC conference, deploring their participation as "a naked intervention in Nepalese affairs".

But contrary to the expectations of the panchas, all the left leaders were highly appreciative of the articulated support of Indian leaders to the aims and objectives of the opposition movement being launched in Nepal. The panchayat regime once again changed the way it tried to portray the opposition movement. From a week after the agitation was formally launched, the government began alleging that it was the work of communist extremists. This line was taken in order to discourage external support to the democratic movement in Nepal but the opposition regarded it as a new trick to sabotage the movement. Opposition leaders – though under house arrest or having gone underground – remained in close contact with the national and international media. They, therefore, individually and jointly, warned the people to be aware of this new move of the regime that it was a "conspiracy and mischievous device directed to disrupt unity between the NC and the ULF and also to spread false notions". Ultimately the tactics applied to weaken the unity between the Congress and the Communists proved futile.

As has already been noted, the panchayat regime pursued a policy along two mutually contradictory lines with regard to India's role in the anti-panchayat struggle in Nepal. To alienate the people from the movement and to divide the NC and the ULF, it tried to depict the opposition movement as backed by India. At the same time, in order to discourage the movement, it gave high coverage and exaggerated emphasis to the non-interference approach of the Delhi government. Additionally family relationships between certain sections of the elites in Nepal and India, together with the religious leverage which Nepal's status as a Hindu Kingdom commanded in India were manipulated behind the scenes lobbying in the south of the border. Moreover, the government developed an understanding with the V.P. Singh government in regard to the impasse in Nepal-India relations with a commitment that Nepal would wholeheartedly respect India's sensitiveness in the future. Two-rounds of talks were held in Delhi and Kathmandu between the Governments of India and Nepal at the time when the Nepalese people were coming out on the streets against the panchayat system. But the rapprochement at the governmental level between Nepal and India did not have much effect on the democratic movement in Nepal.

The ruling elites were equally sensitive to the Western support for the opposition movement. In addition to lobbying and manoeuvring behind the scenes, they attempted to diffuse external pressure in various ways. First, the panchayat system was claimed to be a democratic system. The verdict of the referendum held in 1980 and two general elections were specifically mentioned in the reply letter by 13 members of the National Panchayat (NP) to the US senators who had written in protest against the government's actions. Next, they played the 'communist card' alleging that the movement was fully controlled by communist extremists, in the hope of exploiting the anti-communist sentiments in the West. Perhaps this was one of the major reasons why the US pressurized the king and the NC to resolve the problem through a compromise by enlarging the scope for democratization within the system. Accordingly King Birendra, in his address at a pancha rally in Pokhara on 16 March 1990, publicly announced a proposal to introduce reforms in the existing panchayat system. This announcement however should not be viewed exclusively as a response to external pressure. However, in the absence of any follow-up action after the announcement it as believed that the proposition of reformation had mostly been put up to satisfy the Western world.

"We'll eliminate them," said Kamal Thapa, Minister of Communication in reference to the opposition. This statement not only manifested individual dogmatism, but was also indicative of the government's strategy to counter the movement. Within the first three days of the movement, a dozen freedom fighters lost their lives in Bharatpur, Bhaktapur and Janakpur. Thousands of people both party activists and commoners were put in detention under very inhuman conditions. The opposition demonstrations augmented especially by unemployed youths and campus students against the government's suppression had given a real spark to the popular agitation. A foreign observer after watching the first few days of the movement concluded, "Nepal, one of the world's truly beautiful places, is fast becoming a land of the midnight knock" (Brown, 1990). As the movement gained momentum and spread far and wide, the panchayat regime's repressive measures also became harsher and more brutal. Consequently, many people were shot and thousands were put behind bars. But from the very beginning, there was every likelihood of a backlash against the government's suppressive policy. The brutal suppression by the government aroused indignation among the people and also aroused concern in the international community.

The loss of lives of unarmed demonstrators provided an additional reason for the early involvement of different professional groups in the movement. The people from different walks of life, especially doctors and lawyers took to the streets to fight against the panchayat system. A small section of teachers and lecturers, engineers and overseers, and artists and writers also got actively involved in the movement later. However, in consideration of the slackening of the momentum after its first stage, the opposition followed another way to bring the people to the streets. Rumours, like the offices of the Provision Fund and Banks were going bankrupt due to massive drawing out of funds by the government succeeded in raising the ire of the employees of public enterprises. Moreover, superb examples of courage were demonstrated by school-going boys and girls against the panchayat system in the interval between the second and third stages of the movement. The movement, then onwards, rapidly gained a revolutionary character that never flagged. In the third phase that began from 24 March, the movement assumed a new shape: a true people's movement. Day after day, the crowds of the people chanting "democracy and human rights" multiplied within and outside Kathmandu valley. In reaction to the firing in Patan and Kirtipur where six persons were shot on the spot, the people from each household in these cities including even housewives and children took to regular marching on the streets brandishing various kitchen utensils and agricultural tools. In the final phase corporation staff and civil servants also took part in the struggle against the panchayat system.

Since the movement was moving towards revolutionary resolution in terms of popular participation and the style of the agitation, King Birendra was compelled to realize the limitations of his options and the possible repercussions for the institution of monarchy if the policy of suppression was further intensified. Even weeks before the movement began, G.M. Singh (leader of the NC and supreme commander of the mass movement), had rebuked the palace for its role as protector of the panchayat system. The king's active patronage to the panchayat system had become a focal point of public criticism throughout the movement. In every corner of the city, there were cartoons and wall-paintings showing popular resentment against the palace. A foreign newspaper reporter also commented, "There are... striking similarities in the lead up to the recent eruption against the authoritarian rule of the king of Nepal and the revolution in Iran in which the Shah became the prime target" (*South China Morning Post*, 12 March 1990). In fact the anger against the palace grew spontaneously in proportion to the repression employed by the government. But for the NC, hitting the palace was only a strategy to pressurize the king for early resolution of the problem in favour of the objectives of the movement for the restoration of democracy. In its conference on 18-20 January, where the date for the movement was announced, NC's supreme leader Ganesh Man Singh had clearly stated, "Abolition of the monarchy is tantamount to the end of democracy in Nepal". While forming the ULF on the eve of the movement, the involved left parties also had tacitly accepted the retention of the king (Interview with Shyam Koju, 18 July 1990). But ideologically they are virtually pro-republican. Therefore, the institution of monarchy might have been jeopardized had the movement intensified to such an extent that the NC could no longer command the movement.

Perhaps, realizing the imminent danger, suddenly the palace changed its hard-line into a conciliatory overture to stall the movement. In the early morning of 6 April, King Birendra unexpectedly announced his decision to form a Constitution Reform Committee and an Inquiry Committee. By the same proclamation, he made the Marich Man cabinet the scapegoat for the turmoil in the country and replaced him by a former loyal Prime Minister (PM) Lokendra Bahadur Chand as the head of the new cabinet. The king also added that the new cabinet would consult people holding different political views.

In fact most of the former PMs and chairmen of the NP and many rank and file panchas had been repeatedly urging an early resolution of the political crisis in the country. A statement in the name of 40 members of the NP, three of whom disowned it later, demanded a political solution for the political crisis. There was a constant flow of statements, individual or collective, and everyone requested King Birendra to pursue a dialogue with the opposition to resolve the problem. Even earlier former PM Surya Bahadur Thapa had declared some months before the opposition movement was formally launched that "the day could prove very bad for the rulers if the system failed to acknowledge the existence of the opposition and to encompass their aspirations" (*Nepal Press Digest*, 25 December 1989). But the reshuffle of the cabinet on 1 April, a council of minister comprising hardliners, manifested the usual mood of the palace even at the eleventh hour of the movement. When all the cards played to suppress the popular struggle failed and were as a matter of fact backfiring, the palace was compelled to initiate an alternative strategy, the reconciliatory approach, which was indeed the last straw for the panchayat system.

However, it came too late. The hard repressive measures followed by the government to deal with the movement had already brought home the irrelevance of reformation to the people. Consequently, the orchestration of events reached a climax on 6 April, the day of final confrontation for both the pro and the anti-panchayat groups. This was the day the king announced possible reformation in the panchayat framework, but hundreds of thousands of people in different parts of the Kingdom spontaneously poured out into the streets to express their indignation over the inadequacy of the king's step. The regime in a last act of desperation ordered the army units, which had been ordered to fire on the unarmed crowd and consequently eleven people in Butwal lost their lives. On the "Black Friday" the king's regime bared its fangs in Kathmandu resulting in a street massacre on the Durbar Marg around the statue of the late King Mahendra, the architect of the panchayat system. The loss of scores of lives of people on this day proved too costly in the sense that it marked a turning point in the struggle; from this point onwards the people's expectations overtook the limited objectives of the movement, jointly set forth by the NC and the ULF.

The political parties and their leaders also rejected the palace's proposals. G.M. Singh angrily denounced it stating that it was a mischievous attempt to dent the democratic aspirations of the people sweeping over the country. The ULF also issued a statement appealing to the people to continue the movement peacefully. Repeatedly throughout the movement, party leaders individually or jointly had forthrightly made clear that the struggle against the panchayat system would continue till the objectives of the movement were fulfilled. On the night of April 8 after talks between the king and the party leaders, the four leaders K.P. Bhattarai and G.P. Koirala of the NC and Mrs. Sahana Pradhan and Radha Krishna Mainali of the ULF called off the movement following a compromise with the palace that 'partylessness' would be deleted from the constitution and the lifting of the ban on political parties.

Forces of the Movement

When the ban on political parties was lifted and partylessness was promised to delete from the constitution on 8 April 1990 by a notification of the press secretariat of the king, the *desire of the Nepalese people* and *international environment* were explicit in the notification. The opposition leaders had already expressed optimism regarding the changing internal and external scenario and their impact on the democratic movement in Nepal. G.M. Singh during his nationwide campaign for the preparation of the movement had stated that, "the national and international situations have never been as favourable to the cause of democracy as now".

Political Conflicts

The conflict between the palace and the parties had begun soon after the success of the 1950-51 revolution. The revolution had ended the century long autocratic Rana rule and achieved a political system based assuredly on constitutional monarchy and parliamentary democracy. But the achievement of the revolution had gradually become diluted because of the king's refusal to confine his role to that of a formal head of state. The weakened and fragmented political parties gave their consent to King Mahendra's decision not to go for the Constituent Assembly election promised earlier by his father King Tribhuvan. Instead, King Mahendra himself granted a constitution in 1959. However, under the NC government, which had secured a two thirds majority in the elections to the parliament in 1959, the king's role had once again been reduced perhaps not in substance but in form to that of a nominal head of state. It was unpalatable to the assertive and ambitious King Mahendra. Ultimately even before the expiry of two years he abruptly ended the experiment with parliamentary democracy by a royal coup on 16 December 1960.

The hijacking of democracy had led the NC to launch a mild violent movement. But King Mahendra successfully tackled the challenge. He devised the panchayat system as the infrastructure to perpetrate his absolute rule. At the time of initiation of the panchayat system, it was said that the arrangement was "experimental". But later, by the first amendment to the Constitution of Nepal 1962, the panchayat system was declared "partyless" and a system to which there was no alternative. King Birendra moved a step further to make the panchayat system more rigid. By the second amendment to the constitution, the Back to Village National Campaign was made extremely powerful in all respects: from recruitment to retirement of the rank and file of panchas. The panchayat system, then from onwards began to function as a totalitarian one party system gradually eliminating the room for systemic opposition. The role of the banned political parties became very unpredictable. The NC, which had launched an armed insurgency against the panchayat system in the early 1960s, had offered 'cooperation' to the king and declared its faith in the leadership of the king by a statement of Subarna Shamsher, Chairperson of the NC, in 1968. But B.P. Koirala after his release renewed the line of confrontation with the unequivocal statement that "an armed revolution is the only way to topple the panchayat system and thereby restore democracy" (1990: 15).A section of young communists who were inspired by the Cultural Revolution in China and the Naxlite movement in India also followed the path of violence in the name of liquidation of the class enemy. The violent movements, whether launched by the NC or the communists, had been suppressed. Ultimately B.P. Koirala and his colleagues returned to Nepal from exile in India in 1976 with a "national reconciliation" policy, arguing that the NC had a twofold responsibility of safeguarding democracy and nationalism. The oppositions however were divided. The communists had equated the panchas and the Congress as two parts of a coin. While the NC also frequently used the communist card as a bargaining chip with the king, Subarna's "cooperation" and B.P.'s reconciliation policies had this stance in the background. The panchayat system placidly continued with the divide and rule policy. But when the students, with democratic and left affiliations had jointly launched an agitation against the panchayat system, King Birendra was compelled to announce a referendum on 24 May 1979, the choice being between two alternatives: reformed panchayat or the multiparty system. The verdict of the referendum went in favour of the panchayat system by a margin of 10 percent, securing 54.7 percent against the multiparty system's 45.3 percent.

The verdict of the referendum gave the stamp of popular legitimacy to the panchayat system. While appealing to all sections of the Nepali people to join the "singly national mainstream", King Birendra promised to give due respect to the minority. Indeed, the third amendment to the constitution incorporated some features of the parliamentary system, i.e. direct elections to the national legislature, election of the PM by the legislature and responsibility of the cabinet to the legislature. But paradoxically the referendum had sharpened and intensified political conflict in the country. B.P. Koirala had visualised:

> The panchayat system is breathing its last. It will come to the end of its life because of the following three contradictions. The first contradiction will manifest itself in the National Panchayat in the form of personal differences which will come to the fore given the lack of party discipline or because of the lack of concrete principles and a strong centre.... The second contradiction will rise from the conflict between the palace and the National Panchayat. Prior to the referendum, if nothing else, there was a strict command of leadership. This is no longer possible. The third contradiction will rise from the two-decade long conflict between the admirers of the panchayat system and the democrats, outside the system. This conflict will intensify further (1981: 12).

Though there was an ideological division between hardliner and liberal panchas, factionalism among them, from top to bottom, was merely based on the politics of one-upmanship and the politics of aggrandizement. There was a tendency of polarization among panchas as between "official" candidates and "non-official" candidates. The frustrations and anger generated by the elections would seemingly come to the fore from the very beginning of the NP session. Many members of the NP frequently shifted their loyalty from one group to another, apparently motivated by the aspirations for post, power, privilege and easy money. By the time of the dramatic removal of the first ever elected panchayat government headed by S.B. Thapa, the house had become permanently divided between pro- and anti-government factions. Moreover, the no-confidence motion became a major obsession of the legislatures.

From another perspective, the conflict and conspiracy among the ruling elites was a by-product of a bundle of controversies and contradictions within the system. The third amendment had produced an odd mix of authoritarian tendencies and democratic procedures. Adult franchise and cabinet responsible to the legislator could, with good faith, be used to produce popular leadership, to foster competitive politics and to the evolvement of an organized opposition. But all these contravened the active leadership of the king and partyless character of the system. The palace was well aware of the cost it would have to bear if the potential for democratization was permitted to be developed fully. The palace was, therefore, sometimes overtly and generally covertly involved in efforts to sabotage the spirit of adult franchise and responsible government. The unopposed election to the post of PM and Chairman of NP, the unprecedented removal of the government of S.B. Thapa and the rejection of a no-confidence motion against PM Lokendra Bahadur Chand even after it had been officially tabled at the house, were all examples of the behind-the-scene manipulations of the palace. In such circumstances an invisible centre of power, popularly known as the "underground gang" (patronized by the palace) emerged as a critical political factor. It was obvious that this gang monopolized court politics, amassed commissions and tenders, ran big business houses, indulged in large-scale smuggling, etc. The more the gang's grip tightened the more certain their final destruction became. B.P. Koirala rightly observed that the referendum had made the panchas like cannibals. Prof. Baral also advanced a general argument that, "In traditional regimes, intra-elite conflict plays a significant role in destroying the system" (1986: 5). The internal discord among the ruling elites contributed a lot to weakening the panchayat system.

The conflict between the admirers of the partyless panchayat system and its opponents had been intensified by post-referendum politics. Except for B.P. Koirala who accepted the result of the referendum however *unexpected* and *inexplicable* (Baral, 1983: 104), many of his party followers and most of the communist leaders rejected the verdict as "manipulated and rigged". Consequently all political parties, except Rohit and Rayamajhi groups of the left and the 'Group of 38' of democrats, boycotted the first general elections under the panchayat system held after the referendum. But none of them could provide an effective way out of the political impasse. The *satyagarha* launched by the NC in 1985 drove home a lesson that prospects of extra systemic opposition were not bright at that time. In fact the incorporation of the idea of popular participation and responsible government by the panchayat system after the third amendment widened the scope for systemic opposition. By the time of the second general elections, mainly communist factions including the Communist Party of Nepal, Marxist-Leninist (ML) and the Fourth Convention had made changes in their policies deciding to abandon the non-effective strategy of boycott with the view that "the struggle against the panchayat system could be intensified within the system" (Baral, 1987: 174)." However there were many restrictive provisions[2] in the constitution that obstructed the participation of political parties with dignity. In consideration of such constitutional bars, the NC laid down some preconditions[3] for their participation in the elections. But the palace discouraged all possibilities of systemic opposition. That was why the NC had to face a humiliating defeat when it took part in the local elections without fulfilment of its preconditions. After the result of local elections, G.M. Singh declared. "The Nepali Congress will not participate in any panchayat elections so long as the party remains under my command" (*Nepal Press Digest*, 16 November 1987). The confrontation between the NC and the panchayat system culminated on 16 December 1987 when the NC followers, who had been elected in the local panchayat elections, boycotted the King Mahendra Memorial and Constitution Day and subsequently the government suspended them. On the whole, the party secretary G.P. Koirala in his address to the historic conference of the party on 18-20 January 1990 made it clear:

> In the hope of achieving a national consensus for democracy the late B.P. Koirala, till the end of his life, favoured solving the problem through dialogue with the king. Hence, the endeavour was continued by myself and finally by Ganesh Man Singh. But time showed that such meetings alone would not solve the problems of the country... (This, however, does not mean) the NC has abandoned

> the idea of talks and mutual understanding. But we feel that talks or dialogue are worthless unless and until substantial change comes into the politics of the country (NC [a] 1990).

Unity Between Congress and Communist

The most important factor behind the success of the recent mass movement was unity between the NC and the ULF. In the early 1960s, Pushpa Lal Shrestha, the leader of the Communist Party of Nepal (CPN) initiated the idea of bringing the Congress and the Communists together on a single platform against the panchayat system. The idea was revived during the referendum and thereafter by some left leaders, especially Man Mohan Adhikari worked hard for unity among the anti-establishment forces. But both the leaders mentioned were then branded as 'traitors' and the 'tail of the Congress' by the extremists and radical communists. The proposal set forth by the moderate communist leaders for unity between the Congress and the Communists was sceptically refused by the NC under the leadership of B.P. Koirala. The NC's anti-communist phobia was further aggravated because of the boycott of the referendum by the ML and the Mashal (emerging influential leftist groups) and its consequences. On the other side, the NC's national reconciliation policy limited its options for working in harmony with the left. Because the gist of this policy, as defined by B.P. Koirala and his followers, was a mix of cooperation and confrontation with the king: cooperation for nationalism but confrontation for democracy. The orientation of this policy was, by and large, towards the palace. The leftists also strongly suspected that the NC's two-track reconciliation policy amounted to virtually aligning with the king against the communists. Even Bala Ram Upadhyaya, a leader of the Man Mohan group, which had better relations with the NC than any others, made this clear:

> It is our policy to seek unity with the B.P. group. At the same time, it is our policy to oppose the Nepali Congress if it pursues a line of seeking compromise with the panchayat system. This explains why we have been consistently opposing its line of national reconciliation. We want them to abandon this line and forge unity with all anti-panchayat forces for the restoration of democratic rights (*Nepal Press Digest*, 31 May 1982).

The NC's reconciliation policy remained unchanged. But, though there was some inconsistency, it moved towards confrontation rather than cooperation after the death of B.P. Koirala. G.M. Singh in his capacity as supreme leader and K.P. Bhattarai as the acting president of the party argued that B.P.'s acceptance of the result of the referendum was done in his individual capacity and was not binding to the party (*Nepal Press Digest*, 27 February 1984; 12 March 1985). Still there was divergence of perception among the top leaders of the party: G.P. Koirala was strongly in favour of 'reconciliation' with the king and participation in the panchayat elections, while Ganesh Man Singh clearly saw the inevitability of the struggle with the help of the communists. During the interval between the death of B.P. Koirala and the recent mass movement, the party tested both options. In 1985, it had launched a *satyagraha* on the basis of unity in action with five left groups.[4] Later in the general elections of 1986, the NC offered its participation with certain preconditions. Ultimately it was compelled to boycott the elections since the regime did not fulfil the demands of the NC. However, the party took part in the local elections in which its candidates suffered a humiliating defeat. On the whole, though the importance of the NC's reconciliation policy to liberalize the politics of the country to a certain extent could not be overlooked, the policy of national reconciliation as a medium for seeking systemic opposition was not well responded by the panchayat regime. Consequently, the NC was compelled to move towards the struggle against the panchayat system in cooperation and unity with the communist.

Besides, it was the change in strategy and perceptions among many communist splinter groups in Nepal that led to parallel efforts towards forming a joint front among themselves and also to seek unity between the NC and the left front. On account of the constant improvement in relations between the two communist giants, the USSR and China, the relevance of division along Soviet and Chinese lines narrowed down. Again, internal changes in the politics of the Soviet Union and China reduced the importance of the international communist movement which helped in shifting the orientation of the Nepalese communists towards a more nationalistic and less internationalist outlook. On the internal issues, the Nepali communists had different approaches mainly on the questions of acceptance of the Maoist ideology, participation in panchayat elections, alliance with the NC, and so forth. Still there was consensus among them to the need of struggle for the multiparty system in the country. Even those who strongly advocated the "new people's revolution" supported the multiparty system as a bourgeois pre-requisite for moving ahead to the path of socialism and communism.

The consensus among the leftists on the multiparty system helped to gloss over other differences. The most important issue was unity among themselves and with the NC which wanted the communists to accept the multiparty system as a commitment not just as a strategy.[5] The Man Mohan, Tulsi Lal, Manandhar and Verma groups were initiators for unity between the Congress and the Communists. The NCP, led by Sahana Pradhan came later, but readily into the fold. However, the Maoists, especially Mashal and ML, seemed intransigents. In course of time, Nirmal Lama of the Mashal group urged cooperation with the NC and consequently his group split with the Mashal, an extremist communist party of Nepal led by Mohan Bikram Singh. Previously, at the time of Satyagraha in 1985 two Maoist factions, led by Rohit and Nirmal Lama had shown eagerness for unity among anti-panchayat forces for an effective mass movement. The ML was also of this opinion but it was cautious and reluctant to work with the NC. This party also stayed outside the left front formed by the five communist groups during the Satyagraha in 1985. Still, there was an influential moderate group within the party which constantly and forcefully pleaded for an alliance with the NC at least for identical interest against the panchayat system. Besides, the multiplication of ML's activities in the post-referendum period through electoral participation in the panchayat system, joining human rights organizations, and similar front bodies made its leaders more pragmatic and prepared for democratization and liberalization in the party's outlook. By its fourth conference in August 1989, the trend towards liberalization propelled the party into dropping Maoism, abandoning the old concept of "dictatorship of the proletariat" and totalitarian one-party rule (Interview with Ghanshyam Bhusal, 25 February 1990).All these developments made it possible to achieve a broader unity among opposition forces, notwithstanding the rhetoric of the Mashal and similar other marginal groups which opposed this step. In conformity with the preconceived plan to launch a joint mass movement by the Congress and Communists, the ULF was formed on 15 January 1990 consisting of seven splinter groups.

The constant forward looking change in the attitude and behaviour of Nepali leftists was tremendously influenced by the massive erosion of communism in the Soviet Union and Eastern Europe. Gorbachev's policy of openness and reform changed the old face of communism. Adopting the slogan of "socialism with a human face and democracy", many communist parties in Eastern Europe renamed themselves as "Social Democrats". This new wave largely affected the way of thinking of the Nepali communists despite their strong rejection of the possibility of mechanical duplication of such international developments in the Nepalese context. Very significantly and boldly, the ML at its central committee meeting in October 1989 decided to accept the multiparty system as an indispensable part of the principles of the party.

The changing strategy and perspectives of the Nepali communists was widely appreciated by the NC as the leftists wholeheartedly welcomed the wish of the Congress to launch a joint mass movement. G.M. Singh on the eve of the movement stated optimistically, "The present is not the age of Stalin. The world's situation has changed. There have been changes among the communists accordingly. They have understood well that socialism or communism follows democracy" (*Nepal Press Digest*, 23 October 1989). Similarly, Bal Krishna Khand, the president of the NC student wing, Nepal Students Union, expressed the view that it would be unfair to regard Nepali communists as still within the framework of 1979-80, because they have reformed towards democratic socialism in line with the modification in communist philosophy all over the world (Interview, 15 March 1990). The unity between the Congress and the Communists, in totality, had been formed on the ground of their identical interest against the panchayat system and their mutual appreciation of increasing pragmatism on both sides. This augured well for the movement for restoration of democracy (MRD) in the country.

Role of Middle Class

The success of the MRD in Nepal once again proved that the middle class is a change agent. Though the struggle against the panchayat system affected rural dwellers also, it was largely a middle class urban movement. It was perhaps the first movement in Nepal in which different professionals, i.e. students, lawyers, doctors, nurses, para-medicals, lecturers, teachers, corporation staff and civil servants became openly involved. These middle class people played a prominent role in the movement making three principal contributions: giving continuity to the movement, paralysing the machinery of the regime and motivating the rest of the population. The involvement of the middle class in recent MRD was generated mainly because of stagnation in economic development, imbalance in economic development between one sector and others, the gap between expectations and attainment, and hopelessness in regard to the future under the panchayat system.

Nepal's economy had suffered from a prolonged state of stagnation. During 1960-85 the per capita growth rate was only 0.1 percent. The basic structure of the economy remained unchanged. Agriculture continued to contribute 60 percent of the population; the contribution of manufacturing to GDP hovered around 4 percent (Pandey, 1989: 321). Industrial development was held back because the pattern of investment was highly concentrated in the trade sector. Worst of all, a parallel economy grew massively in the post-referendum period. The trade deficit increased rapidly. Dependency on foreign aid also increased. The state of Nepal's economy, on the whole, was miserable, as the then US ambassador pointed out:

> A hard reality is that Nepal has been living beyond its means, that without major increases in external assistance, Nepal cannot even afford to operate and maintain the existing level of government provided goods and services (*Nepal Press Digest*, 7 September 1987).

However, relatively speaking, the fields of education and communication achieved some progress during the panchayat system, which helped the growth of the middle class. This class is highly ambitious in both political and economic areas, and also widely exposed to national and international developments. They are/were quickly affected and inspired by international trends and also equally frustrated when they compared the situation of their own country with others. "This frustrated middle class has emerged as a stronger and more dominant force than the traditional forces, and this led to bring an invisible change in the previous balance of power of Nepalese politics" (Interview with D.P. Adhikari, 20 March 1990). The increasing middle class naturally required enlargement in the scope of the political dissent to accommodate changing aspirations. But the panchayat system granted only licensed dissents. "This gap between the desire for change and accomplished change would create frustrated expectations about political life, which in turn could lead to riot, rebellion and revolution" (Goldstone, 1986: 6).

As already noted, the MRD was an urban class movement. Two grievances stand out as the main factors behind revolutionary urban tumults: the cost of food and the availability of employment (Goldstone, 1986: 612). The gap between population growth and the dismal economic growth rate posed a chronic employment problem. The problem of educated employment had also steadily worsened in proportion to the growth of educated people. "The number of school leavers increasing at least four times faster than new jobs are being created" (Shah, 1988: 945). Besides, the living standard of the Nepalese people had declined partly because of steep price rises and inflation. The average price rise was 10.4

percent in the five years from 1983/84. Viewing objectively, the index of price rise, between 1986 to 1990, in food grains, the increase ranged 22 to 32 percent in rice, 33 to 84 in pulses (mas), 65 in milk and 31 to 35 in cooking oil (MF, 1990). In addition, the Nepali rupee was devalued twice in the aftermath of the referendum, which also caused a decline in the per capita income and purchasing power of the people. All these created hardships in the day-to-day life of the people, the most affected group being urban dwellers and the middle class. The already bad situation further deteriorated because of the prolonged deadlock in Indo-Nepal relations. The consequence of India's trade embargo on Nepal as admitted by the then Finance Minister was: "The Indian economic blockade would cause loss of goods and services worth Rs. 2000 million during 1988-89. Revenue is likely to go down to Rs. 1000 million and inflation which was expected to come down from 11 percent in 1987/88 to 8 percent in 1988/89 is likely to remain in two digits. The GDP which had expected to grow by 5.3 percent is likely to grow by 1.6 percent" (*Nepal Press Digest*, 8 May 1989). Besides, the government could not adequately supply the shortages of essential commodities and sky-rocketing prices were out of the reach of the poor Nepalese. In such troubled times, thousands of unorganized workers who were previously engaged in construction and other industries lost their jobs as these sectors immediately began feeling the consequences of the trade embargo. Prolonged hardships generated anger and frustration among the people that suddenly exploded when the NC and the ULF jointly called for a mass movement against the PS.

International Environment

The international environment was also favourable for the democratic movement in Nepal. The global relaxation in east-west tensions reduced the room for manoeuvre by the authoritarian panchayat system. At the time of the Cold War in the 1960s, the panchayat regime had exploited the situation of the "decline of ideology" in international relations. Both the East and the West had also granted protective support to the panchayat system at least as a part of their global strategy to contain the influence of one against other. Gorbachev's commitment to the spirit of *glasnost* and *perestroika* and also the US's global concern for human rights and democracy encouraged the opposition in Nepal to struggle for multiparty democracy. Besides, given the increasing rapprochement between the two super powers, there was no logic for both countries to give active protective support to the panchayat rulers against the popular aspirations of the people as they had done during the period of hostility when each sought to counter the other.

Moreover, the detente in Sino-Indian relations had substantially weakened the panchayat system's elbow room. The panchayat system was established at the time when the relations between China and India were tense. King Mahendra had played off once against the other to sustain his regime. The statement of Chen Yi, in response to the reaction of Nehru on the royal coup of 1960 as "a setback for democracy" could be recalled here: "If any foreign force attacks Nepal, we Chinese people stand on your side." Similarly India seemed happy after the 1965 secret agreement with Nepal obviously entered into for its support to the panchayat system. The role of China and India vis-a-vis Nepal to counter one against the other was anticipated to continue on the issue of MRD in Nepal. Hemanta Rana, one of the members of the think-tank of the panchayat establishment who perceived India's hand in the recent anti-panchayat struggle, expected Chinese support to the regime against the movement (Interview, 25 March 1990). But China was surprisingly silent on the movement in Nepal. As India had adopted a non-interference policy at the time of the movement, China had no basis to interfere. The indifference of neighbours even at the time of crisis to the panchayat system manifested the decline of the manoeuvring capability of the regime.

The external strength of the panchayat system was severely affected by its strained relations with the southern neighbour. Tensions were aroused by a number of issues, i.e. the work permit system, bilateral trade and tariff, the engagement of Chinese technicians in Tarai, imports of arms from China by Nepal, etc. The crisis reached its culminating point on 23 March 1989 following the expiry of the trade and transit treaties, India's abrupt decision to close 13 out of 15 entry points into Nepal and its consequences led both sides to talk about the need to review the whole gamut of their bilateral relations. Nepal insisted on two different treaties on trade and transit and also asserted independent views on other issues. The prime focus of India was on the acquisition of Chinese arms by Nepal. Because it was viewed in India as the completion of the chain of China's arms transfer relationship in South Asia in addition to the arms deployed in Tibet along the Sino-India border (Kumar, 1989: 17). But political developments in both Nepal and India brightened the hope of sorting out the problem as the date of the movement approached. The National Front government in Delhi also showed signs of change from the past coercive attitude of the Rajiv Gandhi government to a conciliatory approach towards Nepal. The way of dealing had changed from irreconcilables to friendly overtures between the governments of Nepal and India. But by then the prolonged stalemate in trade relations with India had considerably helped in preparing the Nepalese people psychologically for the MRD in Nepal.

Besides, Nepal could not remain isolated from the tidal wave of democracy and human rights sweeping all over the world. In this regard an Indian MP, M.J. Akabar rightly observed, "The struggle for liberalization knows no boundary; the idea of democracy, the soul of freedom romps in impunity across the borders" (NC [c] 1990).The sudden collapse of communist regimes in Eastern Europe largely inspired and encouraged Nepal to take similar action against the authoritarian panchayat system. It was indeed the tragic end of 24 years "iron rule" of Ceausescu in Romania that boosted the morale of the Nepalese people as an example of people's power. Surya Bahadur Shakya, in his speech of welcome at the NC's conference, which decided to launch the movement, remarked:

> The wave of democracy is sweeping throughout the world. In many neighbouring countries, dictatorships are falling one by one, whether they be Marcos of the Philippines or Ceausescu of Romania. If the iron wall of Berlin has fallen into the dust of liberation, how long will partylessness based on corruption stand (NC [b] 1990).

International Support

The MRD in Nepal got widespread humanitarian and political support from the international community, mostly from non-governmental sectors. Almost all papers and magazines that have world-wide circulation gave coverage to the events in Nepal. Similarly the electronic media, especially the BBC and the VOA helped to internationalize the domestic riots in Nepal by highlighting day-to-day developments. Amnesty International and other human rights organizations also forcefully reiterated their concern over the violation of human rights in Nepal. The MRD was further buttressed by the Socialist International, political parties in different countries associated with the Socialist International, and by the Association of Asian Students, all of whom declared their impassioned solidarity with the struggle of the Nepalese people.

With regard to government level support, some of the major countries of the world, especially the Western countries, voiced their concern for human rights and democracy in Nepal. It was believed that they warned the government, through diplomatic channels, the possible consequences of the excessive use of force. Besides, in response to the appeal of party leaders and intellectuals to stop economic aid for the panchayat government, Switzerland and West Germany decided to suspend their assistance to Nepal. Except Japan, none of the donor countries and agencies provided any aid to Nepal during the days of the movement. However, as best as they could, some of the Western countries made an attempt to compromise between the establishment and the opposition. In the Nepalese media, it was reported that the British and Danish Ambassadors specifically worked for this purpose. Interestingly there was a marked similarity between the Soviet Union's approaches with that of the West. On one occasion Radio Moscow suggested that both the panchas and opposition parties should resolve the problem through mutual accommodation and mutual understanding.

The US and MRD in Nepal

The US was the first country that explicitly called for a compromise between the panchayat regime and opposition, and at the same time it granted a constant humanitarian support to the MRD in Nepal. Within four days of the agitation, the US government, a group of Congress members and Asia Watch, a human rights organization, put pressure on the government to avoid the excessive use of force. Above all, six influential members of the US Congress in a joint letter to King Birendra voiced their political support to the democratic movement in Nepal stating, "While we understand there are strong differences of opinion in Nepal on the issue of a multiparty system, we believe that all persons should have the right to express their opinion on this and other political issues" (*Text of letters jointly sent by six members of the US Congress to King Birendra,* 22 February 1990). The US's stand was however ambiguous. On the one hand, from the beginning to the end of the movement, John Kelly, the Assistant Secretary of the State Department, forthrightly reiterated the US support to "freedom of expression" and "respect for human rights". But after the unprovoked massacre of more than a dozen freedom fighters, the same official shockingly remarked that his government appreciated the patience shown by the Nepali police to control the opposition's demonstration. Besides, he used phrases such as "the verdict of the referendum", "traditional Nepalese way of ruling", "internal affairs of Nepal", when Sephen Solavz asked him to clarify the reluctance of the Bush administration to support the multiparty system in Nepal. Mr. Kelly further stated, "We certainly support parliamentary democracy, but as to the organization of a party system certainly there has to be room around the world for flexibility and countries have to decide their own path. We are not the judge of the world" (*Text of statement of John Kelly on the US's position on the MRD in Nepal*, 16 March 1990). The US government again changed its stand when the movement reached its climax. In contradiction to the earlier approach, the spokesman of the US government insisted, "The US never supported one-party or a partyless system. It was in favour of establishing human rights and freedom of political organization and political freedom" (*Nawaras Weekly*, 4 April 1990).Whether it was because of the US's good relations with both sides, the king and the Congress, or because of its scepticism regarding the success of the movement, or because of its apprehension of being caught on the wrong foot. The flip flop in the US stand could hardly be said to be behaving as a forthright champion of democracy in the world.

India and MRD in Nepal

India's role vis-a-vis the democratic movement in Nepal was distinctly divided and ambiguous. At popular and party levels, it provided active support, but the Indian government steadfastly followed a "non-interference" approach. The V.P. Singh government did not support the movement. It was partly because of increasing rapprochement between the government of both countries and the Nepal government's willingness to respect Indian sensitivities and also partly because of India's doubt of the success of the MRD in Nepal. A Nepali scholar who was in Delhi in the first half of the movement and also the NC activists who stayed in India to mobilize public support found that journalists, bureaucrats and intellectuals of India were sceptical of the success of the struggle of the Nepalese people against the panchayat system.[6] Moreover, the Government of India was really in a dilemma owing to the polarization between two wings of the government: Bharatiya Janata Party (BJP) versus the rest. The BJP, one of the dominant political forces in India, was naturally an ally of the Hindu Kingdom. On the issue of sending an Indian government delegation to Nepal, when the MRD had already been launched, 60 MPs, mostly from the BJP, issued a joint statement urging the early conclusion of a treaty with Nepal. To counter this line, 207 MPs issued their own statement supporting the struggle of the Nepalese people against the panchayat system. Moreover, Chandra Shekhar warned, "If you can sign the agreement (with Nepal) by-passing the people then this sovereign parliament has every right to reject that as well" (*Telegraph*, 31 March

1990). Despite the opposition from a majority in the house, an Indian delegation visited Nepal on 2 April, to advance the negotiation between the two countries. This delegation handed over an 80-page document which identified India's security sensitivities under five headings: joint Indo-Nepal surveillance of the border between Nepal and Tibet; training of Nepalese military personnel by India alone; no foreign aid project along the open 500-mile Nepal-India border without Indian concurrence; binding respect to property rights of Indians in Nepal; and Nepali laws not in conformity with the 1950 treaty to be terminated (*Hindustan Times*, 14 May 1990). From this document one could easily assume that the sole objective of Delhi's non-interference approach was directed to extract maximum concessions from the government of Nepal at the time of instability in the country. However looking at matters from another perspective, it could be said that the Government of India deliberately confined the process of negotiation with Nepal to the bureaucratic level and also consciously delayed the resolution of the bilateral problems despite both countries' agreement to respect each other's sensitivities on the Delhi visit of the then Foreign Minister of Nepal in January 1990. India's approach of non-interference in the battle between the panchayat regime and the people of Nepal was cast in favour of the regime, and it did help the regime to deal with the opposition. However, India's stance disappointed the political parties of Nepal and India. G.M. Singh reacted angrily, "We agree that it is not possible for India to distance itself totally from the government of Nepal. The problem is India has done nothing for us" (*India Today*, 15 March 1990). More vocally, Chandra Shekhar alleged, "India was helping a "Shahenshah" in Nepal like the US once had in Iran" (*Telegraph*, 31 March 1990).

There was, however, consensus among the people and parties of India to the support of MRD in Nepal. An Indian MP, M.J. Akbar was of the view that "It was a terrible mistake to compromise on fundamentals no matter what the excuse; Indians and even Indian national interest could better be served by a commitment to democracy rather than a commitment to a mere set of rulers perceived to be friendly" (NC [c], 1990). Even the BJP could not deviate formally from this broader consensus supporting the MRD in Nepal, though many of its leaders, directly or indirectly, revealed their sympathy to the king's regime. The party Secretary of the BJP, J.P. Mathur, issued a statement that, "In full sympathy with the democratic aspirations of the people of Nepal, we in India wish that a multiparty democracy would come to prevail within the constitutional monarchy in Nepal" (*Text of Statement of the Secretary of the BJP*, n.d.). Other political parties, the Janata Party, Janata Dal, Congress (I), Congress Party of India (CPI) and Communist Party, Marxist (CPM), independently or collectively, exerted pressure on their government to assist the movement in Nepal and condemned the Nepal government for state repression of a peaceful movement. To uplift the morale and spirit of the movement, they displayed solidarity through demonstrations on the streets of Delhi, picketing at the Nepalese Embassy, blocking the border on one occasion, opening refugee camps, etc.

In fact, the MRD in Nepal did not receive direct government level support from abroad. But concern shown by many countries on the issue of human rights in Nepal and also their condemnation of the use of the force by the Nepal government on the peaceful movement contributed to the fall of the 30-year old panchayat system. However impassioned solidarity with the MRD in Nepal given by various non-government organizations of the world helped a lot in mobilizing international opinion in favour of the anti-panchayat struggle. The overall sympathy and support received by the movement in Nepal from the international community was highly significant in achieving the target of the movement: the fall of the panchayat system and restoration of multiparty democracy.

Epilogue

The multiparty system was restored and the leaders also called off the movement. Yet there followed a week of significant and rapid developments before the future course of Nepali politics became clear. The seating of the four leaders of the movement and all four members of the Chand cabinet on either side of the king during the meeting at the palace was in contrast to the hooting which greeted G.P. Koirala the next day at the open-theatre when he remarked contradictorily that what the people had achieved was a "victory of the people as well as the panchas and the king". The two events symbolized the divergent attitudes between the palace and the people and also between the party leadership and the general people regarding the final result of the movement. The high expectations of the people uncompromisingly voiced worked as dissatisfaction on the people's faces. Speaking at the open-theatre, all Congress and Communist leaders, including those who called off the movement the previous night, spoke in the same vein and spirit stressing that the movement had completed one phase gaining partial success, and that it would continue further but by different methods. G.M. Singh argued that the removal of the ban on parties was a "step forward in opening the door to democracy." J.N. Khanal, representative of the ML sought the continuation of the struggle for safeguarding the freedom of party politics. It was, in fact, the living revolutionary spirit of the people that prompted the parties to go beyond the stated objectives of the movement. The NC and the ULF, therefore, called for the immediate fulfilment of 8 demands. They included dissolution of the NP and the Council of Ministers, formation of an interim government, dissolution of all panchayat units, proper representation of the NC and the ULF in the proposed constitutional reform commission, etc. Aiming for complete abolition of the panchayat system, the people encircled the Academy Hall, where the last round of talks was going on between the panchas and the opposition on 15 April. These developments dashed the hopes of the palace which thought that it could accommodate the panchas as a living political force within the framework of the minimal objectives of the movement. The king was seeking to protect the panchas and had wanted to use the Chand government as the interim government for this purpose. The haste shown in the withdrawal of suspension of Hari Bol Bhattarai and Tirtha Ram and others who were suspended from their posts because of their boycott of Constitution Day in 1987, together with the convening of meetings of different NP's committees on 15 April indicated the intentions of the palace regarding the survival of the panchas in a new guise.

Lokendra Bahadur Chand, the then PM, in his first meeting with the press after the removal of the ban on parties, claimed that his cabinet was the interim government and declared that people from the multiparty side would be accommodated in his cabinet and also in the forthcoming constitutional reform committee (*The Rising Nepal*, 10 April 1990). Furthermore, he stated that the proposed reforms in the constitution would be directed towards the building of "pluralistic democracy" and avoided to use the term multiparty system. But all these efforts proved in vain against the people's determination to abolish the panchayat system altogether. After the Academy Hall incident, L.B. Chand resigned from his post on 18 April and the king accepted G.M. Singh's proposal to appoint K.P. Bhattarai as the PM of the interim government.

The formation of a coalition government including the representatives of the king, the NC and ULF marked culminating as well as a turning point in the politics of Nepal. At the oath taking ceremony of the new council of ministers, Ganesh Man Singh, the commander of the mass movement, emphasized the continuation of unity between the Congress and the Communists to preserve and promote newly achieved democracy in Nepal. In the way of consolidating the achievement of the mass movement, PM K.P. Bhattarai gave priority to frame a democratic constitution and to hold an impartial election.

NOTES

1. The ULF, formed on 15 January 1990, consisted of seven communist parties: Marxist, Marxist-Leninist (ML), Fourth Convention, Verma, Manandhar, Amatya, and Rohit (NWPP) groups.
2. There were a number of restrictive provisions in the constitution such as the arrangement of a coordination council as a super cabinet, the revival of the BVNC in the modified guise of the Panchayat Policy and Investigation Committee, 25 percent royal nominees out of the total members of the NP, requirement for membership of any class organization to qualify as a candidates, the wording of the prescribed oath, etc.
3. Some of the major demands put forward by the NC as a precondition for its participation in elections were: interim government, a single manifesto and the same symbol to pro-party candidates, campaign in the name of the party, removal of the compulsion of the membership of a class organization, etc.
4. Five left groups consisting of Man Mohan, Tulsi Lal, Verma, Rohit and Nirmal Lama factions unitedly launched a "Political Movement" as a complement to the NC's *satyagraha* on the basis of unity in action.
5. Part of the national reconciliation policy of B.P. Koirala was perceived as anti-communist strategy, but once he stated, "I am ready to live together with them (communist) if they accept the multiparty system and put their faith in it", *Punarjagaran*, Push, 2038 (1981).
6. Informal talks with Dhruba Kumar, Hari Sharma, Kishore Nepal, Kausal Raj Regmi in April 1990.

CHAPTER 2

NEGOTIATION BEHIND CONSTITUTION MAKING, 1990

Democracy in Nepal first attained in 1951, through an armed revolution against the autocratic Rana Regime, was shortlived. By a coup d'etat in 1960, King Mahendra dismantled the parliamentary democracy and introduced the partyless panchayat system. After 30 years of the Panchayat Raj, the movement for the restoration of democracy (MRD) was launched jointly by the Nepali Congress (NC) party and the United Left Front (ULF) in February-April 1990. The mass movement terminated successfully in its objective to restore the multiparty system. The lifting of the ban on political parties on 8 April 1990, however, opened up new conflicts between the king and the movement leaders on several issues, with its focal and culminating point in constitution making.

Did the dawn of the multiparty democracy mean the end of the panchayat system? Would the king continue to enjoy his traditional

---

* This paper extensively uses the information collected through interviews, conducted in October-December 1992, with the key actors involved in negotiation of constitution making, i.e. Ganesh Man Singh (supreme leader of the NC and commander of the 1990 mass movement), Bishwanath Upadhya (chairperson of CRC), members of CRC: Madhav Nepal (ULF), Mukunda Regmi (NC) and Ramananda Prasad Singh (king's nominee), ministers of interim government: Sahana Pradhan (ULF), Nilambar Acharya (ULF), Kesharjung Rayamajhi (king's nominee) and Devendra Raj Pandey (independent), and others: Pashupati Shamsher Rana (Minister of the Chand cabinet) and Padma Ratna Tuladhar (ULF).

prerogative to grant the constitution in the changed context? What would be the nature and content of the new constitution? During the negotiations held on each of these issues, the palace and its allies made every possible effort to minimize change in order to sustain most of the king's traditional power, position and privileges. On the other side, notwithstanding the democratic movement's initial simple objective of legalizing party politics in the country, the parties involved in the democracy movement made four successive upward revisions in its goals during the period between 8 April and 9 November 1990. First, legalization of political parties; second, abolition of all panchayat institutions; third, formation of a constitution drafting commission on the recommendation of the Prime Minister (PM) against the traditional prerogative of the king; and, last, constitutional monarchy.

This paper tends to analyse negotiations held between the king and the movement leaders on the following political issues: removal of the ban on political parties; dissolution of the panchayat institutions; formation of a constitution drafting commission; drafting of the constitution; revision of the draft constitution by the cabinet; counter-draft constitution submitted by the palace; and finalization of the constitution. The paper focuses on the goal set by the contending parties, bargaining techniques and strategies applied to assert their own points against the others, development that influenced the negotiations, skill and style of the negotiators, reconciliation of differences, accommodation of each other's views, compromise, etc.

One Agenda Three Perspectives

The mass movement was formally started on 18 February 1990. At the moment when the popular struggle was gaining a revolutionary character,[1] King Birendra abandoned the suppressive line, and sought for dialogue to resolve the political problem in the country. The agenda was obviously the two-point demand of the mass movement: multiparty system and interim government. But the king, on his part, proposed political reform within the panchayat structure, while the NC pursued the goal of freedom for political parties. Besides, the ULF sought for the dissolution of the panchayat institutions along with the restoration of the multiparty system.

King: For Political Reform: By a proclamation on 6 April 1990, King Birendra put forward a three-point proposal for starting negotiation. First, Marich Man Shrestha's cabinet was replaced by a four-man Council of

Ministers headed by Lokendra Bahadur Chand. The movement leaders were offered accommodation in the new government. Second, the agenda was 'political reform'. The proposed reformation was confined to the panchayat structure. The proclamation harked back to the national referendum of 1980 which had endorsed the panchayat system. Besides, the same proclamation issued a notification to convene the session of the National Panchayat (NP). Third, the Chand government was deputed to hold talks with the movement leaders. The PM following instructions invited Devendra Raj Pandey on 6 April and Padma Ratna Tuladhar on 7 April to his office where he requested them to convince Ganesh Man Singh (commander of the mass movement and supreme leader of the NC) and the ULF leaders for sincere dialogue to resolve the political crisis in the country.

Devendra Raj Pandey said that Ganesh Man Singh rejected outright the PM's offer for negotiation with the words. "I refuse to meet even the king without the announcement of the multiparty system". Hundreds of thousands of people marched on the street to display their fury against the royal proclamation on the morning of April 6. The palace was put in an unenviable position by the loss of the lives of scores of demonstrators in front of the palace in the afternoon from indiscriminate firing by the police and the army personnel. The hope of tackling the situation at the government level and through the proposal for reform within the panchayat framework soon proved to be a miscalculation. Minister Pashupati Shamsher Rana said that the king and the Chand government, therefore, changed the strategy straight away on the night of the same day, April 6. Accordingly, the agenda shifted from the king's earlier proposal for political reform to the demand of the popular movement for the multiparty system. Instead of the Chand government, the king himself would talk to the representatives of the movement. The cabinet members shared the responsibility of contacting and consulting each senior leader of the NC and the ULF separately, Minister Rana said that he found the president of the NC, Krishna Prasad Bhattarai, and some of the ULF leaders – i.e. Man Mohan Adhikari, Radha Krishna Mainali – responsive in his meeting with each of them on 7 April 1990.

NC: For Freedom of Political Parties: On 7 April 1990, the NC troika – Ganesh Man Singh, Krishna Prasad Bhattarai and Girija Prasad Koirala – met during the curfew after they received the signal that the demand for the multiparty system could be fulfilled. They had two alternatives. First, they had to satisfy the major demand of the mass movement – the multiparty system – and then they had to respond to the king's offer for talk. Second, the magnitude of the mass movement had spurred additional demands. It was thus quite natural that the target of the people exceeded the previously settled two-point demand. But the NC faced a dilemma. What would happen if the king refused to meet the additional demands? Two possibilities were inevitable. The movement would be radicalized violently. The king, on his part, might impose martial law. In such a foreseeable scenario, the NC might lose its grip on the popular movement.

In all anxiety, the NC avoided taking the risk of putting up additional demands. Its troika's meeting on 7 April therefore unilaterally decided without consulting the ULF to talk to the king for the announcement of the multiparty system. Their fear-psyche acted all the while when they changed the line the next day, April 8, in favour for putting additional demands in response to the pressure by the ULF leaders. In response to the ULF leader's demand for dissolving the NP, an eyewitness, Padma Ratna Tuladhar said, the NC president Bhattarai tried to dissuade them, "What will be left to struggle in the future if we gain all at one stroke?" Tuladhar said that Ganesh Man Singh later accepted the ULF's demand, after the ULF leaders relentlessly insisted, with the words: "This issue can be put up before the king."

ULF: For Dissolution of Panchayat Institutions: "The end of the panchayat system", the ULF put it up as the agenda for talks during Minister Rana's visit to the ULF meeting place on 8 April 1990. This happened under typical circumstances. First, the ULF meeting was going on at loggerheads. One of the participants of the meeting, Padma Ratna Tuladhar observed that the moderate section of the Front, like the Amatya, the Verma and the Manandhar groups urged participation in talks with the king on the point of the multiparty system. The radical wing, such as the Marxist-Leninist (ML) and the Fourth Convention urged "the end of the panchayat system" as the agenda for negotiation. But the problem was that the ULF could make a decision only in unanimity. Second, before the ULF meeting came to any conclusion, its leaders were informed of the NC's decision to meet the king to put up the demand for the multiparty system. This influenced the ULF to take its own decision. Minister Rana – who read the demand of the ULF to end the panchayat system as an indication of the communist willingness to continue the movement – said that the communist leaders came in line to participate in the negotiations only after Ganesh Man Singh threatened to alienate them if they refused to enter into dialogue. Ganesh Man Singh conceded this, "I suggested that the communist leader should accept the offer for talks since the main demand of the mass movement – the multiparty system – was going to be fulfilled."

Judging from the prevailing circumstances there was a risk of alienation of the radical wing of the ULF from the NC and even from the moderate sections of the Front by seeking an alternative to dialogue. Ultimately, the ULF meeting decided to enter into dialogue on the condition of achieving the multiparty system.[2] However, the representatives selected by the ULF for this job were instructed to put pressure on the NC, at least, to raise the demand for dissolution of the NP before the king. The ULF representative succeeded in convincing the Congress leaders on this point.

The movement side strengthened its position vertically. The king was forced to change the content from its 'political reform' within the panchayat structure into multiparty democracy. And, the NC and the ULF agreed to put up an additional demand for dissolving the NP. The establishment also adroitly made the situation favourable horizontally. The Chand government capitalized on the curfew for around 55 hours (6-8 April 1990) controlling the communication channels. It managed to meet both the NC and ULF leaders separately only after the individual consultation of ministers with the movement leaders had already progressed. After the NC agreed to meet the king and the Nepal Television recorded the interview of the NC president, the government arranged for a joint meeting between the NC and the ULF leaders in the afternoon before they visited the palace in the evening of April 8. The NC was in a hurry for talks and the late decision of the ULF helped the establishment in its plan to bring the movement leaders to the negotiation table[3] without allowing them time for a thorough working out of the details.

Two participants in the April 8 negotiations - Minister Pashupati S. Rana and the ULF president, Sahana Pradhan – said that King Birendra fully exploiting the lack of preparation of his opponents brought additional issues beyond the multiparty system like constitution reform commission, the interim government, etc. to seek commitment of the movement leaders in favour of primacy of the erstwhile establishment in post-agreement politics. The representatives of the movement took a defensive position vis-a vis the king's proposal. However, Sahana Pradhan claimed that the representatives of the movement suggested that the king should constitute a new government and dissolve the panchayat institutions, but the king hedged. Neither the movement side nor the establishment was in a position to assert their respective points. The former had the disadvantage of the lack of good preparation. The king dreaded to think of the consequences if the talks failed. So both sides felt comfortable buying time to review the situation later with an understanding that their differences would be amicably resolved through negotiations in the coming days. But the enthusiasm for the announcement of the multiparty system came as an anti-climax, both in content and level. By a royal notification on April 8, the word 'partyless' was deleted from the panchayat constitution.

Abolition of Panchayat System

The April 8th understanding for subsequent negotiation actualized on 15 April 1990 between the Chand government and the representatives of the NC and the ULF.[4] To ensure minimal change in the absolute power of the king in the changed context after the restoration of the multiparty system, the palace sought for the protection of panchas and the panchayat institutions. But the people and the movement leaders exerted pressure for maximum change.

Palace and Government: Protection of Panchayat Institutions: In the first interview, after the removal of the ban on political parties, on April 10, PM Chand claimed his government as the 'interim government', and undervalued the spirit of the popular movement saying that "objections had been raised against the working style of His Majesty's Government under the panchayat itself" (*The Rising Nepal*, 11 April 1990). Showing pleasure in sitting for talks again soon, he boasted, "The panchayat would continue to fulfil its role and adjust to the new situation" (*The Rising Nepal*, 11 April 1990). This suggested that the palace and the panchas were searching for a way to settle the problem reminiscent of the 1951 experience. By the armed revolution in 1950/51 the Rana regime was overthrown but the last Rana PM Mohan Shamsher was retained as the head in the post-revolution Rana-Congress coalition government.

The panchayat establishment wished to defuse the political crisis with a minimum loss. But the king and the Chand government conceived that the situation, which emerged in the demonstration of the people's power on April 6 followed by the movement leader's quest for rapid and radical change, demanded more than they wanted to give up. But on April 8, the representatives of the movement gave a sense of relief to the panchayat establishment. Minister Pashupati S. Rana said the panchayat camp read the euphoria of the representatives of the mass movement that spilled over shortly after the agreement to lift the ban on political parties as a hope to resuscitate the panchayat machinery in the changed political context. But the NC and the ULF changed their line soon after their representatives left the palace on the night of April 8. Minister Rana said that not only did the movement leader refuse outright the Chand government's offer for their accommodation in the cabinet; they increased their demands during the informal consultations with the Congress and the Communist leaders. Though the palace and the panchas contended the new demands before the movement leaders, they relinquished their earlier hope of propping the panchayat institutions. The people were aggressively poised for sweeping change. "King Birendra could not overlook the situation," said a dispatch of Mark Tully's BBC broadcast in the evening of April 14, otherwise, "the time is ripe for another revolution that will be against the monarchy". Since the king and the Chand government were bewildered by the fluidity of the situation unfavourable to them, persuasions for formal negotiations dragged on for a few days.

People: Total Political Change: For the people, the triumph of democracy mingled with acrimony that the notification of the deletion of 'partyless' from the panchayat constitution did not represent what the change meant for them. Greeting the reconciliatory remark of Girija Prasad Koirala, general secretary of the NC, that the movement's outcome was 'a victory of the people as well as of the king and the panchas' with an uproar at the mass meeting on April 9, the people showed their wish that they wanted to understand the dawn of multiparty democracy as the demise of the panchayat system. In fact, the popular expectation of and articulation for radical change followed from their pivotal role in the mass movement which gained a revolutionary character later. Almost all the leaders who addressed the meeting took the position that the achievement of freedom of parties was just a prelude to full-fledged democracy. The assurance of the leaders for the continuation of the struggle spearheaded the popular demand for the abolition of the panchayat system in its entirety. The movement leaders thus had to reset their goals beyond the previously settled two-point demand.

Leaders: Reset the Goal: The NC and the ULF upheld the popular voice for more change. On the night of April 9, after the April 8 agreement, Ganesh Man Singh issued a statement, "It is wrong to say that the NC regards the pro-democracy movement as having been completed...the struggle will continue... until democracy is restored.... Since the term partyless has been deleted from the constitution, the present panchayat constitution has become an anachronism and its operators have lost political legitimacy (*Naya Nepal*, 12 April 1990). At the ULF meeting, held the next morning after the April 8 agreement, Lila Mani Pokharel (Fourth Convention), Shyam Koju (NWPP), and Padma Ratna Tuladhar (independent-left) observed that the agreement was made at a point less achievable than the circumstances offered (*Mulyankan*, March-April 1992: 37). The ML – the most influential member of the ULF – reacted to the April 8 agreement as "feeble, weak and inauspicious" (*Nepali Awaj*, 15 June 1990).

The primary focus of the movement leaders was initially directed at replacing the Chand cabinet with another consisting of the representatives of the NC, the ULF and the panchas headed by the king. But by the evening of April 11, the demand transformed from the dissolution of the NP into the abolition of all panchayat institutions. In order to push for new demands, the NC and the ULF jointly formulated an eight-point demand.[5] They had two advantages in moving their new demands. First, the purposeful non-participation of the commander of the mass movement Ganesh Man Singh in the April 8 agreement[6] so that he could submit the eight-point demand to the king on April 13. Second, Ganesh Man Singh said that he offended the king by saying that "people moved ahead faster than the demands of the mass movement" when the king told him that "these are not demands of the mass movement." Ganesh Man Singh noted further that the king instructed him to settle the issue of the eight-point demand through negotiation with the Chand government.

Negotiations held between the representatives of the multiparty side and the Chand government on April 15, continued for fourteen hours. The negotiators from the panchayat side were already demoralized for two reasons. First, the initial hope for the survival of the Chand government was already sunk by an understanding reached between King Birendra and Ganesh Man Singh to form a new government in the presence of the PM Chand on April 13. Second, as Pashupati S. Rana saw the king was bewildered, so he was unable to give clear guidance to the government; the government was also in disarray that it could not properly advise the king on how to tackle the situation.

The situation was favourable for the multiparty side in more than one way. In the negotiations held between the victorious movement leaders and vanquished panchas, the agenda also consisted of the eight-point demand put forth by the multiparty camp. The leadership was under pressure from the people and party workers to push the demand in a way that could not be subject for bargaining.[7] Ganesh Man Singh said that the leaders for the negotiation were strictly instructed to be intransigent on the eight-point demand. The open location of the talk in the Academy hall allowed a crowd to form and exert overt pressure on the negotiations.

Nilamber Acharya, one of the negotiators from the multiparty side, said that the panchas initially tried to protect the panchayat institutions. But they gave up their stand as the crowd frequently entered into the negotiation hall, and the multiparty negotiators threatened to break the discussions. Minister Pashupati S. Rana confirmed that after PM Chand contacted the king by telephone, the panchayat side agreed to consent to all the demands of the opposition except for the dissolution of the local panchayat units. Nilamber Acharya said that the panchayat side accepted all demands but refused to sign the document of the agreement. The multiparty side therefore declared the failure of the negotiations. Yet the April 15 negotiations concluded with a general agreement on the demands of the multiparty side. Minister Rana maintained that the Chand government advised the king that night to make a unilateral declaration of fulfilling all the demands as agreed.

On April 16, King Birendra proclaimed the dissolution of NP, Panchayat Policy and Evaluation Committee, class organization and also accepted the resignation of the Chand government. The entire panchayat system was dismantled at one stroke. After consulting Ganesh Man Sing, King Birendra accepted Singh's proposal to appoint the NC president, Krishna Prasad Bhattarai, as the PM of the country. PM Bhattarai then formed a coalition government including the representatives of the king, the NC, the ULF and the independents.

Constitution Commission

After the dissolution of the panchayat institutions, no more options were left to the king for retaining his traditional power except one – exerting his prerogative in forming a constitution commission. But the success of the movement forces to install their primacy in the composition of the interim government had reset their target. The immediate target was directed against the king's prerogative to grant a new constitution.

Parties: Reset the Goal: The NC and the ULF had made upward revision on their goal relating to the constitution. Previously, as incorporated in the eight-point demand, they pressed for the repeal of all provisions of the panchayat constitution that contradicted the multiparty system and the formation of a constitution drafting commission with adequate representatives of the NC and the ULF. These demands did not challenge the prerogative of the king to grant a new constitution. But

Ganesh Man Singh's meeting with the king after the proclamation dissolving the panchayat institutions marked the genesis of a new demand, constitutional monarchy. The press note issued by the NC in this context stated that during the meeting with the king, "Ganesh Man Singh repeatedly emphasized the great benefit the country would derive if His Majesty gracefully accepted the role of a constitutional monarch in a parliamentary democracy" (NC [d], 1990). The NC's central committee meeting on 25-27 April 1990 endorsed this new demand that "We want to make it clear that constitutional monarchy under parliamentary democracy is our declared policy" (NC [e], 1990). Though most of the communist parties propagated their ideological identity as republicans, the ULF's immediate objective was also to change the status of the king from that of an absolute monarch to a constitutional one. Its fourteen-point programme prescribed that "A tradition requiring His Majesty to act on the advice of the Council of Ministers must be adopted immediately" (*Daily Diary*, 9 May 1990). The NC and the ULF wanted to see the formation of the constitution commission in accordance with the practices of constitutional monarchy through the recommendation of the Council of Ministers.

Government: Ambivalence: PM Bhattarai requested holding up of the announcement of the CRRC on 11 May 1990. Because "certain things have to be sorted out with His Majesty" (*Gorkhapatra*, 5 May 1990), he informed the press. The problem consisted of inadequate representation of the NC and the ULF, in the view of the chairman of the CRRC Bishwa Nath Upadhyaya. Minister Keshar Jung Rayamajhi confirmed that the PM wanted to delay the announcement of the CRRC because he was under pressure from within and outside the cabinet to change some of the names on the list of members of the commission. The meeting of the NC general secretary, Girija Prasad Koirala, with the king on May 6 did not bring a solution. Then the PM evoked the communists. The ULF issued a statement on May 9, two days before the announcement of the CRRC, that, "the proposed constitution commission be formed soon with equal representation of the NC and the ULF, along with adequate representation of legal and constitutional experts recommended by both sides" (*Gorkhapatra*, 10 May 1990). But the PM's indirect persuasion was unable to bear any fruit.

PM Bhattarai briefed the press that, "His Majesty categorically said that it was his job to nominate the members of the commission" (*The Rising Nepal*, 12 May 1990). Besides the assertion of the king's prerogative, there was additional ground for justification. According to the chairman of CRRC, Bishwa Nath Upadhyaya, "consultations and general agreement had taken place in the formation of the commission" (*The Rising Nepal*, 13 May 1990). The PM therefore shamefacedly condoned the formation of the CRRC. Moreover, Chairman Upadhaya said that the PM assured him that he would tackle the situation (i.e. the people and the parties' resentment against the CRRC) when he conveyed his intention to resign.

In a volte face, PM Bhattarai bowed to popular feelings to discredit the CRRC. With his presence in the capacity of the president of the party, the 12 May 1990 emergency meeting of the NC demanded the reconstitution of the constitution commission in consultation with the interim government. Moreover, the PM publicly denied that he had been consulted before the announcement of the CRRC. The NC and the ULF capitalized this point. They denounced the commission with the logic that it had been formed contrary to the spirit of constitutional monarchy under the multiparty system; it was, therefore, "undemocratic and disgraceful." In support of the demand for dissolution of the commission, Bharat Mohan Adhikari and Daman Dhungana resigned from the commission. Nevertheless, the king appeared stubborn. He dissuaded Chairman Upadhyaya from resigning, as mentioned by Chairman Upadhyaya. But after a widespread display of resentment by the public and parties against the commission, Chairman Upadhyaya submitted his resignation on May 14. The king then had no option but to dissolve the commission and reconstitute a new commission.

Ministers Devendra Raj Pandey and Nilamber Acharya said that the palace had put pressure for the inclusion of a greater number of former panchas in the proposed reconstituted constitution commission. This was further confirmed by the offer of a position in the commission to a former panchayat stalwart, which was turned down.[8] Against the pressure of the palace in camera to retain its greater say in the constitution-making process, the political parties radicalized their demands on the streets. The NC General Secretary Girija Prasad Koirala demanded an interim act as a pressure tactic. The ULF vocally carried this issue for quite long as a means to put pressure to lessen the palace's role in the constitution-making process. Besides, some dominant ULF partners, i.e. the ML and the Fourth Convention, raised the idea of final approval of the draft constitution by the elected government (ML [a], 1990; FC, 1990). After long weeks of pulls and pressures between the palace on the one side and the NC and the ULF on the other, a nine-member Constitution Recommendation

Commission (CRC) – in which the combined representatives of the NC and the ULF was twice that of the king's nominees – was constituted on 31 May 1990 by the king but in accordance with the recommendation of the Council of Ministers.

Drafting the Constitution

Though the king was forced to give up his prerogative to form the constitution commission in accordance to his own discretion, the palace's interest to retaining the king's sovereign power in the proposed new constitution remained intact. Some traditional forces were therefore reactivated, with the military on the forefront to suggest the CRC, "the retention of the king's sovereignty, army under the command of the king" and a "Hindu state" (*Kanun*, 1991: 317-358). The NC suggested that the CRC should frame the constitution based on constitutional monarchy and parliamentary democracy. The dominant ULF partner (who had their representation on CRC) emphasized the consideration of their two-layer objectives in their recommendations to the CRC. First, in regard to the position of the king, they pushed too far too fast. Second, they sought for a provision by which constitutional monarchy and parliamentary democracy could be altered through amendments in the constitution (ML [b], 1990; CPN [Marxist], 1990).[9]

The drafting of the constitution was begun against the background of the open manifestation of conflicting goals among the forces involved in this task. Many factors influenced the work of constitution drafting, but only three major factors would be highlighted here. The first was the nature and preparation of the negotiators on all the three sides. Second was the decision by a majority on all contentious issues, adopted as a modality by the CRC, which led the points of common interests of either two groupings among the representatives of the king, the NC and the ULF to prevail on each issue. Third, an understanding made in the CRC that a decision taken on each issue was not subject to reappraisal or reopening allowed the CRC to resist pressure from the outside to change the provisions that had already cleared the table.

For the preparation of the draft constitution, negotiations among the representatives of the king, the NC and the ULF revolved around three major issues: (1) the position of the king: powerless or vested with some powers? (2) fundamentals of the constitution: irrevocable or amendable? and (3) government: strong or limited?

Position of the King: Consolidation of constitutional monarchy and the multiparty system was the term of reference for the CRC. A thin voice to define constitutional monarchy as vested with power in the king arose from panchayat nostalgia. Some of the king's nominees in the CRC said that the king had instructed them and the conservative elements had put pressure on them to seek for retention of the king's residuary, prerogative and sovereign powers in the draft constitution. But, sources close to Chairman Upadhyaya opined that he was not swayed by such pressure. Because of his position and also from the way he had been reselected in the reconstituted CRC, after the request not only from the king but also from the Congress and the Communist leaders, he was morally bound to separate himself from a hard partisan line. His role as the chairman would have definitely influenced the king's nominees. One of them, Rama Nanda Prasad Singh, said that he had informed the king during his audience about his commitment to frame a democratic constitution. Another of the king's nominees, Pradymna Lal Rajbhandari, was mostly absent because of his ill health. In the days he attended the CRC's meetings, a ULF member of the CRC, Nirmal Lama, observed, "He was in favour of drafting a democratic constitution" (*Kanun*, 1991: 343).

The independent perception of the king's nominees – different from the interests of the palace – brought them closer to the NC on the question of the status of the monarchy. The NC tended to grant higher status and privileges to the royal family for the sake of the king's consent in his position as the head of the state. The representatives of the NC and the king therefore insisted upon the adoption of the "King in Parliament" as the principle of the constitution. The problem was the different approach taken by the ULF's representatives relating to the position of the monarchy. A ULF member of the CRC, Madhav Kumar Nepal, said that the ULF representatives proposed for (1) the reduction of the size and privileges of the royal family, (2) the exclusion of the king's name from the executive, legislative and judiciary and (3) the provision to make the actions of the king and his family questionable in parliament. The ULF's suggestion for the reduction in the size of the royal family was reconciled, but the NC's representatives and the king's nominees opposed the ULF members for their other two points. As a reaction, one ULF partner in the CRC, Nirmal Lama's Fourth Convention went on to the extent of disclosing the secrecy of the CRC with a provocative statement that the "palace had hatched a conspiracy." Ultimately, the king and the NC representatives' joint persuasion for constitutional monarchy with higher status and privileges prevailed through majority voting.

Fundamentals of the Constitution: The early recommendation made by the NC and those left parties which had their representatives in the CRC were contradictory on this issue. The NC opted to make the basic features of the constitution irrevocable, while the left suggested the opposite. For the NC, the problem was the divided opinion among its representatives in the CRC on the issue of the fundamentals of the constitution, as observed by Chairman Upadhyaya and member Madhav Nepal. During the debates, some urged for the perpetuity of constitutional monarchy and parliamentary democracy. But a two-member team constituted by NC representatives Mukunda Regmi, and the other ULF representatives Madhav Nepal, recommended a provision by which even the fundamentals of the constitution could be changed. Mukunda Regmi (NC) admitted that it was his conscience, perhaps inculcated by his educational background and profession, which sought that the sovereignty of the people should not be limited, and which motivated him to go against the guidelines of the party while opting for the divergence of opinion among the NC representatives on this issue reflected a lack of proper consultation among themselves. In fact, the arrogance of the NC representatives – all of them were/are reputed and well-known senior advocates – made them oblivious to the need for homework and proper coordination. Chairman Upadhyaya gave a further insight that he had timely informed PM Bhattarai about the problem among the NC representatives, and he went on to say that he had advised the PM to inform his party representatives on the guidelines of the party. But the chairman said that he did not find any improvement in the presentations of the NC representatives in the CRC. Consequently, the position of the NC weakened in the negotiations over the drafting of the constitution.

The negotiations from the other side – the ULF representatives – spoke in one voice to make their points. The ULF prudently selected its representatives in the CRC from the leadership level, because the party leaders were deeply committed and more assertive in their political principles and objectives than mere professionals. Moreover, even Chairman Upadhyaya admiringly accepted that the strength of the ULF representatives in the CRC laid in their proper homework and perfect coordination in the work of drafting the constitution, notwithstanding that they belonged to different political parties. They therefore succeeded in insisting on the provision of amendment in the fundamentals of the constitution. The king's nominees shared a common perception with the ULF members on the question of the fundamentals of the constitution, but their motivations differed. The ULF representatives took it as a gain in their quest for their anti-monarch and anti-bourgeois identity, while Chairman Upadhyaya urged that "nothing was without alternative and immoral, everything was changeable." Ultimately the provision for amendment in the fundamentals of the constitution was duly passed unanimously.

Government: The issue of government was less debatable in the CRC, but it was more sensitive and controversial. The provision of 'Judicial Committee', 'Constitution Committee', and 'Defence Council' had curtailed the executive prerogative. Moreover, the constitutional monarch was vested with the preventive power that the king, according to his discretion, may refuse to abide by the recommendation of the Council Ministers on the declaration of emergency and dissolution of parliament. The ULF representatives, who had attempted to push the monarchy too fast and too far, accepted and even advocated in vesting the king with preventive power.[10] Why was there such a paranoiac attitude towards the executive branch of the government? Chairman Upadhyaya explained exactly how it was justified in the *Analytical Note of the Draft Constitution*: "It is necessary to have a check over the executive to prevent a dictatorial tendency from abusing emergency power" (CRC [b], 1990). The leftists saw it differently. All the three left members of the CRC remarked that they were certain that the NC would form the government after the elections. This obsession also worked to generate another controversial provision. Chairman Upadhyaya said that initially there were fourteen items in the list which were later reduced to four (peace and friendship, strategic and security, boundary, and natural resources) that a treaty or agreement concluded with foreign countries must be passed by a two-thirds majority of parliament. In justification of this provision, all the three ULF members referred back to the 1950 treaty, Koshi and Gandaki hydro project agreements with India (*Kanun*, 1991: 340-358). Even the chairman was of the opinion that this provision provided a guarantee against the repeat of secret agreements like the 1965 agreement with India. After a mild debate, the report jointly prepared by Daman Dhungana (NC) and Nirmal Lama (ULF) containing the ratification by a two-thirds majority in parliament of treaties in the aforementioned four areas was passed unanimously. The ULF and the king's nominees in the CRC did not need to work hard to convince the NC representatives. By profession, all the three representatives of the NC were lawyers; and the lawyers and jurists are generally ardent advocates of limited government.

At the last moment, the CRC was forced into an impasse after inroads from outside. It obviously meant that the parties involved in the negotiation forced their representatives to review earlier agreements on some issues. In such a situation, the representatives usually lost their independence and they would change the line as instructed by their respective bosses.

A ULF member of the CRC, Madhav Nepal, said that the chairman changed his line after pressure from the palace. Chairman Upadhyaya conceded this in different language saying that he was obliged to draft the constitution so that it would be digestible to all the forces, including the king. He, therefore, urged (1) the de jure sovereignty of the king, (2) the vesting of power to the king in an extraordinary situation and (3) increasing the size and privileges of the royal family. But the NC and the ULF representatives got united to isolate the proposal of the chairman. However, Chairman Upadhyaya said that the problem was resolved in the way that he got a mandate for reconsideration on the question of the size and privileges of the royal family if the king insisted on it.

The NC sought changes on two points: the provision of amendment in the fundamentals of the constitution, and the provision of treaty ratification by a two-third majority in parliament. The king's nominees also changed their mind after they were informed that the palace was disappointed by the provision of an amendment on the fundamentals of the constitution. Consequently, against the earlier unanimous decision to make the basic features of the constitution amendable, the fundamentals of the constitution were framed as unamendable by a majority vote. But the ULF representatives refused to abide by the later decision, and they exerted counter pressure of abstaining from the CRC.

Hence, Chairman Upadhyaya said that the problem was thrown into the courts of the NC and the ULF to find an acceptable solution. Before the NC and the ULF sat together for this purpose, a meeting of the central committee of the ULF was held. An eyewitness, Padma Ratna Tuladhar, said that the ML and the Fourth Convention pleaded that, being communists, their ethic would not allow them to accept the proposal of perpetuating the monarchy and parliamentary democracy. The *Gorkhapatra* reported, "The representatives of the ULF maintained that they had no faith in multiparty democracy and constitutional monarchy but had joined the CRC as part of their strategy" (1 September 1990). The possibility of deadlock or submission of more than one draft of the constitution appeared. But neither the NC nor the ULF was prepared to bear the cost of choosing either option. This factor brought both the NC and the ULF to settle the issue through a compromise. The early understanding made in the CRC – that the decision taken on any issue was not subject to being reopened – was ascribed to the ULF for its resistance against the pressure of the NC. Consequently the provision of treaty ratification by a two-thirds majority remained intact. The NC consented to the ULF's stand to retain the provision of amending the basic nature of the constitution. The ULF also agreed to the NC's proposal to make the procedure complex on the basis of a three quarters majority vote in the legislature and a national referendum. Chairman Upadhyaya as well as all the members of the CRC were of the opinion that the CRC solved the problem in a compromise through a middle way, but also with ambiguity.[11]

Though the draft constitution was a product of compromise among the representatives of the king, the NC and the ULF, the popular spirit of change that had been manifest in the mass movement dictated even more. It transferred the sovereignty from the king to the people, and it guaranteed the fundamental and human rights of the citizen. The draft constitution granted a polity based on the democratic principles that the sovereign people choose their representatives, the party which enjoys majority in parliament forms the government and the executive is responsible to the legislature. It provided a bicameral legislature, representative government and independent judiciary.

Several limitations were imposed on the government. The draft constitution put the popular sovereignty in absolute terms as much as the absolute rights – even right to suicide – because most of the provisions of the draft revolved around two fundamental principles: constitutional monarchy and parliamentary democracy. But at the same time, the basic features of the constitution could be altered by amendments to the constitution (CRC [a], 1990).

Draft Constitution: Revision and Approval

A compromise had been made to enable the CRC to prepare a single draft, but it did not clinch the dispute among the king, the NC and the ULF on some crucial provisions of the draft constitution. It simply shifted the stage for renegotiation from the CRC to the cabinet. King Birendra openly exhorted for the revision of the draft constitution on the occasion of the CRC's formal submission of the draft to him on 1 September 1990. Even before the draft was formally submitted, the NC leaders revitalized their quest for the change in two provisions – amendments of the basic features of the constitution and treaty ratification by two-thirds majority in parliament. The stubborn determination of the NC went to the extent that Ganesh Man Singh said, "The NC troika leaders once thought of throwing out the left minister from the cabinet."[12] But they soon dismissed this idea and followed the line of persuasion. Some ULF members, particularly the ML and the Fourth Convention, demanded the immediate promulgation of the draft constitution without any changes. They took to the streets to exert pressure. But later they reluctantly consented to revise the draft constitution. The ML enlarged the volume of its discontent over provisions in the draft constitution from 6 to 29.[13] The ostensible strategy behind the bulk of their dissent was to ensure minimum change in the draft.

The change of stage and the actors on the constitution issue was favourable to the NC. In the CRC there was equal representation of the NC, the ULF and the king, but the cabinet was headed and dominated by the NC. Again, out of the three ULF representatives in the CRC two had belonged to the hard-line factions, but in the cabinet with three left ministers, two ULF minister were soft liners.

Furthermore, PM Bhattarai adroitly made a favourable position when constituting the three-minister (Keshar Jung Rayamajhi, Yog Prasad Upadhyaya and Nilambar Acharya) cabinet sub-committee for the recommendation of the final draft constitution before the cabinet. The cabinet sub-committee was constituted by equal representatives of the king, the NC and the ULF, in the manner of the composition of the CRC. The difference was that each of the parties had selected their own representatives to the CRC, while the members of the cabinet sub-committee were chosen by Bhattarai, the PM and the president of the NC. The PM selected the most moderate left minister, Nilambar Acharya, as the representative of the ULF in the cabinet sub-committee. Both he and his party – Manandhar group – took quite a soft line towards the NC.

While revising the draft constitution, the NC's prime target was the provision of amendment in the basic features of the constitution. The palace had also manifested its discontent over such a provision since the latter half of the drafting of the constitution by the CRC. There was therefore no problem from the king's nominee minister Keshar Jung Rayamajhi to revise the draft constitution in favour of making the fundamentals of the constitution unamendable. This line was also supported by the left minister Nilambar Acharya and his party. But some ULF members, particularly the ML and the Fourth Convention, were against any change in the draft constitution. During the revision of the draft constitution, the position of the ULF was weakened by differences among its own members who held a position similar to that of the NC representatives during constitution drafting in the CRC. The NC was gaining strength from the warm embrace by some ULF partners of the NC's view[14] for the revision of the draft constitution to make the fundamentals of the constitution irrevocable. The manifestation of a split among the ULF members[15] strengthened the NC's stand. Minister Acharya said that ultimately the ML itself relented to make the fundamentals of the constitution irrevocable after PM Bhattarai met and convinced its two leaders, Minister Jhala Nath Khanal and CRC member Madhav Nepal. The cabinet unanimously revised the draft constitution so that the basic features of the constitution embodied in the preamble were made unamendable.

The NC wanted to change the provision of treaty ratification by a two-third majority in parliament. But the equation was against the NC on this issue. Both the cabinet sub-committee members, Ministers Acharya and Rayamajhi said that they refused the proposal of the other member, Minister Yog Prasad Upadhyaya (NC), for the provision of ratification of all kinds of treaties by a simple majority of the Lower House. They went on to say that they had however relented to Minister Upadhyaya's proposal on two areas – peace and friendship, and natural resources – if the nature of treaty would not have an extensive, severe and enduring effect upon the country.

On the basis of the recommendations made by the cabinet sub-committee, the interim government reportedly made over 20 changes in the draft constitution prepared by the CRC (*Nepal Press Digest*, 15 October 1990). The most important changes were made in three provisions: the basic principles of the constitution embodied in the preamble were made unamendable; treaties or agreements of an ordinary nature relating to peace and friendship and natural resources were subject to ratification by a simple majority in the Lower House; and the Kingdom of Nepal was specifically identified as a 'Hindu state' (*Text of Draft Constitution* [revised and approved by the cabinet], 1990).

The revision and approval of the draft constitution by the cabinet resolved the conflict between the NC and the ULF over the constitutional provisions. But did it consider the points of the king who had suggested the revision of the draft constitution incorporating the suggestions received from various conservative elements? The king's nominee Minister

Rayamajhi said and the left Minister Acharya conceded that the cabinet had overlooked the volume of suggestions that prescribed the retention of many powers of the king – emergency, prerogative, residuary and sovereign. A negotiation between the palace and the cabinet was therefore anticipated to give the finishing touches to the constitution.

Palace's Draft Constitution.

On 11 October 1990, the cabinet submitted the constitution to the king for promulgation. But the king's intention to revise the constitution as per the suggestions of the conservative elements, which had been overlooked by the cabinet, was clearly manifest in the royal notification issued on the same day: "His Majesty would now study the draft in order to determine ... in what manner it had considered suggestions put before the cabinet for finalization" (*The Rising Nepal*, 12 October 1990).

Previously, the king's postponement of the submission of the draft constitution four times from 13 August to 10 September 1990, revealed his antipathy towards it. An intensification of erosion in the unity between the NC and the ULF[16] concurrently appeared, fortifying the palace's attempt to consolidate its position. The king pushed for the revision of the draft constitution accordingly before its formal submission. But he was convinced by the logic of the chairman of the CRC that, "any amendment or revision in the draft should be made at the political level itself" (*Gorkhapatra*, 17 September 1990). On the occasion of the CRC's submission of the draft constitution to the king on 10 September 1990, the king handed it over to the PM with the instruction that, "As demanded by constitutional organs, and political parties not represented in the commission, the prime minister should... consider the suggestions put forth by them" (*The Rising Nepal*, 11 September 1990). This was a clear direction of the king to revise the constitution in a different direction from that of the draft prepared by the CRC.

Ministers Keshar Jung Rayamajhi and Nilamber Acharya said that the cabinet received suggestions from the conservative elements – the army, the police, the heads of constitutional bodies, most of the new mushroom political parties, including both the Rashtriya Prajatantr Party (RPP) formed by former panchayat stalwarts. Both ministers said that the main content of the suggestions was to perpetuate the institution of monarchy, to retain the king's sovereignty, and to keep the king as the ultimate source of power. Minister Rayamajhi, who himself admitted that he had worked in consultation with the palace secretary, Rebati Raman Khanal, said that he fought in cabinet meetings to make the king the symbol of unity, independence as well as sovereignty of the country, and also to vest all residuary, emergency and prerogative powers in the king, but he said, and Minister Acharya conceded, that the cabinet overlooked the suggestions of the conservative elements and also ignored the view of the king's nominee, Minister Rayamajhi. But the palace did not capitulate. Rather, its activities went into high gear. On 22 October 1990, the *Gorkhapatra* reported that a copy of the constitution drafted by the palace had been submitted to the PM for consideration.

Against the constitution drafted by the CRC and approved by the cabinet which clearly mentioned 'sovereignty vested with the Nepal people', the palace draft constitution stated, 'sovereignty vested in the Nepali people, including His Majesty'. Though the phrase used relating to sovereignty was ambiguous, the following clause in the palace draft made the king sovereign. In the exercise of executive power, the constitution drafted by the CRC, ensured that the king would act according to the advice of the cabinet, using the binding phrase, "by and with the recommendation and consent of the Council of Ministers". But the palace draft put this in a different way – "with the assistance and consultation of the Council of Ministers". It meant that the king would not be bound to act only in accordance with the advice of the cabinet. Indeed, according to the palace draft, all executive, legislative and judiciary power would also emanate from the king and the residuary power would also be vested in him (*Text of the Palace's Draft Constitution*, 1990). The sole objective of the palace draft constitution was to make monarchy superior to democracy.

The king simultaneously applied multiple strategies. The palace draft was moved from the highest level – the king himself. Aware of the fact that the popular forces were afraid of the loyalty of the army to the institution of the monarchy, the military was mobilized again. Ganesh Man Singh and PM Bhattarai both said that the chief of the army and several generals met each of them separately and suggested to them that the power and position of the king should remain intact. Hoping to capitalize on the strong concern of the NC to hold the elections on schedule, Ganesh Man Singh said that the chief election commissioner had informed him at that moment that the election might be postponed for one year if the constitution could not be promulgated in time. Intending to nullify the work of the CRC and the government with the charge that they worked on negative premises[17] both RPPs demanded immediate promulgation of the constitution after the release of the palace draft.

Moreover, in order to give impetus to his move, King Birendra used the name of PM Bhattarai. The cover of the palace draft as reported mentioned that it had been prepared in consultation with the PM. "It has been circulated after continuous discussion and consultation" with the PM (*Gorkhapatra*, 23 October 1990), was the press statement issued by the palace in its defence after the PM absolved himself from this incrimination.

PM's Negotiation Style

A person, who had formerly been involved in constitution making, said that in response to his query to the PM whether the palace draft was made in consultation with him, the PM explained, "I am not a legal expert. King Birendra read this draft in my presence. I made no objection. It is up to you to say whether I consented or not." But the next morning the PM denied his involvement in the palace draft before all the three ULF representatives of the CRC. He, indeed, assured, "I would not give up my stand; I prefer to resign otherwise", as conveyed by Madhav Nepal. More interestingly, in response to the ULF leaders' request to publish the palace draft constitution, the PM said, "That is why I give it you" (Kanun, 1991:344).

The ambiguity of PM Bhattarai in showing two contrasting approaches revealed how he tackled the situation. Minister Nilamber Acharya observed that PM Bhattari, by his nature and character, avoided direct confrontation with the king. The avoidance of confrontation and his style of persuasion seemed idiosyncratic. He did not insist on his point, and even he would not directly reject the view of an opponent, but he plotted in such a way that his opponent was forced to change his mind and hence lose his stand. In his own words, the PM said, "The king thought that he could pressurize me, but I did not give in. I referred to my cabinet and the communists, saying that it was not for me to decide" (Raeper and Hoftun, 1992).

Besides, there were some things that he concealed. Minister Devendra Raj Pandey and Chairman Bishwa Nath Upadhyaya gave an insight that the PM, in the meantime, emphasized making the precedent of popular supremacy through political process – election – rather than confronting the king on constitutional issues. This epitomized a capitulative tendency of the PM in which he had always opted for shrinking away from confrontation.[18]

Yet, PM Bhattarai was amendable. He later realized his mistakes and corrected his stand accordingly. Ministers Nilamber Acharya and

Devendra Raj Pandey observed that the PM put the points he had concurred with the king at the cabinet meeting to ask the opinions of his colleagues. But it was the advantage of the coalition government that the cabinet suggested that the PM should correct and review his line, and the PM honestly followed the suggestion. Besides, there were the ULF, the NC, and the CRC, and above all, the people that backed up the PM to renegotiate with confidence. The concern shown by the Nepal Aid Group against the palace draft which the PM had supposedly put before the king gave additional strength to the PM.[19] Mukunda Regmi told an interesting story of how Ganesh Man Singh had connected on the PM Bhattarai's way of dealing with the constitution issue: "If somebody gives a death warrant to Kisunji, he will say 'okay' but he will buy time saying that he has to polish his shoes and iron his clothes. At that moment, if someone advises him against the death warrant, Kisunji has the skill to change his line in a way acceptable to the man who had brought the death warrant."

The NC and the ULF leaders denounced the palace draft constitution. The left took to the streets, but the PM prevented the NC from following this path in order to keep room for negotiations with the king open. The king also dreaded to think of prolonging an amorphous situation because the popular indignation against the palace draft had spread speedily. The palace abandoned its hope of retaining more power which had arisen with the conflict between the NC and the ULF but died when they patched up later. Its initial hope of manipulating the PM was also relinquished. But King Birendra seemed embarrassed by the volatile and unpredictable dealing of the PM. In the eyes of the king, the PM Bhattarai was unreliable. To give a finishing touch to the constitution, the king therefore met the NC's troika on October 24. Ganesh Man Singh noted that the meeting concluded with an agreement on major issues, and that some peripheral issues were under consideration (*Gorkhapatra*, 30 October 1990). PM Bhattarai affirmed that he had the mandate of the cabinet to consider some grievances of the king, keeping intact the major provision of the constitution as approved by the cabinet (*The Rising Nepal*, 23 October 1990).

The cabinet re-finalized the constitution, incorporating some of the palace's points. Accordingly, the king was vested with some powers that he could exercise on his own discretion, especially regarding the business of the royal family and the succession to the throne. The king's insistence on his role regarding the army was also reconciled. The institution of the monarchy and some of its symbols were put in perpetuity.

The cycle of negotiations on the constitution was completed in four rounds: drafting by the CRC, approval by the cabinet, revision by the palace with a different draft constitution, and re-finalization of the draft by the cabinet. Most of the provisions as drafted by the CRC were retained, but some substantial changes were made during the course of the negotiations and renegotiations.

Future Projection

On 9 November 1990, different from general expectation that the king would promulgate the constitution by reading its preamble, King Birendra appeared on Nepal Television (live broadcast) with a strained face and read a piece of paper prepared by the palace. His displeasure over the inauguration of the new democratic constitution epitomized the fact that the institution of monarchy in Nepal had never reconciled itself with democracy on its own conviction. Let alone the late King Mahendra, who had dismantled parliamentary democracy in 1960. Even the late King Tribhuvan, who was decorated as the 'father of the nation' because of his contribution to the anti-Rana revolution in 1950, laid the foundation of royal absolutism (Gupta, 1964: 85) through an amendment to the 'Interim Act 1951' in 1954. After the restoration of democracy through the mass movement in 1990, King Birendra had openly made every possible effort to retain his position as the benevolent monarch and not a constitutional figurehead. Perhaps this is the reason, why the fear of the palace persisted in the psyche of the Nepalese people.

Despite reduction the formal position of the king from absolute ruler to constitutional monarchy, the 1990 constitution equipped the monarchy with discretionary power in some areas, i.e. succession of throne and employees of the royal palaces. It indeed acknowledged the constitutional role of the palace in a crisis situation, i.e. at times the need of a dissolution of parliament, declaration of emergency, mobilization of army, etc. These constitutional loopholes might invite the palace for political manipulation when democracy suffers with instability and crisis. At the outset in the 1950s, the palace regained power as much as the popular forces became weak. The history was repeated in the 1990s, particularly since the royal takeover of October 2002 (see Chapter 8).

Some ULF members, particularly the ML, led the quest for making monarchy and parliamentary democracy alterable during the constitution making. The ML greeted only a "critical support" to the constitution and

TABLE 2:1
Contentious Issues in Negotiations: Sustained and Change

	A	*B*	*C*	*D*
Issues	*Draft of CRC*	*Approved by Cabinet*	*Palace Draft*	*Final*
Above the Preamble	-	-	*Swasti Shree...* (King as incarnation of God)	same as 'C'
National Anthem	valid till the law does not change	same as 'A'	cannot change	same as 'C'
Nepal	Hindu constitutional monarchical kingdom	Hindu, constitutional monarchical kingdom	same as 'B'	same as 'B' and 'C'
Constitution promulgated by His Majesty	on the advice and with the approval of Council of Ministers	same as 'A'	in accordance with the constitutional laws, customs, usage and tradition of Nepal	same as 'A' and 'B'
Sovereignty vested in	Nepali people	same as 'A'	Nepali people, including His Majesty	same as 'A' and 'B'
His Majesty: symbol of	Nepalese nation and unity of the people	same as 'A'	Nepalese sovereignty, national integration and unity	same as 'A' and 'B'
His Majesty	-	-	has right to consult, encourage and warn the Council of Ministers	may offer suggestions, encouragement and alert the Council of Ministers
Executive power be	vested in His Majesty and Council of Ministers that shall be exercised by and with the advice and	same as 'A'	emanated from His Majesty that shall be exercised by and with the advice and assistance of the Council of	same as 'A' and 'B'

	consent of the Council of Ministers		Ministers	
Legislature	constitutes His Majesty and by-cameral houses	same as 'A'	be emanated from His Majesty	same as 'A' and 'B'
Judicial	be exercised in accordance with the provision of this constitution	same as 'A'	be emanated from His Majesty that should be exercised according to the constitution	same as 'A' and 'B'
Residuary power	-	-	vested in the King	-
Emergency be exercised	by the King on the recommendation of the Council of Ministers	by His Majesty (on advice and consent of the Council of Ministers)	by His Majesty	same as 'B'
Army operation	on the recommendation of Defence Council	same as 'A'	on consultation of the Defence Council	same as 'A' and 'B'
Appointment of army chief	-	by the King with the recommendation of PM	by the King with consultation of DC	same as 'B'
Constitutional Committee, consisted by	PM, Chief Justice, Chairman of Upper House, Speaker, Opposition leader	same as 'A'	PM; Chief Justice, chairman of Standing Committee of Raj Parisad	same as 'A' and 'B'
Fundamentals of the constitution	can be changed through amendment	Unamendable	same as 'B'	same as 'B' and 'C'
Treaty ratification (on peace and friendship, boundary, security	by two-third majority of joint session of both Houses	same as 'A', but also by simple majority of Lower House on	same as 'B'	same as 'B' and 'C'

and natural resources)		peace and friendship and natural resources if no grave conseque-nces		
Council of Ministers transition	should be taken as constituted pursuant to this constitution	same as 'A'	King may sustain or change	same as 'A' and 'B'

underrated the parliamentary democracy as "limited democracy". But it changed its line later. The first central committee meeting held by the ML after the enactment of the new constitution, endorsed the multiparty system in its goal of New People's Democracy (ML [c], 1990). Its slow and steady moderation towards liberalization culminated in the Fifth Convention of the UML,[20] held in January-February 1993, when it passed the line of *Janatako Bahudaliya Janabad* (Multiparty People's Democracy) by an overwhelming majority. The components of liberalism in its programme of Multiparty People's Democracy is reflected in its commitment to the guarantee of human and fundamental rights of the citizen, peaceful competition among political parties, periodic elections, rule of the majority, and the rule of law (UML [a], 1993). The UML appeared as a contestant of power politics rather than a force committed to alter the present political system.

But there are radical Maoist parties, one (Fourth Convention) participated in the 1990 constitution-making process but others stayed out from it. All Maoist parties, including the Fourth Convention, took a non-conformist position vis-à-vis the 1990 constitution. The threat from the extreme left was felt since the launching of an armed insurgency in 1996 by the CPN [Maoist] (see Chapter 7).

NOTES

1. The democracy movement ran up towards a revolutionary resolution, with republican slogans at the last moment. Let alone students and professionals who openly involved themselves from the days the movement started, the government corporation employees, civil servants and people in general took to the streets from the beginning of April 1990. In Patan and Kirtipur, adjoining the capital, the people from each household, including housewives and children, took to regular marching on streets brandishing various kitchen utensils and agricultural tools. On April 6, several lakhs of people spontaneously demonstrated in Kathmandu and other parts of the country.
2. Bishnu Bahadur Manandhar, leader of the Nepal Communist Party (Manandhar), said that the ULF meeting on 8 April 1990 gave a mandate to its representatives to make compromise with the king at least on the point of announcement of the multiparty system; the leader accredited for this job was instructed to make efforts for maximum gain if possible. The Fourth Convention leader, Lila Mani Pokharel viewed radically that the ULF meeting on April 8 framed the following points for agreement: (a) to lift the ban on political parties, (b) to dissolve Panchayat Policy and Evaluation Committee, class organizations and all tiers of panchayat units, at least the NP, (c) to replace the Chand cabinet with an all-party interim government.

3. Participants in the 8 April 1990 negotiation were King Birendra, PM Lokendra Bahadur Chand, Ministers Pashupati S. Rana, Achyut Raj Regmi and Nayan Bahadur Swanr from the establishment side and Krishna Prasad Bhattarai and Girija Prasad Koirala (NC president and general secretary respectively) and Sahana Pradhan and Radha Krishna Mainali (the chairman and a member of the central committee of the ULF respectively) from the movement side.
4. Negotiations held on 15 April 1990 between the panchayat camp – represented by PM Chand, Ministers Rana and Regmi, panchas Padma Sundar Lawati and Keshar Bahadur Bista – and the movement side – represented by Yog Prasad Upadhyaya and Daman Nath Dhungana (NC), and Nilambar Acharya and Krishna Raj Verma (ULF).
5. The eight-point demand consisted of the following: (1) dissolution of the Chand government and the NP, (2) annulment of the articles and the clauses of the constitution which ran counter to the changing context of the multiparty system, (3) dissolution of panchayat units from the district to village levels, (4) nationalization of the property of panchayat units and class organizations, (5) release of all political prisoners, (6) granting honour and financial assistance to martyred families, (7) formation of a CRC having proper representatives of the NC and the ULF, and (8) impartial investigations of recent violence in the mass movement and punishment of guilty persons.
6. Ganesh Man Singh said he refused to participate in the 8 April 1990 negotiation for two reasons. First, he was abiding by his stand for 'no meeting' with the king before the announcement of the multiparty system. Second, he wanted to preserve himself as the last foil if the negotiations could not bring the desired results.
7. The soft tuning remark of Ganesh Man Singh towards the panchas after his meeting with the king on 13 April 1990, as broadcast by Nepal Television, did not coincide with the revolutionary mood of the people. This was manifest in the April 14 gathering of a crowd – mostly professionals and party workers who were just released from prison – at Ganesh Man Singh's residence where the meeting between the NC and the ULF leaders was being held inside to frame the strategies for negotiations to the next day. At that meeting, Devendra Raj Pandey said that he pleaded for perceiving the situation as poise for power transformation rather than power sharing. In sum, both the NC and the ULF leaders were pressured to present the eight-point demand as unnegotiable. As a result, the meeting decided for non-participation by senior most leaders in the negotiations of April 15.
8. Pashupati S. Rana was of the view that the panchas should not be involved in constitution- making for two reasons. First, the panchas as the defeated force could not dictate the nature and content of the constitution. Second, they solely would be blamed for any defect in the constitution.
9. The Fourth Convention showed its antipathy to monarchy and democracy by refusing to make suggestions to the CRC.
10. The Democratic Constitution of Nepal 1990, separately prepared by the ULF representatives of the CRC because of the possibility that the CRC might have been unable to make a single draft because of conflicting stands taken by the representatives of the king, the NC and the ULF on some of the substantial issues. This left-made separate draft vested the king with preventive powers.

11. One of the senior persons of the CRC said that the conflict regarding the preparation of a single draft constitution was managed applying the theory of ambiguity. The theory of ambiguity meant, he said, "Any law or constitution should not make it clear if its articles and provisions invite difficulties putting them in unambiguity. It should, therefore, be put ambiguously, because the future course of political development would interpret them according to the situation." Here are some of ambiguous clauses on major issues of draft constitution. (1) In *Analytical Not of the Draft Constitution*, the objective was stated as to consolidate constitutional monarchy and multiparty democracy. Analytical note did not define the basic features of the constitution. (2) The draft constitution mentioned the king as constitutional monarch, but the constitutional monarch here did not mean the 'rubber stamp' because it enjoyed preventive power to refuse the recommendation of the government on the subject of dissolving the parliament, and declaring emergency. (3) It put the identity of the country in these words: "Hindu Constitutional Monarchical Kingdom". It neither made Nepal a Hindu nor a secular state. (4) It provided a Defence Council consisting of five members having a majority of popular representatives. But the king was vested with the right to mobilize the army.
12. The idea of throwing out the left ministers spilled over into the NC's leaders' statement denouncing the communist stand. Insisting on the NC's determination to change the draft constitution making fundamentals of the constitution unamendable, the party general secretary Girija Prasad Koirala said, "If the ULF does not accept this stand, it must quit the Council of Ministers and take to the street." Ganesh Man Singh also spoke in the same spirit, "If they (ULF's leaders) wish to do so, we have our own path, and they too should choose their own path".
13. The ULF representatives in the CRC registered note of dissents on six broader issues. That was broken down into 29 to make them colossal by the ML. The content of both the 6 points and the 29 point of dissents cover mainly three areas: (1) reducing the size and privileges of the royal family, (2) excluding the name and sign of the king from all the active state institutions including the army, and (3) making the institution of the monarchy and its symbols changeable through constitutional means.
14. Two member groups of the ULF, Manandhar and Verma, did not recommend a provision to change the basic nature of the constitution to the CRC. Besides, Padma Ratna Tuladhar informed that in the ULF meeting on this issue, only two out of seven, the ML and the Fourth Convention, insisted on a provision that the fundamentals of the constitution should be subject to change by amendment. Krishna Raj Verma (Verma group) and Man Mohan Adhikari (Marxist) came out openly to denounce the demand for the promulgation of the draft constitution without change. Verma advocated in favour of making the basic principles of the constitution inviolate, and Adhikari said he had no objection to revising the draft this way. He highlighted the need to revise the draft so that treaties could be ratified by just a simple majority in the parliament.
15. The split among the ULF members was seen from the very beginning on diverse points. The first was perspective that three of the ULF partners – Verma, Manandhar and Amatya groups – shared a perception more in common to that of the NC than the radical wings of the ULF. In contrast to the ML and the

Fourth Convention's insistence on bringing an end to the panchayat system as agenda of dialogue on 8 April 1990, they suggested to go for talks on the point of achieving the multiparty system. These three groups, including the Marxist, acclaimed the announcement of the removal of the ban on political parties as a historic achievement. The rest of the ULF members perceived it as a lesser achievement. Nilamber Acharya disclosed that even the proposal of demanding an interim act was not at first endorsed in the ULF meeting. He viewed that the ML and the Fourth Convention had subsequently manipulated the passage of the agenda of the interim act at the moment when most of the senior leaders of his party and some other parties were outside the capital. Unlike the ML, the Marxist and the Tulsilal group, the Verma and the Manandhar groups did not recommend the CRC to make the fundamentals of the constitution amendable. The Fourth Convention and the NWPP demonstrated their disbelief in monarchy and democracy by refusing to give any suggestions to the CRC. In a great debate over whether constitutional monarchy and parliamentary democracy be made perpetuate or changeable, the communist parties were polarized. The moderate left took sides with the NC's stand on making the constitutional monarchy and parliamentary democracy unalterable. The hardliner Maoists, allied with the United National People's Movement (UNPM), backed the ML in its quest for a provision in the constitution by which monarchy and parliamentary democracy could be changed. The second factor behind the split among the ULF partners was realignment. The Fourth Convention worked to return the hardliner Maoist camp through the Unity Coordination Committee formed in June 1990, by some of the UNPM members. The Verma, the Manandhar and the Amatya groups had also worked out for their unification, possibly with the Marxist and the NWPP also. The third and the most important reason behind disintegration in the ULF was power sharing. The ULF was allocated three seats in both the interim government and the CRC, but all the seven members aspired for a chance in both or at least in one. The ULF changed its modus operandi – the decision through unanimity in favour of election for selecting its representatives in the interim government and the CRC. The Marxist and the ML secured marks in both the interim government and the CRC; the Fourth Convention for the CRC and the Manandhar group in the interim government. The Verma, the NWPP and the Amatya groups were overlooked.

16. The NC - ULF alliance had begun to erode with the revival of mutual suspicion between the NC and the radical wings of the ULF. The left regarded the NC with suspicion from the day the NC unilaterally decided to talk to the king on 8 April 1990, oblivious to the need of pre-consultation with its movement partner, the ULF. The ULF suspicion of the NC was aggravated by a conflict over the nature of transformation. The ULF opted for radical transformation of power from the king to the people through the enactment of an interim act. The NC opposed the demand for an interim act as it found the king responsive to its reconciliation overtures. The left interpreted the revival of the NC's reconciliation policy with the king as a nexus directed against the communists. The NC also did not treat the left as a viable long-term ally. It also suspected the ambiguity of the communists' position. Were they propagating for their declared objective of *naulo janbad* or working to strengthen liberal democracy? The NC-ULF conflict deepened over the issue of the constitution. The former was determined to make

constitutional monarchy and parliamentary democracy unchangeable; the radical left presented its own counter proposal; nonetheless all subsequently relented to the NC's stand. However, the possibility of regaining strength by the traditional forces, and its repercussions to the constitution, on the bedrock of total disruption in the NC-ULF alliance, forced both the NC and ULF to maintain a sort of unity throughout the constitution-making period.

17. Concurrent to the release of the palace draft constitution, the president of the RPP (Thapa group), Surya Bahadur Thapa, issued a statement on 21 October 1990: "The constitutional provisions being made on the basis of negative belief would promote a lack of confidence in the relations between the institutions of the crown, the executive, the legislature and the judiciary". By a statement "the central office of the RPP (Chand group) wondered how the undemocratic step taken in the process of framing a democratic constitution could help to consolidate democracy." It indeed harked back, "The agreement signed on 8 April 1990 between the forces of the movement and the palace must be presented before the people. According to our information, removal of the term "partyless" from the constitution and lifting of the ban on political parties were the main terms of the agreement".
18. Krishna Prasad Bhattarai constantly displayed his non-confrontationist nature from the very beginning. Anxious over the possibility of sabotage in the dialogue with the king to fulfil the demand for the multiparty system, he advised the communist leaders to hold back the new demand of dissolving NP. He condoned the announcement of the CRRC on May 11; notwithstanding that he himself had accepted that the process was wrong. When the draft constitution framed by the CRC was in the court of the cabinet for revision, he shrank away arguing, "If we add or omit one thing, the left would seek ten times, the king may add double that of the left. So whatever we have to do, it should be done in the parliament after the election." His thinking to make a precedent of popular supremacy after the elections through moving away from confronting the king over the constitution was the culminating point. However, he corrected himself in all phases throughout the transition period.
19. Finance Minister Devendra Raj Pandey said how international support was mobilized against the palace draft constitution. He said that he had received a fax in Paris, where he was on a visit to attend the meeting of Nepal Aid Group, of the *Gorkhapatra's* reporting of the palace draft. He circulated the fax with a remark that the palace was trying to sabotage the making of a democratic constitution. Each donor country of the Nepal Aid Group showed its concern against the palace draft constitution. He sent all the concerned statements to the PM through fax. He later found that PM Bhattarai had shown the fax to the king.
20. The UML was formed in January 1991 after the unification of the ML and the Marxist party.

CHAPTER 3

POLITICAL PARTIES

Brief History

Nepali political parties have entered a new phase after the success of the 1990 *Jan Andolan* (mass movement). In the past, they existed as movements. They came into being with the birth of the democratic movement, which originated in the 1930s and 1940s in opposition to the century-old Rana oligarchy (1846-1951). The history of origin of the Nepali political parties is markedly different from the history of political parties in the West, where parties evolved within the parliament as a consequence of the extension of popular suffrage (Duverger, 1964). The genesis of political party in Nepal is also different from stories of other Third World countries, where parties first appeared as part of the nationalist movement against colonial rule (Randall, 1988).

The Praja Parishad, formed in 1935, was the pioneer political party in Nepal, but it could not survive the Rana repression. The Nepali Congress (NC) Party and the Communist Party of Nepal (CPN) were founded in exile in India in 1947 and 1949 respectively. The mission of the NC, at the time of its inception, was to overthrow the oligarchic Rana regime, a goal later directed against the partyless panchayat regime. It was only in 1956, that the NC proclaimed its ideology of democratic socialism. Unlike the NC, the CPN adhered to Marxist ideology, i.e. class struggle, armed revolution, dictatorship of the proletariats etc. The NC was instrumental in launching a successful armed movement against the Rana regime in 1950-51.

In 1951 when democracy was ushered in[1], a promise was made that election to constituent assembly would be held, but this promise was never fulfilled. When parliamentary election was finally held in 1959, the NC won a two-third majority and formed a government under the leadership of B. P. Koirala. The Gorkha Parishad, created by the former Rana rulers and their cohorts, became the major opposition party in parliament. But before and after the 1959 election, the CPN was a dominant actor in oppositional politics outside parliament. Despite its participation in the political process, it took the oppositional role, politically as well as ideologically, against the parliamentary system.

The evolution of the party system was, however, cut short when King Mahendra, through a royal coup in December 1960, banned all political parties. Among the several political parties that emerged before and after the 1950-51 revolution, only two, NC and some splinter groups of the CPN, could survive in difficult days under the partyless panchayat system (1960-1990). During the authoritarian panchayat regime, political parties were forced to recast themselves in their original format, as movement organizations working in exile or underground. The NC and some communist groups had constantly shown their presence in society through exerting anti-establishment struggles, sometimes violently and at other times peacefully.[2] For a short period of one year (1979-80) from the announcement of referendum to the election of choosing one between the two, multiparty or partyless panchayat, they were legally allowed to opt for public campaigns and mass mobilization. The partyless panchayat won by a margin of ten percent votes. The NC and the communist parties failed to unite in the referendum.

The communist movements had been fragmented for long.[3] The dominant factions in the different time period was: pro-Soviet Rayamajhi group versus pro-Chinese Pushpalal group in the 1960s, between Naxalite and non-Naxalite lefts in the 1970s, and in the 1980s between one arguing for replacement of the partyless panchyat by the multiparty system at least for transition towards people's democracy and the other pleading for a direct jump to people's democracy. Realignment among the splinter communist groups to fight against the authoritarian panchayat regime in alliance with the NC surfaced with the formation of the United Left Front (ULF, consisting of seven splinter left groups) on the eve of the 1990 mass movement.

As a result of concerted efforts both the NC and the ULF jointly launched a mass movement in February-April 1990. The movement ended the three-decade-old panchayat system (1960–1990) and restored the multiparty system in the country. Subsequently a new constitution was promulgated in November 1990.

The enactment of a new Constitution – framed by the representatives of NC and ULF along with the king's nominees for the Constitution Recommendation Commission – attempted to translate the spirit of the mass movement into a legal document which would become the supreme law of the country. By this constitution, the sovereign power of the state was transferred from the palace to the people for the first time in the history of Nepal. The constitution attempted to ensure the stability of the newly established democratic regime by stating categorically that popular sovereignty, constitutional monarchy, multiparty parliamentary system, and fundamental rights of the citizen were unamendable. The avowed commitment to the fundamental principles of the new constitution by the rightist Rashtriya Prajatantra Party (RPP) – a party formed by the followers of the dismantled panchayat system – as well as by several leftist splinter groups, including the Communist Party of Nepal, Unified Marxist-Leninist (UML), irrespective of their ideological stands in the past, demonstrated the assimilation of the major ideological and political forces of the country into the mainstream of the parliamentary process.

The 1991 general elections for the 205 members of the House of Representatives (HOR) – the first parliamentary elections held after the restoration of democracy – had its own significance in introducing the democratic process based on popular mandate. The 1991 general elections created a two-party dominated system with the NC in the government and the UML as the major opposition party. This is generally considered as an ideal situation for political stability and institutionalization of democracy. The second parliamentary elections held in 1994 produced a hung parliament, bringing a reversal in the parties' position. The UML moved from the opposition to the Treasury bench as the largest party in the HOR and the NC was relegated to the opposition as the second largest party. The NC, however, regained its original position with a comfortable majority in the HOR after the third parliamentary elections 1999.

Political transition in its initial phase – demolishing of the partyless panchayat structures and setting up of democratic institutions – was smooth and the political parties won some of the credit for that task. But, the parties were soon blamed for the rapid emergence of political instability and erosion of democracy in its functional attributes.[4] The first elected majority government of the NC led by Girija Prasad Koirala collapsed earlier before the end of its prescribed five-year tenure owing to internal conflicts in the ruling party. The same reason eventually led to defeat of the NC in the 1994 mid-term elections, which produced a hung parliament. The UML, as the largest party of the parliament, formed its minority government, but it also fell from power after nine months due to internal dissension over the choice of a coalition partner. During the second parliament (November 1994- May 1999), Nepal experienced eight governments of different types. The frequent change in the government led people to believe that Nepali politics degenerated into a naked struggle for power. The problem of government instability remained as before in spite of the fact that the 1999 general elections brought a return to a two-party system. Krishna Prasad Bhattarai was compelled to resign after holding the post of Prime Minister (PM) of the NC majority government for ten months. Long before he finally resigned in July 2001, Girija P. Koirala had to face endless speculation that he would face the same fate as his predecessor. In fact, the party system in the post-1990 period was dominated by intra-party conflicts over access to power as well as by unhealthy inter-party competitions, which created a sort of political crisis, impeding the consolidation of newly achieved democracy.

This paper makes an attempt to explore party-people relations in Nepal in the post-1990 period. For conceptual clarity, I have borrowed the "linkage theory" which defines political parties "as agencies for forging links between citizens and policy makers" and suggests two general modes of linkages: through penetration in society and through reaction to public opinion (Lawson,1980). In addition, I have used the 'party transformation' approach (Kirchheimer, 1966; Panebianco, 1988) to comprehend the changing nature of party-people relations. Indeed, I have refereed India's experience of party building through party local leaders' involvement in non-political activities (Weiner, 1967; Kohli, 1991). Party-people relations are shaped by interaction of respective interest. People's involvement in party politics is generally motivated either by personal gain or by public benefit or by both. An individual seeks, in return for his/her vote, the favour of the party in order to fulfil their personal interests, i.e. money, job or other opportunities. The interest of public benefit, another motivational factor, relates to the people's adherence to the party's ideology, goal, policy and programmes, and their trust in the party's ability to deliver service to society in terms of development.The interest of the party is to maximize its votes through the distribution of collective incentives (identity, solidarity, ideology, policy and programme) to the people in general as well as selective incentives (power, status, money, job and other material rewards) to the party's clients.

This paper covers only the NC and the UML, the two dominating parties representing two different ideologies: the NC is a liberal democratic party but with a socialist trademark and the UML is a communist party but with allegiance to multiparty democracy. I examine party-people relations under four major headings: the setting of ideological goals, formulation of public policy, development related performance, and patronage distribution.

IDEOLOGICAL PLATFORM

The initial period after 1990 was a euphoric phase followed by mass enthusiasm for joining political parties. Individuals with vested interests had different considerations in joining a political party, but the choice of the party by most ordinary people was largely determined by two factors: the result of the mass movement and ideological preference. Though the mass movement was mainly an urban middle class movement, the people at large, including the rural masses, had retained the habit of Nepali society, namely'follow the victor', when choosing a political party. A large section of the people, therefore, was attracted to the Congress and the communist parties, the perceived winners of the 1990 mass movement. In choosing between them, the party's policy and performance in terms of social change and economic development was the least important factor in the formative phase of democracy, because parties and the interim coalition government (April 1990 – May 1991) were overwhelmingly preoccupied by specific political objectives, viz. constitution making and general elections, rather than by establishing socio-economic programmes. Thus, the people's emotional and sentimental attachment to broad ideological identity –to the NC as democrat and UML as communist – worked as the guiding factor in their choice of the party.

Nepali Congress

The NC is closely associated with the main achievement of the 1990 mass movement: the restoration of multiparty democracy. Because of its long struggle, since its inception, for the parliamentary system and constitutional monarchy, the NC has long been considered as the main protagonist of democracy in Nepal. Thus, the party was ideologically in

TABLE 3:1
Ideological Platform of NC and UML

Contents of Ideology	*NC*	*UML*
Party, representative of	People of all classes and castes	Proletariat and working class
Nepali state, at present	Poor and developing country	Semi-feudal and semi-colonial
Goal	Democratic socialism	Communism
Political system	Parliamentary democracy	People's multiparty democracy
Economic system	Mixed but open economy	Mixed but protective economy
Monarchy	Constitutional monarchy	Republic
Religion:	Freedom of religion	Secular state
Language	Nepali as national/official language	Equal status for all languages
Main slogan	Peace, stability and development	Food, clothes and shelter for all

Source: NC (1991[b]), UML (1993[a])

an advantageous position against the UML's non-conformist stand on the parliamentary system in the initial phase of democracy. As was suggested by NC propaganda during the 1991 parliamentary elections: "Vote for RPP: vote for partyless system; vote for communist: vote for one party dictatorship; vote for NC: vote for democracy" (IIDS, 1993).

When defining the party's ideology of democratic socialism, almost all Congress leaders and workers referred to what the late B.P. Koirala said and did. Some policy measures taken against the feudal landlords, i.e. the abolition of *birta, jagirdari, jamindari and raja rajouta* forms of land tenure by B.P. Koirala's NC government in 1959-60 were used to project the NC as a bona fide socialist party. B.P. Koirala equated socialism with mixed economy, different both from the Western capitalist system as well as from a communist state-controlled and centralized economy (Koirala, 1979). He encapsulated the party's socialist goals in the slogans "rural development" and "upliftment of the poor". In order to convince people that the NC's socialist ideology is for the cause of the poor, the NC leaders and workers frequently quoted a famous conversation that B.P. Koirala had with the late King Mahendra,

> Each and every Nepalese family should at least have a house like mine; like me they should have plenty of food to eat; their children should go to school like my children; and when sick, they should be able to get medical treatment, and further, let them have cows and buffaloes in their courtyards (Koirala, 1979).

The NC's socialist image was exclusively personalized with the image of B.P. Koirala to the extent that most of the party leaders and workers were found to be unaware of how the authors of the party's election manifesto had defined democratic socialism in terms of a "mixed economy", "equitable distribution of national product", "participation of labour in production management", "equal dignity and rights to all the people", "government's service to the oppressed and poor people", and "social security for the old, disabled and helpless people" (NC [b], 1991). Without the symbolic figure of B.P. Koirala the NC appeared ideologically an orphan so far as the party's vision about its proclaimed goal of democratic socialism was concerned. Owing to lack of clarity in thought and vision on its avowed goal of democratic socialism, the NC was unable to give any radical policy and programme for the development of the country.

On the political front too, the NC seemed heading away from the centre to the right. Though the objective of the mass movement was not for a republic, it was a fight against the king for the transfer of sovereignty to the people. The palace was, therefore, generally perceived to be hostile to the spirit of the mass movement. The NC had revived and reaffirmed its policy of reconciliation with the king. Its reconciliatory stance appeared the moment the ban on the political party was lifted in a remark of party President Krishna Prasad Bhattarai "His Majesty is a very gentle person. His liberal disposition and his love for his people is truly deep. That is why he accepted our request for the multiparty system" (*The Rising Nepal*, 9 April 1990). The popular sentiment immediately following the mass movement was against the NC's reconciliation with the king.

The change of political regime through a mass uprising naturally raised the people's aspirations for change in other areas as well. The advent of democracy in Nepal raised in its wake the voices of different groups of people who had hitherto been silent. The demands of the minority and disadvantaged sections of the society became increasingly apparent soon after the restoration of democracy. But the NC supported the retention of Nepali as the national and official language. Its principle of "freedom of religion" was reduced into an affirmation that Nepal should continue as a "Hindu state".

Though the NC made an outstanding contribution to the transformation of the political structure towards parliamentary democracy and constitutional monarchy, at the same time it resisted pressures for radical change, preferring to retain some of the old symbols and traditional structures. It is, therefore, generally considered to be a liberal and centrist party, but oriented towards the right in the political spectrum of the country. This ideological identity has both advantage and disadvantage in mobilizing public support.

Communist Party of Nepal (UML)

The UML officially designated Nepal as a "semi-feudal and semi-colonial" state. Its declared objective is "to abolish feudalism, comprador, bureaucratic capitalism and imperialism." With adherence to Marxism and Leninism as the guiding principle of the party, the UML identifies itself as the "representative of the proletarian and working class." Nationalist capitalists, middle class, intellectuals, etc. are its allies (UML [a], 1991).

The UML stands on the left of the political spectrum of the country. In the Nepali understanding, this means to advocate radical change and greater equality among the people. The party appeared broadly successful in symbolizing itself "as a party of new ideas" (POLSAN, 1991:14) espousing "rapid and radical change", and also in projecting its image as a champion for the cause of the poor and the disadvantaged sections of the society.

The projection of Nepali communists as "radical, nationalist and pro-poor" is nothing new. Such credentials had long been established since the foundation of the CPN in 1949. The UML, the most dominant among several splinter communist groups, acquired a new identity as a supporter of the multiparty system. It actively participated in the 1990 mass movement and spoke out for the consolidation of its achievement. Despite the party maintaining its communist identity, the UML, immediately after the promulgation of the constitution, took a decision to endorse the system of multiparty competition as the means to achieve its goal of *Naulo Janbad*(New People's Democracy). It tried to convince the people that the ideology of communism and multiparty system – generally conceived as two antagonistic principles – could become complementary and supplementary. Its communist trademark remained valuable in attracting the majority of the poverty-stricken people of Nepal, particularly in the early days after 1990 when the national psyche was yearning for rapid and revolutionary change.

The transition to democracy in Nepal ended with the logical conclusion: the restructuring of the polity on the basis of constitutional monarchy and a parliamentary system. But mere change of political regime, though concrete and substantial, did not satisfy the people at large. The popular feeling that political reform on its own was inadequate came to the surface in different ways. The interim period was featured by mob manhandling some *Mandale* (notorious henchmen of the panchayat regime); there were squatters' movements which forcibly took over public places; ethnic activists demanded a secular state and for equal status for all languages; industrial workers and government and corporation's employees went on strike and demonstrated for increase in their salaries and other facilities. All segments of society demanded a better situation and some quick benefits after the demise of the panchayat system (Hoftun et al., 1999).

The UML fuelled the people's resentment arising from their frustration at the slow pace of change. It tried to give an impression that whatever had been achieved during and after the mass movement was less than it wished for. The UML also instigated movements to radicalize social needs and interests. It projected itself as a quick provider of "bread for hunger, jobs for unemployed, land for landless, and shelter for homeless". The party machinery, local leaders/workers, and the party-run news media in particular, actively sought the confiscation of land from landlords and redistribution so there would be "four *bighas* per family". Such populist slogans and propaganda raised the hopes of the poor and the disadvantaged sections of the society. The UML tried to combine the class interest of the poor with the ethnic interest of the minorities while generally radicalizing both people and society.

POLICY PLATFORM

Nepali Congress

Though the ideological factor predominated in the people's choice of party in the initial phase of democracy, the NC and the UML provided separate policy platforms in order to sustain and expand their support base in the society. Since the 1991 parliamentary elections, they brought out their policy platforms related to social change and economic development to win the support of a larger number of people. The NC's policy position on several areas of development, i.e. agriculture, industry, social security, foreign policy, etc. were spelled out in its documents, i.e. speeches, statements, resolutions, etc. But the key points included in its election manifestos (provided in the first, second and third parliamentary elections) and in the Congress government's first annual policy (presented to the parliament) had been primarily considered to map out its policy position on the overall development of the country. The highlights of NC's policies and programmes are presented in the table below 3.2.

An overview of the NC's policies embodied in its election manifestos suggested that the party covered wide areas of development, including the protection and promotion of newly established democracy through free elections, impartial administration, independent judiciary and decentralization. Rural development was its priority and the party, therefore, proposed to invest 70 percent of the available resources in this area. In the agricultural sector, unlike its own policy in the 1950s and unlike the communists' ongoing propaganda on redistribution of land, the NC's proposed land policy appeared growth-oriented: it focused on providing irrigation and other facilities. The end of dual ownership of land remained as one of the targeted goals of the Congress government, but the protection of the rights of the tiller (mentioned in the 1991 election manifesto) was missing in its government's annual policy statement when in government as well as from the party's 1994 and 1999 election

TABLE 3:2
NC's Policy Commitments

Areas	*Election Manifestos, 1991, 1994 and 1999*	*Government's Annual Policy*
Democratization	— Protection / promotion of democracy — Free and impartial elections, impartial administration, independent judiciary, decentralization — Political stability**	— Protection and promotion of democracy — Decentralization
Agriculture Development	— Provide rights to tiller (x) — End of dual ownership in land — Expansion of irrigation — Establish fertilizer industry (x) — Provide all facilities to farmers — Agriculture revolution**	— End of dual ownership in land — Irrigation to 38,000 hectares of land — Establish fertilizer industry (x) — One window system in providing facilities for farmers
Industrial Development	— Emphasis on small-scale, agro-based, labour-intensive and cottage industries — Industrialization**	— Emphasis for small scale, agro-based, labour-intensive and cottage industries
Infrastructure Building	— Link road to all 75 districts — Postal service to each village, and expansion of telephone services — Rural electrification	— Road to districts having link with highway — Postal service to each village — Rural electrification
Privatization Liberalization	— Encourage private sector mainly in industry, commerce, tourism, hydroel-ectricity, tele-communication (+) — Encourage and protection to joint venture and foreign investment — Liberal economy and privatization**	— More emphasis on private sector, joint venture and foreign investment — Small hydroelectricity through private sector — Hand over of unwanted public owned industries into private sector
Social Service and Welfare	— Pure drinking water to all — Free education up to secondary level — Radical change in education**	— Provide pure drinking water — Free education up to secondary level — Primary health service to all

	— Health care in each village — Price control — Free legal service to poor — Abolition of bonded labour system — Distribution of land to squatters	— Price control — Special programme for women, children, disabled and the people of remote areas — Distribution of land to squatters
Minority and Backward Communities	— Primary education in mother language, consideration of minority language in state-run electronic media — Special consideration for ethnic groups and backward communities (+) — Special concession for women in education, health and employment, increase women's participation in politics and in decision-making (+) — Women's equal right to parental property**	
External Relations world peace	— Based on principles of democracy, human rights and world peace — Greater friendly relations with both neighbours, India and China — Foreign assistance in accordance with national priority	— Based on principles of democracy, human rights and world peace — Greater friendly relations with both neighbours, India and China — Foreign assistance in accordance with national priority
Others	— 70% national investment for rural development (x) — Human Development (+) — Employment and poverty alleviation (+)	— More national investment in rural areas

Key: + added in 1994; ** added in 1999; (X) omitted either from the 1994 or from the 1999 election manifesto or from both.

manifestos. The party gave emphasis on agro-based and labour-intensive small and cottage industries in conformity with B.P. Koirala's thought. The same words, if not in spirit, were copied in the Congress government's annual policy paper. The NC's election manifestos and its government's annual policy promised to provide relief for the people from price rise and assured a number of social welfare programmes to the disadvantaged sections of society. Distribution of land to squatters was a top priority. But the party withheld its earlier promise to end the bonded labour system. In foreign affairs, the NC and its government kept its stand on the principles of "democracy, human rights and world peace", and improving friendly relations with its neighbours, India and China.

On minority problems, the NC promised to grant citizenship certificate on the basis of enrolment in voter lists of the 1980 referendum, in order to appeal to the Madheshi communities of the Tarai belt. Besides, it undertook to consider enabling the use of minority languages in primary schools and in the government-run media to some extent. Its promise to grant concessions to women in the fields of education, health and employment was upgraded later to include endorsing the need for greater female participation in politics, administration and in the decision-making process. The party committed itself to equal inheritance rights for women in its 1999 election manifesto. But none of these commitments found a place in the Congress government's annual policy paper, though the issues related to citizenship and minority language were implemented. The NC had only a few policy commitments relating to the interest of minorities and backward communities. An observer, therefore, rightly remarks, "A noticeable shortcoming of the (NC's) manifesto was that it failed to highlight the issues related to regional disparities and ethnic problems" (Upreti, 1993).

The NC's approach to development underwent some change. Instead of rural development, the NC election manifestos of 1994 and 1999 adopted the concept of human development as its central thrust. Emphasis was given to employment, poverty alleviation, and harnessing of hydro-electricity. A distinct change appeared in its privatization policy. Previously, the NC election manifesto in 1991 simply considered the role of the private sector under the purview of its mixed economic policy. After the party assumed power the Congress government adopted the policy of privatization and liberalization with great enthusiasm on the grounds that it was imperative to integrate Nepali economy into the global wave of market competition (MF: 1992; NPC, 1992). The Congress Party endorsed the government's new economic policy stating the need of "redefining of socialism to make economic policy of the NC dynamic" (NC [b], 1992). The Congress government wanted more investment to come from the private sector, from joint ventures, and from foreign investments, and it wanted the areas of such investments expanded from industry, commerce,and tourism to hydroelectricity, telecommunication, education, health, etc. Government-owned industries and enterprises which were running in deficit were to be transferred to the private sector. The Congress government's policy of privatization and liberalization was followed in both the 1994 and 1999 election manifestos.

Communist Party of Nepal (UML)

In its 1991 election manifesto, the UML made a number of policy commitments for restructuring Nepali society, economy and politics. The issues of infrastructure building and social services dominated in the UML's election campaigns, just as they did those of the NC. However, the UML gave more emphasis to land reform aimed to ending feudal land ownership by reducing the current ceiling on land holding, ending dual ownership of land, and safeguarding the rights of the tiller. This was continued in its manifesto of the 1994 and 1999 elections. Another issue the UML emphasized in all three parliamentary elections was that of the minority and disadvantaged sections of the society. The proposal for reservations for the backward communities and another to make the Upper House of the parliament an assembly of ethnic minorities and disadvantaged groups were unique to the UML's election manifestos. The UML's policy commitment to bring about a fundamental change in its relations with India through the abrogation of the 1950 treaty was designed to attract the masses. Its policy on social security and welfare included measures such as the abolition of untouchability, distribution of ration cards etc. In the industrial sector, the UML, like the NC, stressed the need for the establishment and expansion of agriculture and forest-based and labour-intensive small and cottage industries. Indeed it characterized its industrial policy as aiming to bringing about "a self-sufficient nationalist economy" – in apparent disregard of its simultaneously expressed policy on privatization. A summary of the UML's policy commitments is given in the table below 3.3.

Though the contents of the UML's policy platform in the areas of land reform, industrial development, infrastructure building, social security and minority groups were retained in its 1994 and 1999 election manifestos,

TABLE 3:3
UML's Policy Commitments

Areas	*Election Manifestos, 1991, 1994 and 1999*	*Government's Annual Policy*
Democratization	— Commitment but amendment in Constitution — Distribution of voter identity card (+) — Delete title of His Majesty before government — Total restructure in administration (x) — Independent judiciary, decentralization — Political stability and good governance**	— Consolidation of multiparty democracy
Agriculture Development	— End of feudal land ownership, land ceiling, land to the tiller, protection of rights of tiller, and end of dual ownership in land — Expansion of irrigation, provide all facilities for farmers	— End of dual ownership in land and land reform
Industrial Development	— Self-sufficient economy — Classification of industry on the basis of ownership: public, private and foreign investment — Emphasis for small-scale, agro and forest-based, labour-intensive and cottage industries — Facilities through one window policy	— Development of all kinds of industries — Single-door system for facility in industrial sector — Expansion of tourism industry
Infrastructure Building	— Road facility to all 75 districts — Expansion of telephone services — Rural electrification	— Link–road to district headquarters — Rural electrification
Privatization Liberalization	— Expansion of private sector(+) — Selective privatization and liberalization in areas, i.e. trade, commerce, industry, tourism and urban development (+)	— Follow policy of privatization — Encourage private sector and foreign investment in industries based on indigenous raw materials, export promotion, import substitution, water power project — Transfer of unwanted public-owned industries into private sector, priority to national investors

Social Security and Welfare	— Pure drinking water to all — Free education up to secondary level — Expansion of health facilities — Price control — Distribution of ration card — Abolition of bonded labour system — Distribution of land to squatters — Special programmes for women, children, old, disabled and backward communities — Abolition of untouchablity	— Free education up to secondary level — Expansion of health services to VDC level — Price control — Abolition of bonded labour system — Distribution of land to squatters — Programmes for children, old and disabled
Minority and Backward Communities	— End of constitutional provision retaining discrimination on the basis of caste, language and religion — Make Upper House an assembly of ethnic and disadvantaged groups — Reservation for the people of backward communities/ areas in education, health and employment — Primary education in mother language — Gender equality — Equal property rights to women (x)	— Uplift womenfolk
External Relations	— No ideology in foreign policy (+) — Equal relations with both neighbours, India and China — Repeal unequal treaty with India — Foreign assistance in accordance with national priority	— Close relations with both neighbours, India and China — Solution to Bhutanese refugee problem — Build Your Village Yourself campaign
Others	— Rural development — Balanced regional development — Employment and poverty alleviation**	

Key: + added in 1994; ** added in 1999; (X) omitted either from the 1994 or from the 1999 election manifesto or from both some new dimensions appeared which indicated a shift in its policies and its election agendas. Its previously stated republicanism and its slogan for restructuring the administration were now omitted. Its call for amendment to the constitution was reduced to one point, directed against the state protection for the Hindu religion and the Nepali language. Support for privatization – though in selective areas only, i.e. trade, commerce, finance, industry, tourism and urban development – was a new development for the UML, allegedly adopted to satisfy Western donor countries. The party stated categorically that there would be "no ideology in formulation of foreign policy". Its high pitched demand for the abrogation of the 1950 Treaty with India was toned down to a need for review and modification of the treaty.

Interestingly, the UML government's annual policy paper appeared to be a rather conservative document. The contents under the index of social security, infrastructure building and industrial policy embodied in its election manifestos were translated into its government's annual policy paper. However, its promised land reform was confined to a programme to end dual land ownership and its several policy incentives, made through its election manifestos, to the minority and disadvantaged groups was completely forgotten, except a phrase "uplift the womenfolk", in its government's annual policy paper.

On economic policy too, the UML government's annual policy paper took the line of liberal market economy pledging greater investment by the private sector, joint venture and foreign investment and pledging to continue the transfer of sick public enterprises to the private sector. But in practice, the policy of liberal market economy and privatization was frozen during the UML government. If the UML government's annual policy was taken as guidelines one could conclude that it had espoused a conservative, reformist, and liberal economic policy. PM Man Mohan Adhikari, in an interview with a correspondent of *Newsweek*, pledged to "take cautious steps, with a minimum reform, a minimum change....Our economic and political programme is adjusted to the present reality" (*Newsweek*, 28 November 1994).

Both the UML and the NC were similar in essence and substance so far as their policies relating to land reform, social service, minority problems, infrastructure building, and industrial development were concerned. Differences between them were much more noticeable in their different ways and styles of communicating. This led to alternative policy platforms in some areas. The NC put more stress on peace, stability and democracy, whereas the UML campaigned for rapid, radical and revolutionary change. The NC's proposed land reform gave more emphasis to the growth of agriculture production, whereas the UML stood for redistribution of land. The NC supported privatization; the UML was against it. The NC was less sensitive to the minority problems, whereas the UML, at least in its rhetoric, appeared more sympathetic to the ethnic demands. The NC was in favour for the continuing and consolidating close relations with India, whereas UML advocated change through reviewing the 1950 treaty. The NC wished for bilateral cooperation with India to harness the hydro-electricity potential of Nepal but the UML emphasized multilateral cooperation in this sector. The NC made area/sector (i.e. rural, agricultural, electricity) the thrust of its development approach, whereas the UML made the class and community (i.e. poor, peasant, minorities, backward, etc.) the target for development.

PERFORMANCE

Nepali Congress

G.P. Koirala, in his capacity as the first elected PM after the restoration of democracy, envisaged building a "new Nepal" by eradicating aberrations left behind by the past regimes, by bringing political stability and sustainable economic development, and by providing immediate economic relief and essential needs to the people. But when he left from power after three and a half years in the government, many things had not changed at all; in other fields better in some sectors but worse in others. The table below 3.4 provides an evaluation by the Congress government itself on its performance.

The table showed poor performance of the Congress government, except in areas of infrastructure building and social service. It had credit for providing one or more of these facilities – drinking water, health, schools, post offices, roads/bridges, electricity and telephones – to the people at the grass-roots level. The expansion of infrastructure facilities the lifestyle of the people but it does not necessarily raise the living standard of the poor. The people need an ever increasing income to pay for the ever-increasing charge of public utilities, i.e. drinking water, electricity, telephones, transportation, etc. The income of the people at the mass level largely depends on the economic growth of the country and equitable distribution of the fruits of development.

TABLE 3:4
NC Government's Performance

Areas	*Self-assessment of NC's Government (May 1992-November 1994)*
Democratization	— Institutionalization of democracy at local level through local elections 1992 — Granting more power and authority to local elected bodies
Agriculture Development	— Drafting of a bill related to land ceiling and end of dual ownership in land — Irrigation facility to 93,737 ha. Land
Industrial Development	— Formulation of new industrial policy and foreign investment policy
Infrastructure Building	— Construction of 2197 km. roads — Postal office in all VDCs — Telephone facilities provided to 1,42,000 lines — Hydro-electricity produced 2,350 kw.
Privatization Liberalization	— Commitment to invest Rs. 40 bn. in joint ventures — Transfer of several public industries/corporations to the private sector
Social Service and Welfare	— Free education up to grade 8 — Provide drinking water to 1,65,600 population — Establishment of healthcare centres in 1,300 VDCs — Land provided to 15,000 squatters
Minority and Backward Communities	— Constituting Language Recommendation Committee — Eight major languages got a place in the public electronic media — Scholarships for 41, 000 girl students — Appointment of 1,400 female teachers
External Relation	— Additional trade facilities from India
Others	— Economic growth rate 5%

Sources: NC (1994 [c]).

The NC government claimed the growth of the national economy by 5 percent during its tenure. For the benefit of the larger number of population, the growth in the agriculture sector is very important since the livelihood of more than 80 percent of the population depends on agriculture. But the production of principal food crops, cash crops and others increased only marginally, leading to constant decline of exports and increase in imports of food items during the Congress government

(MF, 1995). Another question relating to land reform was distributive justice. The NC showed some concern over this issue but it largely appeared insensitive in this matter. Its ideological commitment to democratic socialism, which stressed justice and equitable distribution of resources, was diluted by the Congress government's priority to liberalization and privatization policies.

In this context the Congress government brought out a number of policy measures, especially in areas of trade, commerce, industry and joint ventures. Consequently the number of industries increased and the capital flow committed was Rs. 40 billion in joint ventures. In addition to the sale of some sick public enterprises to the private sector, the effect of the liberal economic policy could be seen in an unprecedented growth of financial institutions and commercial banks. But most of them were confined to urban areas and had minimal impact in the rural and agricultural sectors where the overwhelming population of Nepal is to be found. The question that has to be asked is: who benefited from the growth of the national economy as the result of privatization and liberalization policy. The immediate cost of the Congress government's liberal economic policy was high for the people. Privatization, increase in charges of public utilities, and withdrawal of the subsidy system are some of the major conditionalities tied to the post-Cold War foreign aid/loan flows from donor countries. The Congress government totally failed to resist the flat conditionalities of the donors. Against the government's promise to provide economic relief to the people, the prices of public utilities, i.e. drinking water, electricity, telephone, petroleum products, fertilizers, etc. increased sharply. Besides, the ever increasing price rise in food-grains, consumer items and other essential commodities made the day-to- day life of the people harder. In essence, the Congress government largely failed to link the growth of the national economy with the basic needs of the people.

Communist Party of Nepal (UML)

The UML succeeded the NC and formed a minority government after the November 1994 general elections, which lasted for 9 months till early September 1995. The economic condition of the country and the people largely stagnated despite the change in actors and some changes in the approach to development.

By reintroducing the subsidy system the UML government controlled price rise, even if they could not reduce them. The government was credited for stabilizing prices of essential goods and consumer items. Besides, the

TABLE 3:5
UML Government's Performance

Areas		*Self-assessment of CPN-UML's Government (November 1994-September 1995)*
Democratization		Consolidation of democracy
Agricultural Development	—	Constitution of Land Reform Commission
Industrial Development	—	15% industrial growth
Infrastructure Building	—	Construction of 100 km. motorable roads
Privatization/Liberalization		
Social Security and Welfare	— —	Providing free education up to grade 10, Land distribution to 58,000 squatters, Pension for old, widow and disabled
Minority Communities		
External Relation	— —	Initiating package deal on Mahakali river Proposed to review of the 1950 treaty with India
Others	—	Implementing Build Your Village Yourself programme

Sources: UML (1999).

UML government launched a populist programme, Build Your Village Yourself (BYVY), under which each Village Development Committee (VDC) was entitled to receive a direct grant of Rs.300,000 from the central government. The UML government also initiated some social service/ welfare programmes, including a grant of Rs. 100 per month to senior citizens and distribution of land to 58,000 squatters. The UML government was criticized for its populist economy focusing on the distribution of limited resources of the country rather than growth of the economy. In the fiscal year of 1994/95 (7 out of the total 9 months tenure of the UML government was during this fiscal year) agriculture production declined; import of food-grains increased; and foreign aid also decreased to 7,542 million from 12,877 million in the preceding fiscal year (MF, 1995). The registration of joint venture industries declined from 38 in the previous fiscal year to just 18 in 1994-95 (CNAS, 1996). The real estate business and share market went down sharply, suggesting economic stagnation and regression. This suggested that the UML government deliberately ignored the long-term economic interest of the country when taking up distribution-oriented programmes.

In fact both the NC and the UML were engaged either in in-fighting within their respective parties and or inter-party confrontations on emotional and sentimental issues. As a consequence, the two major parties gave most of their time to unproductive issues of intra-party and inter-party conflicts. They could neither forward their own agenda nor could they properly address the problems of the people. It is suggested that both the NC and the UML were moving closer to becoming a part of state rather than consolidating themselves as 'people's organization'. As they were aware of their failure to deliver "public goods" to the people, both the NC and the UML seemed to be preoccupied with the alternative methods of party building through granting "selective incentives" to their own party clients.

PATRONAGE DISTRIBUTION

One of the ways the NC and the UML tried to sustain and expand their own support base was through the distribution of patronage. This is a system of establishing links through rewards to the party clients for a variety of services – donations, mobilization of voters, and others – to the party. The mass is generally excluded from such benefits since political parties, by their patronage functions, seek loyalty of the affluent sections of society who will thereby mobilize public support in their turn. This is, therefore, like a market-exchange system – "vote for favour" and "favour for vote" – between the power-brokers and the party. The power-brokers may be varied – relatives and friends of party leaders, party workers, intellectuals, local notables and other affluent sections of society who wish to use the party as an instrument to achieve their own personal interests.

One of the main reasons for the emergence of the NC and the UML as patronizing parties was that most of the rank and file leaders have tended to seek power, position and privileges as a deserved payoff for their struggle and sacrifice in the past. A number of other factors have pushed the parties in the same direction, e.g. the erosion of ideology and leadership quality, in-party factional competition for organizational control, increasing election expenditure, candidates' promise to fulfil particular individual interest of voters, and so on. All these contributed to make both the NC and the UML as patronizing parties. The more the party is oriented towards patronage distribution functions the less is the party's commitment to its ideological and policy goals. Of course, favour for party clients is a *sine qua non* irrespective of the party's ability to attract the mass through its ideology, policy and performance, but as the party's dependency on patronage distribution increases so its capacity to distribute collective incentives decreases.

Nepali Congress

The appeal of the NC as the protagonist of democracy, which was strong immediately after the 1990 political change, lessened over time for two reasons: the poor performance of the Congress government, and the change of its immediate rival (UML)'s ideology in favour of the multiparty system. Along with the poor performance of the Congress Party and its government, internal power conflicts among its troika leaders – Ganesh Man Singh, Krishna Prasad Bhattarai and Girija Prasad Koirala – led to considerable erosion of their popularity, because it made them appear selfish and power-hungry in contrast to their earlier image as men of principle. Thus the personalities of the Congress troika leaders, which had been used as assets by almost all Congress candidates in attracting the voters in the 1991 parliamentary elections, figured low in the party's campaign strategy in the 1994 and 1999 general elections. So the NC's capacity to attract the mass through its ideology and leadership personality decreased. Consequently the Congress's dependency increased in another way of party building, i.e. patronage.

Patronage is guided by the personal interest of power holders to consolidate their influence in their own electoral constituency. Realizing what they needed to do in order to be re-elected next time, Congress parliamentarians and ministers did strive more to provide services to the power-brokers in their own electoral constituency. Since the NC is a mass-based party, party activists were not sole beneficiaries of patronage by the Congress government. Others who were relatives, friends or had personal connections with the Congress leaders, benefited more in grabbing opportunities from the state and the government. Each of the Congress leaders, MPs and ministers had records of providing jobs and other favours to several hundred persons during the three-and-a-half year rule of the Congress government. Soon after the NC formed the government, party workers from all over the country flowed to Kathmandu seeking personal benefits and recommendations for jobs and other services to their relatives and friends. Inter-personal relations between ministers and party leaders were largely dominated by a tendency of the party leaders to insist on using government resources for their personal and political interests and more so in distribution of patronage, i.e. for appointments, transfers, and promotions, and for granting contracts to persons they wished to favour. Despite this, the party was defeated in the 1994 mid-term elections. This suggested two things. First, political awareness among the Nepali people has been increasing, and so, the influence of power-brokers among the voters is declining. Second, the "selective incentive" which a political party provides through patronage distribution cannot be a substitution of "collective incentive", i.e. the mobilization of public support through ideology, policy, leadership, and performance.

Communist Party of Nepal (UML)

The replacement of the Congress rule by the UML's minority government brought in its wake massive changes in executive posts at all levels not only in the bureaucracy but also in other public institutions, i.e. corporations, hospitals, educational institutions, etc. Since the UML is a cadre-based mass party practising a strong levy system, the pressure for party-run clienteles was very strong. The UML tried to institutionalize the government's patronage distribution functions. It tended to use the party as an active and powerful state organization through party-run clienteles under the purview of the party's State Affairs Department. The logic behind the formation of the State Affairs Department at both central and district levels was to prepare a profile of civil servants and to control the appointment, transfer and promotion in the bureaucracy and corporations from the lowest to the highest posts. Recommendations from the party channel, at least from the party District Committee, became mandatory in taking decisions regarding recruitment, transfer and promotion in government service.

Thus, once the UML got to power, it bluntly manipulated the state resources for patronage purposes. The formation of the Commission for Landless at the central and local levels was another lucrative avenue for party clients. The UML government distributed land to 58,000 squatters within a short span of time acting along the party's recommendations. The transformation of party loyalists to the posts of Local Development Officer with the power of dispensing funds allocated to the BYVY programme and the provision of an all-party committee at VDC level to spend such funds was one of the several instances which suggested that the UML government even used the development resources in this way. The overall impact of the UML's manipulation of state resources and distribution of patronage exclusively to party clients had not yet come out clearly. But the party claimed that it was able to recruit 10,000 new members during the time of the UML government (UML, 1996). Its rank and file leaders, however, felt selfishness, opportunism, and individualism increased among party leaders and workers, that would be a negative impact on the UML's capacity to distribute collective incentives to the people in general.

Concluding Observation

Following the restoration of the multiparty system in 1990, Nepali political parties have stepped into a new phase of party building. Of the several factors contributing to political parties in gaining public support, their image as 'a change agent' is a vital one. Political parties in Nepal were founded in order to accomplish certain envisaged changes in the social, economic and political affairs of the country. Through their long struggle and sacrifice, both the NC and the UML have already established their separate credentials as 'democrat' and 'progressive' forces respectively. Their broad ideological identity, together with their catalytic roles in the 1990 mass movement and in making the 1990 Constitution, further helped to establish their credentials as change agents. But in the aftermath of the 1990 mass movement, political parties have suffered from several problems. The main weaknesses and shortcomings faced by the NC and the UML in the post-1990 period can be summed up in the following points.

1. The support base of the NC and the UML, built on the basis of their broad ideological identity in the early phase of democracy, is eroding over time. Since ideology and policy contents are missing in their efforts at party building, both increasingly rely on other sources of vote maximization, i.e. money, power and patronage.
2. The more a party depends on money, power and patronage, the less would be the party's capacity to mobilize the mass of the people. Since political parties, by their patronage function, seek loyalty of the affluent sections of society for the mobilization of public support, the ordinary people are excluded from benefits. This, in turn, leads to narrowing down of the political space making it an exclusive domain of power holders and power brokers only.
3. Most rank and file leaders of both the NC and the UML are obsessed by their belief that they can maximize votes through the distribution of patronage rather than contributing to development activities.

4. Both the NC and the UML lack a clear vision, perspective, policy, plan and programmes for national development.
5. Parties are increasingly becoming an instrument for self-aggrandizement of the power elites and the vested interest groups. This has a negative impact on the parties' advocacy of collective interest of the society. Nepali political parties have miserably failed in their basic duty of linking citizens' preference with public policy.

Beset by these problems, the NC and the UML seem headed towards a reverse course as protectors of the status quo rather than instruments of change. Their existence among the people and in the society at the grass roots level is mainly confined to physical presence not in functional activity. So the mainstream parties themselves are creating a vacuum, ideologically and politically, in society.

The main political parties of Nepal remain the principal institutions that link the people and the government because of the lack of other effective intermediatory organizations between the state and society. One can anticipate a healthy party-people relations if they take up appropriate reforms and adopt innovative measures. First of all, they have to assess the ground reality of the party in the changed context and situation. In modern competitive politics, the conduct of party affairs has become more and more an art of management directed towards addressing socio-economic and other problems of the society with special emphasis on the formulation and implementation of realistic policies and effective plans and programmes for development. The changing time and situation demand that each party should advance with new perspectives, new vision, new outlook, and setting new objectives. The formulation of realistic and effective policies and programmes rather than ideological rhetoric and leadership cults could be a new source of strength for the parties in competitive politics. Both the NC and the UML should, therefore, reorient themselves as policy seeking and policy implementing parties. The future of the NC and the UML depends upon their ability to formulate public policy and programmes that match with the people's preferences. Their potential to rejuvenate themselves as the true representative of the people has always been there. If they could expedite the party building process in appropriate ways, balancing their interest in controlling state power with their responsibility to address the problems and needs of the society, there would be no stopping their emergence as the long-awaited change agents in Nepal.

NOTES

1. For details about party politics in 1951-1960 see Gupta (1964); Joshi and Rose (1966); Chauhan (1971).
2. For understandingthe panchayat system and various forms and types of opposition at that time, see Shaha (1982); Baral (1977; 1983).
3. For details about the communist movement in Nepal, See Rawal (1988); K.C. (1999).
4. For details about post-1990 politics, see POLSAN (1992); Borre et al. (1994); Hutt (1994); Hoftun et al. (1999); Kumar 1995; 2000); Brown (1996); Hachhethu (2002); Gellner (2002).

CHAPTER 4

ELECTIONS

This chapter is organized into four parts. Initially it discusses the election as a process of gaining legitimacy to govern the country both in the theoretical perspective and in the Nepali context. The second part focuses on internal dynamic of the party's electoral management. This covers a multiple process and decisions, i.e. candidate selection, resolution of internal disputes and dissents, mobilization of party workers, designing campaign strategy and electoral alliance with other party (ies). The third part highlights the external dynamic of the party's vote mobilization strategy which involves the role of actors and factors, i.e. leadership personality, candidate's popularity, transmission of party's ideology, image and policy into society, election agendas, issues and programmes etc. Finally, an assessment is made on parties' post-elections performance in the light of people's expectations and parties' promises made during elections. This chapter includes findings of some elections related questions that entertained in a broad survey on Election and Governance.[1]

"Do you take this man (or woman) to be your lawfully wedded husband (or wife)"? "I do." This analogy, borrowed from the Christian marriage ceremony, with its twin notions of legitimacy and obligation can apply in politics when we see the election as a mutual trust and contract between the voters and their representatives, between people and political parties, and between society and government. In a competitive system, an election is considered as the only one legitimate means through which contesting parties achieve power and authority to run the government. The acquisition of legitimacy to be in power accompanies obligation and responsibility which is generally phrased like "respect to popular mandate" and "representative democracy" to convey its meanings. To respect and represent the popular mandate means that political parties should be responsible and respond to the interest of people and society. If a party fails to balance between legitimacy and responsibility, the people are likely to choose a alternative party in the next election.

Elections provide a channel of communication between the mass of society and political parties. For citizens, exercise of their voting right may mean many things i.e. political participation, dialogue with the political actors, articulation of individual and collective interest, negotiation/ bargaining with political elite, choice of an individual candidate and or choice of a party's policy and programme, and involvement in the process of government formation. The periodic election links the people's power with political parties' interest. Electoral interest of political parties is obviously to seek the maximum number of votes and seats through which they obtain social consent and political legitimacy to be in power and position in the state apparatus. This involves a multiple process, i.e. candidate selection, political socialization in line with the party's image, ideology and policy, mobilization of party workers, campaigning, and setting of election agendas, and issues thought to have popular appeal.

A system of linking people's expectations with parties' policies in governance has recently been introduced in Nepal after the restoration of multiparty democracy followed by the enactment of a new constitution in 1990. Popular sovereignty in the political sense is ensured by the people's inalienable right to choose their representatives to the local and national government. The 1990 Constitution adopted the first-past-the post (FPTP) system in election for 205 members of the House of Representatives (HOR), the Lower House of the bicameral parliament. A party which obtained majority seats in the HOR through general elections formed the government. In case none of the contending party fails to obtain the required majority of 103 seats, a provision of coalition government of two or more parliamentary parties or minority government of the largest party was prescribed as an alternative system of government formation. To be precise, the constitution properly safeguarded the system of popular elections as the only means of making the state's power and authority responsible to the people.

The formation of government through elections contributes to the consolidation of democracy. Nepal had undergone certain democratic experiences in the 1990s with the successful completion of three general elections and two local elections. The parliamentary elections, held in 1991, 1994 and 1999, had created a two-party dominant system which is generally considered as an ideal situation for political stability and institutionalization of democracy. The 1992 and 1997 local elections were also remarkable for grounding the people's participation in competitive politics at the grass root level. Such electoral practices had multiple positive impacts, e.g. rise of political awareness, people's participation in competitive politics, penetration of contesting parties in the society at the grass-root level, assimilation of previously non-conformist forces into the mainstream politics, legitimization of multiparty parliamentary democracy, etc. Above all these elections significantly stressed the observance of the principle of the people's right to choose and reject the government.

TABLE 4:1
Parties' Positions in the First, Second and Third Parliamentary Elections

Parties	*Number of Seats Elected*			*% of Popular Vote*		
	1991	*1994*	*1999*	*1991*	*1994*	*1999*
Nepali Congress	110	83	112	37.75	33.38	36.14
Unified Marxist-Leninist	69	88	70	27.98	30.85	30.74
Marxist-Leninist	-	-	0	-	-	6.38
Rashtriya Prajatantra Party	1	20	11	5.38	17.93	10.14
Rashtriya Prajatantra Party (Chand)	3	-	0	6.56	-	3.32
Nepal Sadbhawana Party	6	3	5	4.10	3.49	3.13
National People's Front	-	-	5	-	-	1.36
Nepal Workers and Peasants Party	2	4	1	1.25	0.98	0.54
United People's Front of Nepal	9	0	1	4.35	1.32	0.83
Communist Party of Nepal (Democratic)	2	0	0	2.43	0.38	0.05
Independents	3	7	0	4.17	6.18	2.83
Other Small Parties	0	0	0	6.04	5.49	4.54
Total	205	205	205	100	100	100

Source: EC (1991, 1994, 1999)

In the 1991 general election, the NC gained a popular mandate, with 37.75 percent popular votes and 110 in total 205 seats of the HOR, to govern the country. The UML emerged as the largest opposition party with its sizable strength, 27.98 percent popular votes and 69 seats in the HOR. The political equation changed as the 1994 mid-term elections produced a hung parliament. The NC's strength declined to 83 seats in the HOR and 33.38 per cent popular votes. The UML, as the largest party in the HOR with its 88 seats and 30.85 percent popular votes, formed its minority government. The NC restored its first position in the 1999 general elections winning a comfortable majority of 112 seats in the HOR.

The results of the three general elections held in the 1990s established a corelation between the government (non-) performance and election results. The simple logic suggests that the party in the government could renew its position if it has had performance legitimacy. Charles W. Anderson said, "The primary task of the voter is to evaluate the quality of government received in the last period. The decision is between the "ins" and the "outs." If generally satisfied, the voter elects to retain the incumbents. If not, the choice is to "throw the rascals out." (1977: 155). Change of parties' position after each election suggests that elections also mean exercise of the people's right to reject the party in government. This logic sounds more valid, which was also proven by the result of the 1997 local election. The NC captured local governments after the 1992 local elections but its strength was reduced to around 30 percent in 1997. The UML's position changed from opposition to the ruling one in the local government of many areas. In the 1997 local elections, the UML won 50.10 percent seats of the VDCs, along with 55.98 percent of municipalities and 68.05 percent of DDCs seats. It showed that any party in power could influence the local elections in its favour.

Table 4.1 also reveals a glaring fact, the emergence of a two-party dominant system in Nepal. The exception was the second tenure of parliament (1994-1999) in which the RPP played as a balancing force between two major parties, the NC and the UML, to which Baral called it a "two and quarter party system." (1994: 440). Otherwise the first and the third parliamentary elections and the local elections of 1992 and 1997 created a two-party dominant system. The NC and the UML appeared as a alternative to one another for the competitive politics of the country.

A system of two-party dominance appeared as a trend in the party system of South Asian countries. But unlike its bases of social cleavages in India (Chhiber, 1999; Mitra, 2001), the Nepali character of the two dominant party system emerged on different grounds. Except for the NSP championing for the cause of the Madheshi community (people of plains region different from those of hill origin), none of the political parties of Nepal associated themselves with a particular caste, class and community. This shows that most political parties in Nepal are not by-products of social cleavage and economic problems. Rather, they originated along with their broad political mission or ideology. The support bases of the NC, the UML and the other parties cross the social, cultural, religious and

TABLE 4:2
Parties' Position in the Local Elections, 1992 and 1997

Parties	*Local Elections (% of seat)*					
	1992			*1997*		
	VDCs	*Munici-palities*	*DDCs*	*VDCs*	*Munici-palities*	*DDCs*
Nepali Congress	50.24	50.84	64.80	29.47	28.92	14.32
Unified Marxist-Leninist	26.05	22.33	17.94	50.10	55.98	68.05
RashtriyaPrajatantra Party	9.73	10.32	7.63	12.22	8.15	9.94
Nepal SadbhawanaParty	2.94	3.38	1.96	1.21	1.59	1.42
National People's Front	5.09	1.50	3.54	-	-	-
Other parties* and Independent	5.93	11.63	4.10	4.93	5.36	6.27
Total	99.98	99.99	100.	100.	100.	100.

* includes NWPP, UPF and CPN (Democrat).
Source: Maharjan (1998).

caste/ethnic divisions of the people. Though the 1990 Constitution recognized the pluralistic character of Nepali society consisting of diverse cultural and linguistic groups, it took enough care to separate politics from caste, ethnicity, language and religion. Article 112 (3) of the constitution categorically prohibited the formation of political parties on the basis of religion, community, caste, tribe and region. Following this spirit, the election code of conduct stated that "...voters shall not be encouraged to vote on the basis of caste/ethnicity, religion, tribe, and language" (ECN, 1999).

The NC and the UML's domination in Nepali politics is likely to continue in the future. There are some factors contributing to stabilize a two-party dominant system in Nepal. One, the majoritarian electoral system that Nepal adopted in the 1990s was obviously against the minority parties, i.e. despite the ML scored 6.38 percent popular vote in the 1999 general election it did not have single representation in the HOR. Two, the constitution itself discouraged the existence of smaller parties by its provision of rejecting to recognize as the national party to those which failed to gain 3 percent popular votes in general election. Three, Nepali adult citizens, by and large, appeared as stable party voters. The margin of difference in popular votes received by the NC in the 1990s general elections was only 4.37 percent, minimum 33.38 percent in 1994 when it was unpopular and maximum 37.38 when its popularity was at the peak in 1991. The UML's popular votes in the three general elections of the 1990s were around 28-31 percent.

Internal Dynamic of Parties' Electoral Management

Elections provide a fair ground to wage struggle for power among contending parties. Intra-party competition for candidacy precedes inter-party elections. A party, which manages internal competition effectively, will certainly be in a better position in an election battle with other parties. The internal exercises for the preparation of competitive elections start with the selection of candidates. Parties' decision of candidate selection intertwines with their objective of the maximization of popular votes and seats to the elected bodies. This obviously indicates that parties generally select those candidates who are perceived as capable enough to get more votes. Candidate selection is also a task of sending parties' representatives to the local and central government. The candidate's personal ability of holding the post is also taken into consideration. Candidate selection is a complex process and a number of factors, i.e. social background, political socialization, political attitude, social and political environment, party history and time of association, personality, continuity, popularity, lobby, support of party workers, backing of factional group, proximity to party high commands, etc. interplay in the eventual outcome of selection of persons as party candidates for elections.

The question of candidate selection relates to a number of other issues i.e. respect for public opinion vis-a-vis the candidate's popularity and ability, consultation with party workers in account to the need of electoral mobilization of the party's volunteers and possible dissent by other aspirants of candidacy. Election is always a high time for intensifying intra-party conflicts and crisis. Among many aspirants only a few will be lucky enough to get the chance. Managing dissidence is therefore a very significant task to maximize the prospect of victory. Other important challenges are to motivate party activists for election campaigning and vote mobilization work. Besides, a party can score some more seats through forging alliances with other parties.

Candidate Selection

Two important factors related to the nomination of candidates are formal/informal procedures of parties' decision-making process and fixing the criteria for the party's candidacy. The NC and many other political parties set up their own Parliamentary Board to look after the business of candidate selections. The Parliamentary Board of each party is generally constituted by a small number of hard-core central leaders, which has formal authority to take decisions on candidate selection for the general and the local elections (NC, 1995: RPP, 1990). The UML's constitution does not specifically provide such a permanent structure though it constituted an Election Board in the 1991 and 1994 general elections to take a decision on the party's candidates which was done by the party Standing Committee in the 1999 general election. This small structural difference however does not contradict the uniform pattern – centralization – adopted by all competing parties for candidate selections. Despite uniformity among the political parties in following the procedure of candidate selection, some divergences among them were observed, affected by each party's unique organizational character and behaviour.

The NC is basically a personality – based centralized party. The party had long operated under the authority of its troika leaders, Ganesh Man Singh, Krishna Prasad Bhattarai and Girija Prasad Koirala. The party's formal structures, District Committee (DC) and Central Committee (CC), had played just a supplementary role for the troika's actual authority in the nomination of candidates for the elections to the HOR. Even the job of the Parliamentary Board was confined to putting a formal seal on the troika's decision. This pattern remained unchanged despite the exit of G. M. Seig from the party on the eve of the 1994 mid-term elections. But coming to the 1999 general elections a slight change was introduced on account of the decline of the party high command's authority and the emergence of mini power centres inside the party. Next to Koirala and Bhattarai, some other second rank leaders, Sher Bahadur Deuba, Ram Chandra Poudel and Khum Bahadur Khadka with their capacity as members of the Parliamentary Board, appeared as influential in taking decisions of ticket distribution for the elections. Unlike in the past when decisions were made in consultation among only two or three top leaders, the NC Parliamentary Board played a decisive role in selecting candidates for the 1999 general elections.

Unlike the NC, the UML – an organization based party – is not under the exclusive control and command of one or few leaders. It has long followed a system of collective leadership and collective decision-making process. At the same time, the UML has adopted an oligarchic and centralized system. The centralized authority structure in the UML is acknowledged by its prescribed manner of vertical relationship, "Each party member is under the committee, each lower unit is under its immediate higher unit, and all members and organizations are under the authority of the Central Committee" (UML [c], 1993: 7) This was well reflected in the decision-making process of candidate selection that the party Standing Committee, constituted of around 12 top leaders, enjoyed final authority in this regard. This pattern has more or less been followed by other communist parties such as the UPF the UNF.

Since the RPP is the party of multipolar power centres, it had adopted a system of collective discussion among the party central leaders in taking decisions of candidate selections. Many other parties had also followed this pattern except the NWPP and NSP. The decision of one top leader prevailed more in these two small parties.

Centralization is, therefore, a rule of all parties for candidate selection. But in practice, the parties' apex bodies had not exercised all their powers arbitrarily. Particularly in the process of candidate nominations, central leaders consulted local leaders for both defence and better electoral prospects.

TABLE 4:3
Consultation with Party Local Leaders/Workers in Candidate Selection

Total No. of Respondents 163

Variables	*Total*		*NC*	*UML*	*RPP*	*Others*
	No	*%*	*%*	*%*	*%*	*%*
Agree	87	53.4	50.8	54.2	61.8	45
Partly agree	36	22.1	26.2	22.9	17.6	15
Disagree	31	19.0	14.8	18.8	17.6	35
Don't know	9	5.5	8.2	4.2	2.9	5.0

Source: NCCS (2001).

Of the total 500 respondents 163 belonged to party members. Around two thirds of party members said they had been fully or partly consulted by the central leaders before taking the final decision of candidate selection. This general finding was applicable to all political parties. In response to a question on consultation, the respondents belonging to the NC, the UML and the RPP fully affirmed by 51, 54 and 62 percent respectively. Those who partly shared this opinion were 26, 23, and 28 percent respondents of the NC, the UML and the RPP respectively. Only a very few party members (NC's 15 percent, UML's 19 percent and the RPP's 18 percent) disagreed with it. The general finding of this table confirmed that nomination of candidates was made by the party centre in consultation with the party local leaders (Dahal, 1992: 105-113).The question arises here: how were party local leaders/workers involved in the candidate selection process?

In the first general election held after the restoration of democracy, the NC granted the authority to its DC to recommend three possible candidates from each parliamentary constituency. Besides, the party sent its central representative in each of the 75 districts to collect the opinion of party local leaders/workers about the prospective candidates and then submitted the report to the Parliamentary Board. These procedures had been followed as precedents in subsequent general elections held in 1994 and 1999. Besides, the NC, being in power in all the last three general elections, had the additional advantage of receiving information from the local administration. It had been practised that on the eve of elections, the district administration submitted a report to the government with its evaluation about the position of contending parties and prospective candidates. But many felt that the party centre relied more on the opinions of its local organizational leaders than the report of the local administration (interviews with sample local government officials, 15-30 January 2001). It was believed that the NC high command largely respected the recommendations made by the party DC while taking the final decision of candidate selection. But the party organizations at the local level in many districts later failed to be strict on its responsibility to recommend only three prospective candidates for one constituency. Instead, the party DC sent the list of many aspirants from one constituency, which further enlarged the scope for manipulation by the centre.

Like the NC, the UML, the RPP and many other parties allowed the district committee of their respective parties to recommend three perspective candidates from one constituency. And each party deputed a team of central representatives in each district seeking the opinion of local leaders/workers. By way of consulting with the party local organization, the party rank and file got involved in candidate selection process in different ways. Their role would not only be limited in providing their personal opinion to the concerned authority. Particularly in the selection of the party candidates for significant posts at different levels, ranging from VDC Chairman to Member of Parliament (MP), most of the party's local units of different levels and leaders of different ranks had shown their favour to particular aspirants in written form.

The space for the party local leaders'/workers' involvement in the decision- making process of candidate selections was much wider in local elections than general elections. The NC, the UML, the RPP and many other parties delegated the authority to their own party DC in taking decisions of candidate selection for local elections, except for the top posts in municipalities and DDC. In both the 1992 and 1997 local elections, most parties followed a standard format – recommendation of three names for one post by the party lower units (Village/Town Committee, Area Committee, Constituency Committee) and final selection by the party district organization. However, the selection of party leaders for elected bodies, VDCs, municipalities and DDC, was also done top-downwards. The NC usually set up a selection committee – consisting of a small coterie of local leaders including MPs – which took the final decisions in nomination of the party's candidates for VDCs and municipalities. The UML also formed an Election Board constituting a small number of Secretariat members of the party DC, which actually selected all candidates for the 1992, and the 1997 local elections.

Though candidate selection is part of the internal affairs of political parties in which the organizational leaders and workers are involved in different ways, the public opinion is supposed to be respected while doing so. The more the respect to the public opinion the more the vote the party receives. But none of the Nepali political parties had adopted a scientific mechanism to collect the voters' opinions on the party's prospective candidates. Besides, the office bearers of the party organizations at the local level, parties have to rely on information supplied by their own activists, mostly those involved in the party ancillary and affiliated organizations. The accuracy and impartiality of such information has always been questionable and so it would have the least impact in the decision-making process, but the local situation and sentiment cannot be completely overlooked. This implies that the contending parties largely respect the public opinion in nomination of their own party candidates despite lack of the scientific mechanism to undertake this task.

TABLE 4:4
Respect for Public Opinion in Candidate Selection

Variables	*Total*		*Area %*		*Sex %*		*Party Affiliation %*	
	No	*%*	*Rural*	*Urban*	*Male*	*Female*	*Member*	*Non-member*
Agree	218	43.6	44.1	41.6	44.4	41.0	50.9	40.1
Partly agree	108	21.6	19.5	29.7	23.5	15.6	18.4	23.1
Disagree	128	25.6	25.6	25.7	27.8	18.9	28.8	24.0
Don't know	46	9.2	10.8	3.0	4.2	24.6	1.8	12.8

Source: NCCS (2001)

Nearly two-thirds of the total 500 respondents fully or partly responded affirmatively to the question whether political parties respected their opinions in candidate selection. Most respondents of different ages, occupations, castes/ethnic groups, rural and urban dwellers, and male and female shared this opinion. But the majority of respondents belonging to the poor, illiterate, Dalit, Buddhists and Muslims said that their opinions were not considered in candidate selections. This shows the negligence of the unprivileged strata of society by political parties in taking decisions of candidate nomination. Besides, around one-fourth of total 500 respondents disagreed with the view that political parties respect public opinion in candidate selections. But in totality, a positive dimension prevails in relations between public opinion and candidate selections.

The correlations between public opinion and candidate selection link with the choice of appropriate persons for parties' candidacies. While justifying the NC's nomination of candidates for the 1991 parliamentary elections, party President, Krishna Prasad Bhattarai said, "The party had nominated its candidates on the basis of three criteria: their record of struggle and sacrifice, their prospect of victory, and their capacity to play an effective role in the parliament" (*Saptahik Bimarsa*, 29 March 1991). These factors were included in the form, which the NC distributed to all aspirants for MP tickets in the 1994 and the 1999 general elections. The primacy of continuity, personality and popularity factors was, therefore, distinct (Dahal, 1992: 104-113). But many felt changes later in giving weight to particular qualities. The factors like wealth, family and kinship ties, proximity to high command leader, etc. played more important roles than the factors of continuity, honesty, dedication and commitment (interviews with sample local NC leaders, 15-30 January 2001).

The NC developed some positive and negative criteria for the simplification of the selection process. The NC granted MP tickets to all CC members and incumbent Ministers, except those who had voluntarily stayed away from the contest. The party allocated 5 percent of 205 candidates to the former panchas, who joined the NC, in all the last three general elections. For others, the overriding consideration in the choice of the MP candidates was their prospect of victory in the elections. The NC's central representatives who were assigned to recommend candidates from the districts of their deputation for the 1994 and the 1999 parliamentary elections normally recommended those persons who appeared to have the best prospects out of those suggested by the local leaders and workers.

So far as negative criteria were concerned, the NC, in the 1994 mid-term elections, denied tickets to the Upper House MPs, and its representatives holding top posts of municipalities (Mayor and Deputy Mayor) and DDCs (Chairman and Vice Chairman). This was followed in the 1999 general elections as well and two more points of disqualification added, one was misuse of diplomatic passports and the other, violation of party discipline during the 1994 mid-term elections.

The UML developed some criteria to be eligible for the candidacy of parliamentary elections. Accordingly, a person must be of high moral discipline, capable, popular and committed to the party's interest and principles. The similar opinion was expressed by most of the UML's local leaders of the sampled districts (interviews with sample UML local leaders, 15-30 January 2001). Besides, preference was also given to the minority communities in those constituencies where they constituted the majority group. The party CC members were exempted from all criteria it developed for the 1991, 1994 and 1999 elections since it granted tickets to all CC members, except those who voluntarily stayed away from the contest. The UML also developed certain negative criteria. The party denied tickets to its members of the Upper House, Mayor and Deputy Mayor of municipalities and Chairman and Vice Chairman of DDCs. Further more, it disqualified most of its 22 ex-MPs for the 1994 elections who violated party discipline through defying the party whip in the elections of the Upper House held in June 1993 in which a dissident candidate Jaget Bogati won. In the 1999 general elections, the party threw out those members of the second tenure of parliament who were involved in the diplomatic passport scandal.

The smaller parties including the RPP bothered least about the positive and negative criteria for candidate selection due to the lack of serious internal competition for candidacy. Many of them even failed to give their own party candidacy from most areas out of the total 205 parliamentary constituencies. Some parties like NWPP gave candidacy from many districts as possible, irrespective of the personal quality and ability of candidates, just to accumulate more votes, if possible 3 percent in total voting turn out which was necessary to get recognized as a national party. Nevertheless in areas of high internal competition for candidacy and better prospects of victory, the minority parties also considered such factors like continuity and contribution to the party, personal ability and popularity.

TABLE 4:5
Basis of Candidate Selection for the 1997 Local Elections

% Based on Multiple Responses

Variables	*Total*		*Area %*		*Sex %*		*Party Affiliation %*	
	No	*%*	*Rural*	*Urban*	*Male*	*Female*	*Member*	*Non-member*
Continuity/seniority	236	47.2	46.6	49.5	49.2	41.0	54.6	43.6
Caste/ethnicity	159	31.8	32.8	27.7	35.7	19.7	31.9	31.8
Popularity	328	65.6	67.4	58.4	69.8	52.5	76.1	60.5
Rich	101	20.2	19.0	24.8	20.9	18.0	15.3	22.6
Favourite of district leader	153	30.6	28.6	38.6	34.4	18.9	30.7	30.6
Favourite of central leader	63	12.6	10.8	19.8	14.0	08.2	15.3	11.3
Opportunist	38	07.6	07.3	08.9	09.0	03.3	08.0	07.4
Others	03	00.6	00.5	01.0	00.8	00.0	00.6	00.6
Don't know	51	10.2	10.8	07.9	05.8	23.8	04.9	12.8

Source: NCCS (2001).

While responding to two separate questions – What criterion did you find parties considered in selection of candidates for the 1997 local elections and 1999 general elections in your own constituency? – 'popularity' and 'continuity' appeared as the two most important factors in preferential order. The third important factor changed, 'favour of central leaders' for general elections but caste/ethnic consideration for the local elections. Major political parties appeared sensitive to the need of maintaining a certain level of caste/ethnic balance. This was manifested in the selection of candidates for significant posts (i.e. DDC's Chairman and Vice-Chairman) in sampled districts in the 1992 and the 1997 local elections. In the 1991, 1994 and 1999 general elections also, the NC, the UML and the RPP had largely maintained caste/ethnic balance among major communities of the sample districts, e.g. hill ethnic Rai/Limbu community and hill caste groups in Dhankuta, Hindu and Muslim and migrant hill caste and plain caste in Rautahat, hill caste Gurung and Brahmin/Chhetri in Kaski, plain tribe Tharu and the hill castes in Dang, and Brahmin and Thakuri-Chhetri in Baitadi districts.

A small variation appeared among different groups of respondents in identifying the third important factor. Majority respondents belonging to Buddhists and the hill ethnic groups found the caste/ethnicity as the third important criteria even in selections of candidates for the general elections. In contrast, the urban dwellers and the rich class gave low weight to the caste/ethnic factor. The rich considered the money power as the

TABLE 4:6
Basis of Candidate Selection for 1999 General Elections

% Based on Multiple Responses

Variables	*Total*		*Area %*		*Sex %*		*Party Affiliation %*	
	No	*%*	*Rural*	*Urban*	*Male*	*Female*	*Member*	*Non-member*
Continuity	281	56.2	55.6	58.4	58.5	49.2	67.5	50.7
Caste/ethnicity	102	20.4	20.8	18.8	22.8	13.1	20.9	20.2
Popularity	309	61.8	62.7	58.4	64.0	54.9	71.2	57.3
Rich	135	27.0	26.3	29.7	29.4	19.7	24.5	28.2
Favourite of central leader	199	39.8	36.8	51.5	45.0	23.8	40.5	39.5
Opportunist	46	09.2	08.8	10.9	10.6	04.9	09.8	8.9
Others	06	01.2	00.8	03.0	01.1	01.6	03.1	00.3
Don't know	58	11.6	13.0	05.9	08.2	22.1	04.9	14.8

Source: NCCS (2001)

third important factor. The significance of favour of central leaders was reflected in the fact that centralization prevailed in candidate selections for general elections. But this factor appeared least important in local elections, instead 'favour of local leaders' counted more. This revealed decentralization in candidate selections for the local elections.

Resolution of Internal Dispute

Elections often create or intensify internal conflicts of the party since candidate selection is the choice of few among many aspirants. If the dissidence is not managed well; the aspirant candidates, who failed to get tickets, and their followers may become opponents or non-cooperatives or inactive against the party's official candidates in elections. This could have a serious impact in the party's position in elections as witnessed by defeat of the NC in the 1994 mid-term elections.

Despite several hundreds of Congress men claimed for candidacy the NC faced least troubles in the 1991 general elections. At that time the party's troika leadership was cohesive and their authority and decisions of candidate selections was not seriously challenged. The level of tolerance among the party rank and file was also high. But a completely reversal picture appeared during the 1994 mid-term elections that may party members contested elections as rebel candidates. The party largely failed to manage internal conflicts that rooted back to the emergence of two distinct factional groups, one led by Girija Prasad Koirala and the other by Ganesh Man Singh and Krishna Prasad Bhattarai.

The factional conflict in the NC was a prelude to the power struggle within the troika leaders that was intensified by subsequent events, i.e. cabinet reshuffle in December 1991 by the then PM G.P. Koirala without proper consultations with Singh and Bhattarai, internal sabotage against party President K. P. Bhattarai's candidacy for the February 1994 by-elections, absence of the NC's 35 members of the HOR at voting on the government's annual policy and programme leading to collapse of the Koirala government, and PM Koirala's harsh retaliation with his act of dissolving the HOR and calling for a mid-term poll. The internal crisis culminated with Singh's exit from the party and formation of a separate political platform, *Jaana Jagaran Abhiyan*, which openly called for a revolt against the NC official candidates belonging to the Koirala group.

In order to minimize the impact of internal revolt, the NC gave candidacy to almost all incumbent MPs and also warned them to take disciplinary actions against rebels to the extent of expulsion from the party. But these decisions could not become effective; one of the main reasons was Bhattarai's absence as a candidate in the elections. As the NC failed to manage its internal problems the party was defeated in the 1994 mid-term polls. Alane Ware's view can be cited here to explain the defeat of the NC, "When internal conflict becomes too intense a party becomes much less credible as a governing party and its electoral prospect can be reduced" (1987: 158).

The situation changed in the 1999 general elections, yet the dissidence resurfaced in the NC. A number of party leaders, including 33 MPs of the second tenure of parliament and presidents of the party DC of several districts who were excluded from the list of party candidates, vehemently opposed the decision of the Parliamentary Board. As their demands were not met dissidents filed their nomination as rebel candidates from 53 constituencies (Dahal, 2000: 16), but many of them later withdrew. The problem was however managed by reviewing the decision already made by the Parliamentary Board and changed the list of candidates in 22 constituencies. G.P. Koirala as the PM and the party president led the course of internal conflict management. By his decision to keep her daughter Sujata Koirala out of the candidacy and another decision to project K. P. Bhattarai as the future PM of the country, G.P. Koirala earned a hard bargain vis-à-vis K. P. Bhattarai and the anti-Koirala group. Besides, Koirala's public announcement of K.P. Bhattarai as the NC candidate for the PM's post could be seen, from one perspective, as a strategy to pacify the factors of internal dissension in the 1999 parliamentary elections.

The UML's decisions of candidate selections and dissent management had been conditioned by many factors. For the 1991 parliamentary election, the first general elections held after the restoration of democracy, the UML proposed for an electoral alliance among the partners of the 1990 mass movement, particularly with the NC. But the NC refused to make even an understanding for mutual cooperation in some constituencies from which the top leaders of both parties contested. The UML then turned in seeking alliance with all the left forces, which materialized at a limited level with the UPF only. The electoral alliance among the left forces could be very significant. In the 1991 general elections, "The Left's percentage of the total vote was only 1.25 percent behind that of Congress and, if the leftist candidates standing against each other in 14 constituencies had not let Congress win by default, both sides would have had 96 seats each" (Whelpton, 1991: 71). With due consideration to this fact, the UML tried to have a broad alliance among the left parties in subsequent general elections held in 1994 and 1999, but at all times it had to be satisfied with limited achievements. In the subsequent two general elections held in 1994 and 1999, the UML left around 10 of the total 205 constituencies out from the contest for the candidates of other left parties, particularly for those of the UPF and UNF. For the 1992 local elections of DDC, the UML made the RPP as one of its alliance partners. But in the 1997 local elections to the DDC, the RPP and the NSP largely swing to the NC in forging an alliance in many areas despite there being a coalition government of the RPP, the UML and the NSP at the centre.

The problem from inside the party was more challenging for the UML. In the 1991 general elections, one section of the party belonging to the former Marxist group revolted against the party's decision of candidate selections. The conflict between the former ML and the Marxist groups appeared on the ground of not following their earlier agreement, made at the time of unification in January 1991, for equal sharing of power and position. The Marxists felt a sense of deprivation in the nomination of the party's candidates. Most of them who received the party tickets were given from extremely unfavourable constituencies. For the former ML, the unification signified merely acquiring the trademark of the Marxist party (which inherited the identity of the original CPN, founded in 1949) and some of its well-known leaders. The UML, therefore, took disciplinary action against a number of the former Marxists for their *antarghat* in the 1991 general elections that suited the former ML's deliberate plan of displacing them from the party. Ultimately the party dissidents belonging to the Marxist group founded a new party with its name CPN (September).

In the 1994 mid-term elections the internal problems in the UML arose from another factional group led by C.P. Mainali. The Mainali group as a dissident faction had long existed in the party since 1982. The internal conflicts waged on ideological lines during the party's Fifth Nation Congress 1993 in which the programme of *Bahudaliya Janabad* (People's Multiparty Democracy) proposed by Madan Bhandari passed by an overwhelming majority of 77.62 percent votes against 14.49 per cent votes for the Mainali group's proposal of *Pariskrit Naulo Janbad* [Refined People's Democracy] (UML [c], 1993: 4-10). Defying the party whip by 22 members of the HOR loyal to C. P. Mainali in elections to the members of the Upper House in 1993 caused trouble since the party decided to disqualify the violators of party discipline for the candidacy to the 1994 mid-term elections. As a precautionary measure, the UML set a new formula that party candidates were required to submit their resignations from the HOR prior to filling their nomination papers (IIDS, 1994: 25). C.P. Mainali demanded at least 15 percent seats for his factional group in proportion to the strength the minority group showed in the party's Fifth National Congress, but the party dominant section rejected outrightly. Party General Secretary Madhav Nepal's decision not to contest the elections strengthened his bargaining capacity vis-à-vis the minority faction. Eventually the minority faction was compelled to be satisfied with getting a few candidates in the elections. The situation completely changed in the 1999 elections. Because of the split of the party in March 1998 by dissident groups which formed the ML as the new party, the UML appeared as the most cohesive party. The UML's leaders and workers' common sentiment to take revenge against the splinter groups led to neutralizing the factors of internal problems and dissidence. Nevertheless, the UML tracked back to the major opposition party from its earlier expectation to be in power, mainly because of a split in the party in March 1998.[2]

Parties' Vote Mobilization Strategy

Elections provide an opportunity for mutual and active interactions between the people and parties and between the candidates and voters. Though elections are a reciprocal process of meeting people's expectations and parties'/candidates' promises at one juncture, election agendas are always set unilaterally by political parties. The people most often appear as receptive or they reject the policy and programme presented by parties.

The contending parties generally try their best to put forward such policies, programmes and plans, which would have great appeal to the masses. The transmission of parties' ideology, identity and election agendas to the larger mass of the people is another vital part of elections, for which the contending parties/candidates rely on mass media, party workers and other means. Parties' election campaigning can roughly be divided into two broad level, national level and local/constituency level. Campaigning at the national level is general conducted through mass media, parties' election manifestos and public speeches and addresses by parties' national leaders in mass meetings. Parties' candidates and activists mostly carry out the local level campaigning.

National Level Campaign

The NC had tried its best to steer the competitive elections, 1991 general election in particular, on ideological lines. Its political identity is closely associated with the achievement of the 1990 *Jana Andolan* (mass movement): restoration of multiparty democracy, so, it propagated coining the phrase like "Congress means multiparty system" and "multiparty democracy means Congress." Guided by its interest of vote maximization, the NC naturally made high promises at election time. But on the other hand, the party being the protagonist of parliamentary democracy appeared as a symbol of *status quo* in the post-movement period. It resisted social demands for rapid and radical changes. The NC's psychology of "would be ruling party" also impacted in adopting "peace, stability, democracy and development" as its pet slogans in the last three general elections and the two local elections.

The UML, because of its history and communist trademark, had always been ideologically awkward and assured a defensive position in elections under the parliamentary system. But seen in retrospect, its radical and revolutionary image associated with its communist identity proved as an asset to catch the people's sentiment and the national psyche for revolutionary change that appeared in the early phase of democracy. The national psyche for more change that appeared against the background of the 1990 popular uprising affected the people's political judgment. Merely a change of political regime from partyless panchayat to multiparty democracy did not satisfy what the change meant for the people at large. The popular feeling of inadequacy of change surfaced repeatedly in different ways. The advent of democracy in Nepal has in its wake raised the voices of different groups of people hitherto silent. The demands of the minority and disadvantaged sections of the society glaringly appeared soon after the restoration of democracy.

Against the NC which strove to stabilize and normalize the situation against another potential revolution – revolution of the people's rising expectations – the UML urged the radicalization of social demands. The UML had tried to combine the class interest of the poor and ethnic interest of the minorities while radicalizing the interest of the people and society. The UML's general principle for the upliftment of downtrodden people had been moulded with the party's strategy of expanding support bases along ethnic lines through pumping sectarian sentiments among minority groups. The UML, therefore, had adopted a populist slogan: "Bread for the hungry, jobs for unemployed, land for landless, and shelter for the homeless" in all the last general and local elections.

Unlike the UML's presentation as a moderate left, other communist parties, i.e. UPF, NPF and NWPP had fought the elections with their non-conformist stand against the monarchy and parliamentary system. Their election campaigns inevitably also included their anti-India and anti-West posture (UPF, 1991; 1994; 1999; NWPP, 1991: 1994; 1999). The RPP had always projected itself before the voters as the closest party with the institution of monarchy and it inherited the dismantled panchyat's image of being nationalist against India. The NSP had contested the elections in one single banner: uplift the Madheshi community against the age-long exploitation and discrimination by the hill high caste groups. The NSP appeared as a distinct regional party different from others. Its election manifestos, presented to the last two local elections and three general elections, had similar contents, e.g. to turn Nepal as federal state, recognition of Hindi as a national language, reservation for Madheshi in administration, police, army and other state organizations, etc. (NSP, 1991; 1994; 1999).

But divergence of ideological/political identity and posture among the contending parties hardly reflected in their policy agendas presented before the voters, particularly in the case of the three major parties, the NC, the UML and the RPP. All these three contending parties gave emphasis to infrastructure building, rural development, land reform policy, agro-based and labour-intensive small/cottage industries, social security, uplift of minority and disadvantaged sections of society etc. in all the post-1990 elections (NC, 1991 [b]; 1994 [a]; 1999; UML, 1991 [b]: 1994 [a]; 1999; RPP, 1991; 1994 [a]; 1999). One study concluded that, "The two big parties (NC and UML) convey the same message on development, but in different languages" (IIDS, 1994: 25). However some changes were distinct in subsequent elections as far as policy shift was concerned.

The NC largely lost its ideological appeal to the mass in the 1994 mid-term elections since it was a sole outcome of its own internal crisis. As it had no other solid issue the party, particularly its PM G.P. Koirala, pinpointed "political instability of the country created by agitational politics of the left parties including the UML" to rationalize why the NC sought re-mandate from the voters. The party largely adopted the contents of its previous election manifesto for the 1994 elections but with a small revision. Consequently, the agendas of employment, poverty alleviation and human development, harnessing of hydro-electricity and privatization added in the list of the party's priority areas.

Policy shift could also be observed in the case of the UML in the 1994 general elections. Two factors influenced in bringing the party in this direction. One, the UML's tactical and qualified support to the newly achieved multiparty democracy was transformed to its commitment to the fundamental principles of liberal democracy since the party's Fifth National Congress 1993 passed the resolution of People's Multiparty Democracy. Two, owing to the magnitude of *antarghat* in the NC on the eve of the 1994 mid-term elections, the UML seemed confident enough to gain power and so it gave a slogan, "Next government is the UML's government." The changed context demanded the UML to make some policy shift in some areas.

The 1999 general elections also witnessed a change in the parties' election agendas and some issues got more priorities. In the background of this election, there was a hung parliament and change of government eight times between 1994 and 1999, suggesting the political instability in the country. This period was marked by introduction of a number of aberrations, i.e. political corruption, horse trading, manipulation of constitutional loopholes, perennial factional infighting and break-ups of political parties etc. in Nepali politics. The people, therefore, were fed up with such politics. But parties' opinion divided according to their strength. The minority parties, the RPP in particular, stood for the continuation of the coalition system and they blamed the erosion of individual characters of the political elite for all faulty scenes appeared before the 1999 elections. But, the return of majority government had become a common agenda for both the major contesting parties, NC and UML, as it was considered a panacea to all problems facing the country. A system of the majority government was considered as indispensable for political stability, good governance and development. Another notable issue before the 1999 elections was the ongoing Maoists' violent activities, pervasive corruption, unemployment, etc. These major issues and other serious problems facing the nation naturally reflected in parties' election policy and programme. The table below 4.7 shows how the people saw the parties' agendas for the 1999 elections.

The table reveals that political parties raised the problem faced by the average Nepali people and their needs to the greater extent in their campaign during the 1999 elections. The opinions of the total 500 respondents shows that the problems of 'security, control of corruption and price rise', which put in one basket in the questionnaire, scored 76 percent in a list of parties' election agendas. This reflected the state of pervasive corruption and sky rocketing price rise facing by the country and the people, acknowledged by political parties as the most significant problems that needed to be resolved. Moreover this also showed the deteriorating situation of law and order in the country after the Maoists started their violent activities since February 1996.

The respondents also found that political parties gave almost the same weight to the need of infrastructure building when they reached the people to beg for votes. The variable of infrastructure building scored 71 percent in parties' priorities to their election issues. Employment appeared as the third major agenda, followed by uplift of the

Table 4:7
Parties' Main Agendas for the 1999 Election

% Based on Multiple Responses

Variables	*Total*		*Area %*		*Sex %*		*Party Affiliation %*	
	No	*%*	*Rural*	*Urban*	*Male*	*Female*	*Member*	*Non-member*
Political stability	106	21.2	19.3	28.7	24.6	10.7	30.1	16.9
Infrastructure building	357	71.4	73.4	63.4	72.8	67.2	72.4	70.9
Nationality	46	9.2	6.5	19.8	10.6	4.9	14.7	6.5
Land reform	22	4.4	5.3	1.0	5.6	.8	7.4	3.0
Employment	236	47.2	48.1	43.6	51.1	35.2	47.2	47.2
Security, control of prices and corruption	380	76.0	74.9	80.2	79.6	64.8	78.5	74.8
Uplift disadvantaged	172	34.4	32.1	43.6	32.5	40.2	36.8	33.2
Others	09	1.8	2.3	.0	1.3	3.3	.6	2.4
Don't know	26	5.2	6.0	2.0	3.4	10.7	1.2	7.1

Source: NCCS (2001).

disadvantaged (34%), political stability (21%), nationality (9%) and land reform (4%). The cross tab of table by sex, class, occupation and religion reveals a small difference in identifying the third major agenda of political parties for the 1999 elections. Majority among the women, housewives, rich and Buddhist respondents found that parties gave priority to the upliftment of disadvantaged sections of society than the problem of unemployment. This explains the entry of caste, ethnicity, language, religion and other issues of exclusion in electoral politics though at the lower level compared to other significant issues. The candidates across the party indirectly promoted the communal sentiment to collect popular votes on the dominant cluster of minority communities. The question of nationalism and land reform were over shadowed parties' election campaign in 1999. This explained why the radical communist parties, the ML in particular, and the rightist parties, the RPP (Chand group) in particular, which tried to build public opinion against India and the West, failed to cash in on such campaigns.

Local Level Campaign

The local problems and needs prevailed more than national and international issues in the parties' election campaign. A study team of Dang district observed, "Election manifestos of parties do not have much meaning for the purpose of election campaigns. Even educated people do not take much interest in manifestos. So political parties, besides significant

Table 4.8
Issues for Vote Maximization

% Based on Multiple Responses

Variables	*Total*		*Area %*		*Sex %*		*Party Affiliation %*	
	No	*%*	*Rural*	*Urban*	*Male*	*Female*	*Member*	*Non-member*
Party's ideology and policy	217	43.4	42.6	46.5	48.7	27.0	54.6	38.0
Image of leadership	121	24.2	23.3	27.7	25.9	18.9	29.4	21.7
Candidate personality	183	36.6	34.1	46.5	38.6	30.3	46.6	31.8
Assurance of development	416	83.2	83.0	84.2	83.9	81.1	81.6	84.0
Distribution of development materials	192	38.4	39.3	34.7	42.1	27.0	36.2	39.5
Others	34	6.8	6.5	7.9	5.8	9.8	6.1	7.1
Don't know	32	6.4	6.5	5.9	4.5	12.3	1.8	8.6

Source: NCCS (2001).

local concerns and issues, used popular catchy slogans to appeal to the people. Development, security, nationalism, employment are some examples of such slogans (NCCS, 2001)." Parties' strategic issues that used for vote maximization also indicated the significance of local campaigning.

In response to a question that what are the major strategic issues parties generally used for vote maximization, almost all the 500 respondents identified 'assurance for development' as the most important factor. This issue scored the highest mark of 83.2 percent suggesting that the question of development was far more significant than other agendas in parties' election strategies and people's voting behaviours. Even in the 1991 general elections, held in the background of the successful 1990 mass movement, when the ideological factor predominated in vote mobilization strategy, the question of development remained one of the major concerns of the people. Foreign observers cited what one NC candidate for the 1991 elections observed, "We want to teach them (voters) about political rights and freedom, but they want to talk about schools, roads, drinking water and electricity" (Gaige and Scholz, 1991: 1047). The localization of the election campaign in the 1994 mid-term elections too was expressed, "People were more interested in problems of drinking water, canals, roads, food, schools and a range of other issues affecting their villages" (Baral, 1995: 440). The local leaders across the party of the sample districts also identified the development as the key issue of election campaigning. One can therefore conclude that the issue of infrastructure development had been dominated heavily in the elections in Nepal. Most candidates, irrespective of their party affiliation, sought people's mandate on the basis of their promises to provide services like drinking water, schools, health post, transportation, communication, etc.

'Parties' ideology and policy' came as second important issues for vote mobilization. Among the total 500 respondents, 43 percent expressed this view. But the opinion of respondents differed in giving priorities to particular issues. For the majority female respondents, housewives and businessmen, the question of parties' ideology and policy come only after 'candidate personality' in order of priority. The strategy of 'distribution of development materials' by parties ranked to the second important for the majority of rich and poor classes, agriculture, labour and service occupation groups, illiterate and literate persons, Newar, Dalit, Madheshis, and for non-party members. This clearly indicated the decline of the role of ideology in elections despite it remaining as the second most important factor. The convergence of most political parties under the constitutional framework and erosion of ideology in realpolitik explained why the ideological factor increasingly became less relevant for vote mobilization strategy.

Distribution of development materials by contending parties/ candidates came third in ranking of parties' strategies of vote maximization. The practice of distribution of money and material for petty construction or other purposes in the name of development has increasingly became a trend to woo voters. Despite the election code of conduct forbids the use/ abuse of state resources and power from the day of announcement of elections, the party (ies) in power hardly followed it. The NC had always been in an advantageous position since it was in power in the last three general elections. Two of them (1991 and 1999 elections) were, however, conducted by a coalition government of three forces/parties. The excessive manipulation of state power and resources was more acute in the local elections. So the party in power, the NC in 1992 and the UML in 1997, had won the local elections.

Candidate personality and image of party leadership appeared last in preferential order of parties' strategies of vote mobilization. This clearly showed the decline of leadership's popularity in the latest elections. Otherwise the image of parties' national leader was highly saleable in the early phase of democracy. In the early phase of the post-1990 mass movement, the NC organization building followed with highlight of its troika. Along with poor performance of the NC and its government, internal power conflicts among the party troika leaders – G.M. Singh, K.P. Bhattarai and G.P. Koirala – led to considerable erosion of their popularity. Because they projected themselves as selfish and power hungry leaders contrary to the people's perception of them as men of principle. Needless to say that the personalities of the NC leaders, which were used as assets by almost all Congress candidates in attracting the voters in the 1991 parliamentary elections, figured low in the party's campaign strategy in the 1994 and the 1999 general elections.

The UML lacked a charismatic leader except for Madan Bhandari. His popularity picked up due to his victory over the interim PM K.P. Bhattarai in the 1991 parliamentary election but Bhandari died in May 1993 in a vehicle accident. Another least disputed but powerless leader of the UML was Man Mohan Adhikari. His death while campaigning for the 1999 general elections did not bring a wave of sympathy vote to the party. The position of the RPP leaders is mostly determined by their status in the dismantled and discredited panchayat system. So the RPP lacked a crowd puller personality. Besides, the insignificance of image of the party central leader vis-à-vis vote mobilizations showed that most parties suffered from the lack of popular leaders.

In a situation of declining the ideology and leadership factors for vote mobilization, the worth of the local campaigning by the party candidates and activists increased more. The means that parties used for communication with voters further proved it.

The table 4.9 reveals that the modern means of election campaigning through the print and electronic media had been used least in Nepali elections. Instead, 'door to door campaigning' 'mass meeting/rally', 'workers' mobilization' and 'pamphlet distribution' came in preferential order among several means adopted by political parties/candidates in reaching them to the voters. Such observation of the 500 respondents was influenced by the situation of the 1999 general election, which was distinct from previous elections in many respects. It was observed that election *mahol* was noticed least on the street compared to the past elections. Voters were silent before the polling day which was unusual and unprecedented compared to their active participation and involvement in the previous elections. The parties' candidates and campaigners, instead of 'wasting' time on rallies, mass meeting and other demonstrative activities, adopted the most practical way of meeting the voters at their doorstep.

The door-to-door campaign strategy was used heavily in the 1999 elections compared to the previous elections. The direct contact between

TABLE 4:9
Party/Candidate-Voters Communication

% Based on Multiple Responses

Variables	*Total*		*Area %*		*Sex %*		*Party Affiliation %*	
	No	*%*	*Rural*	*Urban*	*Male*	*Female*	*Member*	*Non-member*
Door-to-door campaign	418	83.6	82.2	89.1	85.7	77.0	89.0	81.0
Mass meeting/rally	348	69.6	69.7	69.3	70.4	67.2	73.0	68.0
Pamphlet distribution	223	44.6	44.9	43.6	44.2	45.9	38.7	47.5
Newspapers	11	2.2	2.0	3.0	1.3	4.9	1.8	2.4
Radio/Television	5	1.0	.3	4.0	.8	1.6	.6	1.2
Village elite	96	19.2	21.3	10.9	21.2	13.1	16.6	20.5
Workers' mobilization	304	60.8	60.4	62.4	63.2	53.3	62.6	59.9
Others	5	1.0	.8	2.0	1.3	.0	3.1	.0
Don't know	5	1.0	1.0	1.0	.3	3.3	1.2	.9

Source: NCCS (2001).

the candidate and voters has its own positive dimension in bringing the potential ruler and ruled closer. In retrospect, the dominance of one-to-one meetings between the candidate and voters could have a backlash effect for purity of elections if undue factors influence people's political judgment. It was felt that a tendency of seeking the price of the vote in monetary terms or in the hope of getting jobs was increasing. A previous study also found that the people's individual interest rather than collective interest of society prevailed more in party-people relations during and after elections (Baral et al. 2001: 110-114).The leaders and workers across the party openly realized that the election had become increasingly expensive.

One of the reasons for the election becoming a more expensive affair led to the decline of volunteerism in political parties. The party and candidate generally try to activate the party workers through granting them collective incentive (ideology, policy and leadership) and selective incentive (power, status, money, job and other opportunities). In the early phase of democracy party sympathizers, particularly those of the NC and the UML, were actively and spontaneously involved in election campaigns. But over time, parties had been losing its capacity of workers mobilization through granting collective incentives. The NC workers' appeared relatively least active in the 1999 general elections compared to their mobility in previous elections. This was also a hard reality of the UML, the RPP and the NSP as well. This trend appeared as a consequence of decline of ideology, value and morality in politics. Particularly during the second tenure of parliament featured by hung parliament and coalition government, politics had turned into a cruel game of government making and unmaking in which all kinds of manipulations had been used. Parties have increasingly become an instrument for self-aggrandizement of the power elite and vested interest groups. This had spillover effects in elections that the party workers sought individual benefits, i.e. money, opportunity and other material benefits, etc. as a price for their involvement in election campaigning.

Post-Election Times

Elections can be seen in twin perspectives, one a process of getting people's mandate to rule over the country and, the other, use of state power and resources for the benefit of the larger sections of people and society. For the post-election time, the moot question is whether the parties and people's elected representatives fulfil their promises, made during elections, at least to the minimal level. Whether the agendas they presented before the voters are translated into the government policy and in their functions. Though the people at large seemed critical of the parties' role in post-election time, some appreciation was expressed for parties' initiations in bringing about social reform and economic development.

The restoration of the multiparty system is equated in both the conceptual and operational sense with the citizen's freedom to speak without fear. This has given a sense of empowerment in both subjective and objective ways that reflected with the rise of social movements by disadvantaged sections of society. Social reforms against the untouchability, women's movement against exploitation, ethnic upsurge against deprivation, political awareness and consciousness could be seen spreading all over the country. Credit had been given to multiparty democracy rather than any particular political party (ies) in building people's awareness, confidence, and assertiveness. Other common things observed was development in the sector of infrastructure buildings, e.g. in education, road construction, school building, health, electrification, communication, telecommunication.

But making an assessment of parties' performance in post-election time in totality, the people seemed very disappointed against political parties and their representatives to the elected bodies. The advent of democracy has in its wake brought into focus a number of pervasive socio-economic problems of the country in different forms and shape, i.e. gender issues, minority problems, grievances of the disadvantaged groups, unemployment, corruption, etc. But political parties appeared largely not sincere in addressing such emerging social and economic problems and to give realistic and pragmatic policy incentives. The first tenure of parliament (1991-1994), featured by a bitter confrontation between the NC government and the left-dominated opposition and internal conflicts in the ruling party, ended without any significant achievement. Politics deteriorated to the lowest ebb in the second parliament (1994-1999) marked by the politics of a hung parliament and coalition government. The third parliament appeared as indifferent to resolve a number of problems facing the country and unable to resist increasing the threat to democracy by the Maoists' increasing violent activities. So, despite political parties are conceived as a linkage institution between the state and society (Lawson, 1980), the Nepali political parties appeared to have largely failed to observe their basic duty of linking citizens' preference with public policy.

TABLE 4:10
Post-Election Performance

Total No. of Respondents 500

Variables	*Total*		*Area %*		*Sex %*		*Party Affiliation %*	
	No	*%*	*Rural*	*Urban*	*Male*	*Female*	*Member*	*Non-member*
Agree	11	2.2	2.0	3.0	2.4	1.6	1.8	2.4
Partly agree	113	22.6	23.3	19.8	23.3	20.5	25.2	21.4
Disagree	362	72.4	71.7	75.2	72.8	71.3	71.8	72.7
Don't know	14	2.8	3.0	2.0	1.6	6.6	1.2	3.6

Source: NCCS (2001).

In response to a question about the fulfilment of promise by the parties/candidates after they elected, only 2.2 percent fully affirmed. Those who partly agreed were 22.6 percent. But 72.4 percent of the total 500 respondents completely disagreed with the statement that party/candidate fulfil their promise after they were elected. Even the respondents belonging to party members shared this general filling by an overwhelming majority of 71.8 percent. This shows a vast gap between the people and party in Nepal.

There were long lists of complaints against parties and elected representatives. Most of the party (ies) leaders, once they were elected, hardly looked back and visited their own constituency; they did not care to hear people's grievances; they indulged in power politics and self-interest completely ignoring the interests of society; they were corrupt; they had a loose moral stand and characters.

Once the election is over, the distance between the people and party increases.A number of opinion surveys show that 'poverty, price rises and employment' are the most important problems of the country followed by other issues, i.e. irrigation, drinking water, personal security, etc.(NOCS, 1993; SEARCH, 1994: Khanal et al., 1996). But these problems were put in miscellaneous in parties' agendas and priority lists. The gap between the people and the party has been further widened by the way the political parties perform patronage distribution function. Instead of maintaining direct contact with the masses, the party leaders rely on a small group of party activists, who would supposedly be educated and articulate in their own locality, to consolidate their influence in their electoral constituency. Only these people and not the masses get personal benefits from the patronage of the party leaders.

Conclusion

Of the twin electoral functions of political parties – acquisition of legitimacy and respect for people's interest – the latter has been neglected in Nepal. A decade long democratic experience in the 1990s, during which general elections were held thrice and local elections twice, showed that political parties represented only votes, not the interest of the people. This has a negative impact on the parties' image of change agents. Parties' credentials as change agents remains only in theory, ideological identity, formal documents (i.e. election manifestos and agendas) and promises and assurance to the voters. But parties' potentials to bring about change in social, economic and political spheres have not been transformed into reality. What is wrong?

The candidate selection process, though centralized, is not seriously objectionable so long as the parties respect public opinion and consult their own local leaders in the decision-making process. But the exclusion of marginalized sections of society, i.e. women, Dalit, poor, illiterate shows the candidate selection process as an elitist affair. The process, therefore, needs reformation for broader participation and decentralization for the future. The consideration of continuity and popularity factors while choosing persons for candidacy is admirable. But, at the same time, the entry of money power, family and kinship ties, proximity to party high command and other ascretive factors in nomination of party candidates certainly impede the party's ability to work in post-election times.

The general and local elections held in the 1990s had shown that parties contested and campaigned the elections on general and vague agendas: development, political stability and social security. Lack of specific policy agendas to attract the voters seemed to be an immaturity of political parties. Abuse of state power and resources by the ruling party (ies) is/was another form of manipulation of elections. Moreover, the decline of parties' ability to motivate their own workers and mobilize voters through collective incentive allowed the role of money and muscle power in elections.

Party-people relations have become more problematic in post-election times. Since Nepali politics has perennially been bogged down in intra-party and inter-party conflicts, people's problems and needs have always been sidelined. Conceivably, political parties in general have become too selfish to take up the burning issues concerning ordinary voters. Consequently, political parties appear largely not being sincere in addressing emerging social and economic problems and to give realistic and pragmatic policy incentives.

To rectify such a situation some concrete measures should be taken to improve the overall relations within and among the parties. While doing so one should keep it mind that the smooth functioning of multiparty democracy requires effective leadership, responsible government, constructive opposition, healthy competition, primacy of policy and programme, good governance, etc. Moreover, crisis management within the party is a prerequisite for healthy development of the party system. So, parties may regain their ability to work as true linkage institutions between the people's interest and the government's policy.

NOTES

1. The Nepal Centre for Contemporary Studies (NCCS) conducted a survey on Election and Democracy in January 2001 with a total of 500 respondents from five sampled districts: Dhankuta, Rautahat, Kaski, Dang and Baitadi. The survey also had a component of face to face interviews with local party leaders and stakeholders of the sample districts. This paper also includes the information collected through interviews, conducted on 15-30 January 2001, with government offices: Sambhu Koirala (Chief District Officer [CDO] in Dhankuta), Gupta Bahadur Shrestha (District Superintendent Police [DSP] in Dhankuta), Mahendra Kumar Pokhrel (DSP, Rautahat), Ram Bahadur Gurung (DSP in Dang), Narayan Gopal Malegu (CDO in Dang) and Ram Krishna Bhurtel (CDO in Baitatdi), NC local leaders: Ramesh Amatya (Dhankuta), Majdul Huk (Rautahat), Sukra Raj Shastri (Kaski), Dipak Regmi (Dang) and Narendra Singh Thapa (Baitadi), UML local leaders: Tika Ram Chemjong (Dhankuta), Ram Chandra Patel (Rautahat), Som Nath Pyasi (Kaski), Devi Pokhrel (Dang) and Maya Bhatta (Baitadi), and others: Sarad Shrestha (independent, Dhakuta), Khajanchi Saha (CPN, United, Rautahat), and Tek Nath Gautam (independent, Dang) .
2. The split of the UML in March 1998 had directly affected its position in losing 43 seats by the party. Were the votes polled by the candidates of the breakaway group, the ML, to be added to the candidates of the UML, the party would gain a comfortable majority of 112 instead of the present 69 seats in the HOR. See Khanal and Hachhethu (1990).

Chapter 5

PARLIAMENT AND PRIME MINISTER

> At a time, when I became Prime Minister, I did not have a clear idea about the power and function of the Prime Minister. I asked King Birendra to enlighten me on the role of constitutional monarchy in parliamentary democracy. The King also expressed his ignorance on the position of constitutional monarchy in the changed context.[1]
>
> — *Girija Prasad Koirala*

Girija Prasad Koirala – leader of the Nepali Congress Party (NC) and first elected Prime Minister (PM) of reinstated democracy who held the PM post four times between 1991 and 2001 – admitted that transition to democracy in Nepal began with ignorance of basic tenets of parliamentary system and also of the management of governance. His consultation with King Birendra to clarify the Prime Minister's position vis-à-vis monarchy and the king's reply of his ignorance on this question indicated uncertainty about the future course of Nepali politics: consolidation of democracy or regression.

In the 1990s, Nepal adopted the British and Indian model of parliamentary democracy. The UK – from where a system of constitutional monarchy and parliamentary democracy originated – has developed its political system through evolution. The centuries long power struggle was terminated with the transformation of sovereignty into parliament and hence the monarch never tries to regain power. The British experience suggests that in a monarchical country the king's compliance to the spirit of popular sovereignty is essential for making democracy functional and effective. The UK has built up a strong system – respected by monarchy, parliament, government and others – that any change of party and personality in the helm of power does not make a substantial difference in the party system and political process. Since parties originated to assist the parliamentarian elite, the party organization has placed itself into a subordinate position vis-à-vis elected leaders. The leader of the parliamentary party is also the leader of the party organization. The British system has a good record of following the principle of cabinet responsibility to parliament, which implies the consideration of opposition voices in making major policy decisions. Besides, the stability of the government is ensured by the practice that the opposition does not aspire for power before the next election. To make the system more dynamic, the UK has recently modified its classical model of the two-party system and majoritarian democracy considering the new development, i.e. erosion of two-party electoral domination, class de-alignment within the electorates, the emergence and growth of various minority parties, growth of backbench dissent within parliamentary parties, etc. (Webb, 2000). Since the 1970s, The British system is distinctly heading towards the multiparty consensus democracy.

India is another model for stabilizing democracy in feudal and authoritarian social settings. Unlike the UK where system prevails more than anything else, personality figures more as one of the contributing factors for the stability of democracy in India. Nehru's uninterrupted leadership as the PM for 17 years in the post-independence period under one party Congress dominant system is perceived as a key factor which saved India from political instability. Nehru was a catalyst for introducing the prime ministerial system in India and obviously placing the elected wing of the party in ascendancy over the party organizational apparatus (Kochanek, 1968). He, however, respected the value of the party for the implementation of the government policy and in mobilization of public support for election. By the late 1960s, the Indian party system changed following the end of the Congress domination and personalization of the party by powerful leaders, particularly the Indian National Congress (INC) under the leadership of Indira Gandhi and Rajiv Gandhi (Kholi, 1991). However the prime ministerial system has retained more effectively except during the coalition periods. The PM generally commands the leadership of government and the authority of the ruling party.

British and Indian experiences suggest some points and conditions that require for operating parliamentary democracy in a way as the prime ministeral system. The first point is the personal and institutional capability of the PM to manage the system. The PM's unique and pre-eminent status and power in the parliamentary system is aptly defined by Winston Churchill, "There can be no comparison between the positions of number one and numbers two, three and four" (Quoted in Rose 1980: 54). The general convention is that a minister should resign in two conditions, i.e. if he/she disagrees with the PM's decision and loses the PM's confidence. As both the leader of parliament and chairman of the cabinet, the PM represents the fusion of legislative and executive authority. The PM is overburdened with executive roles and responsibilities. He/she determines who of several hundred MPs will serve as cabinet ministers. He/she generally removes ministers who are not loyal to him. Ministers' proposals generally turn into executive policies and decisions only after the approval of the PM. Getting sanction to the executive's decisions and policies through the legislature is the main parliamentary job of the PM. The executive policies, proposals and decisions are generally approved by the parliament so long as the government enjoys a majority in the House. The PM will always try to retain a majority in parliament either through distribution of patronage or threat to punish the MPs of the ruling party. If the parliament obstructs the government, the PM may use his/her prerogative to dissolve the House. The parliamentary system is, therefore called the prime ministerial system. As being the highest state authority, the PM is the key person and institution in the parliamentary system.

Second, to ensure the institutionalization of the prime ministerial system, it is essential that the head of the state – king in a monarchical country and the president in a republican state – must limit his/her formal power to encourage, to advise and to warn the government. Third, the PM's post should be held by the top leader of the ruling party so that he/she could command the leadership of both the government and the party. Or there should be a system of the party elected wing's ascendancy over organizational apparatus. Fourth, the government should be responsible to parliament that implies the consideration of the opposition's voice in making major policy decisions. The opposition, in turn, should not aspire for power before the next election in order to ensure stability of government.

This chapter is organized in four sections. It starts with a brief note about the attributes of the parliamentary system with references to the UK and Indian experiences. The second section deals with the relationship between the PM and the parliamentary party. The following section concentrates on relations between ruling and opposition parties in parliament. The chapter concludes with an analysis of impacts of the PM's relations with his own parliamentary party and opposition parties vis-à-vis monarchy.

Structure of Parliamentary Party

Each party having representation in parliament should have its own separate structure for its elected members, Parliamentary Party (PP). The PP represents the party in national legislature. It consists of party's members of parliament (MPs) and a leader, elected by the majority of more than fifty percent of the party's MPs in the House. The PP's tasks, as mentioned in the constitution of NC-PP, are: (1) to pursue the party's principles, goal and policy (2) to maintain discipline and cohesion in the party's MPs' role and behaviour in parliament and (3) to develop cooperation and coordination with MPs of other parties in parliament (NC [b], 1994).

For smooth running of the NC-PP in an organized and effective way, it set up an Executive Committee (constituted by a leader, ten elected members, ten nominated members, and other office bearers, i.e. leader of National Assembly, Chief Whip, Whips of both Houses, Minister of Parliamentary Affairs, and the party general secretary) and several subject committees. The organizational structure of other parties in parliament was largely similar to that of the NC-PP. Differences were mainly in name and numbers. For instance, the UML used the name Parliamentary Board for the organization for which the NC-PP called Executive Committee. The UML's parliamentary groups were parallel to the NC-PP's subject committees. The size of parties in parliament also determined for less sophistication in organizational structures of small parties. The constitution of RPP-PP makes a provision that its MPs would automatically become the members of the Executive Committee of its PP when the total number of the party's MPs would be less than 21 (RPP [b], 1994). The number of RPP's MPs in the HOR in the first, second, and third tenure of parliament was 4, 19 and 11 respectively. The Nepal Sadbhabana Party (NSP) – which held 6, 3, and 5 seats in the HOR in the first, second and third tenure of parliament respectively – did not make a distinction between the general body and executive body of its PP, nor did it provide the structure of subject committee/group (NSP [b], 1994).

Ideally the PP is expected to perform as a deliberative organization where diverse opinions of MPs of a party are streamlined into cohesive policy and programme. The BJP in India has set a good example that "its parliamentary party meets every Tuesday when parliament is in session" (Prakesh, 1995). Convening PP meeting frequently and developing it as a true deliberative organization contribute to meet two purposes. One, it provides space, time and freedom to MPs to express their opinion independently on the government's agendas and bills before presentation of these documents to the parliament. It should be taken into account that MPs are normally not allowed to put their conscience voice/vote in Houses of parliament. Two, a system of making decision- earlier in the PP meeting prevents MPs from playing a rebellious role in the House. Though the ruling PP generally helps the government for smooth sailing of its business in parliament, its importance is less significant. Even in the UK, as observed by Paul Webb, "Parliamentary parties are almost entirely subservient to the needs of the elites occupying the executive offices in the state" (Webb, 2000).

In the early 1990s, the NC-PP formed 20 subject committees, each constituting 5-7 MPs, to look after ministries of the government but none of them performed the assigned task as it was proven by using only 4 out of 20 rooms available in the office of the NC-PP (Acharya, 2000). An exception was found in the first nine month of the second parliament (1994-1999) when the NC was in opposition. The NC-PP and its subject committees became active and effective in ventilating the party's agenda and in criticizing the government's policy (NC, 1995). But this was proved a short-term and temporary phenomenon as the structures of the NC-PP virtually became dysfunctional since the party recaptured power from September 1995. The leadership of the NC-PP was changed – G. P. Koirala, S. B. Deuba and K.P. Bhattarai held this position at different times – but none of them gave proper attention to develop it as an effective and deliberative organization in areas of governance and legislation.

The PP had also been undervalued by leaders of other parties, i.e. the UML and the RPP, while sitting in power or in the opposition in the 1990s. Parties' ignorance of strengthening the system of PP could be observed in many ways. One, till the first parliament (1991-1994), parties did not have a written constitution of their respective PP, except the United People's Front (UPF). Two, the UML, as the major opposition party, constituted its Shadow Cabinet at that time, but failed to push forward this system since its oppositional roles were over-weighted in street politics than in the Houses of parliament. The negative projection of the UML's Shadow Cabinet led to lapse of one component of parliamentary democracy in

Nepal, as the subsequent major opposition party did not revive it. Three, many parties did not call the meeting of their respective PPs frequently. The NC-PP hardly convened except during the time of the routine meeting – once in a month during the session of parliament in addition to pre- and post- session meetings and in critical times. The PP of the RPP and the NSP did not assemble regularly. The UML had a relatively good record in this regard that the meetings of its PP were convened in other times, in addition to routine meetings, particularly at the time of deliberation on the government's annual policy, budget, important issues and bills. Last but not the least, both the NC and the UML reset their respective PP committees/groups to make them compatible with committee structures of the Houses, different from previous settings in line with the government ministries. This manifested in realization of parties, based on their experiences, that the structure of PP was least relevant to the governance of the executive.

A survey conducted with 245 out of the total 265 MPs of both Houses[2], including NC's 123, UML's 89 and RPP's 12, revealed of not developing the PP as an effective deliberative structure. Only 12 to 24 per cent MPs affirmed that the PP took 'intensive discussion' on 'party's policy', 'government programme,' and 'bills'. The nature of discussion on given issues was just 'general' (*samanya),* said by majority MPs of all parties, including NC, UML and RPP. Moreover, 29 percent of them stated 'no-discussion' on bills, but the figure of this argument reduced into 14 and 12 percent on 'government programme' and 'party policy' respectively. Party-wise breakdown of data showed the UML's better position, as 39 percent of its MPs claimed that the nature of discussion in their PP was 'intensive' on government bills, but relatively low on party policy (26%) and on bills (12%). Among the NC MPs only 10 to 15 percent affirmed 'intensive discussion' on the given three areas, but those who said about 'no discussion' ranged from 12 to 35 percent.

Insensitivity to the value of the PP for governance and legislation reveals that leaders are authoritarian in their temperaments. In retrospect it also suggests ignorance and incapacity of leaders to transfer collective strength of the PP for the consolidation of the PM's position in governance and in relations with other political forces. The PP is both the source of strength and challenge to the leader. The PM's position will be secure so long as it enjoys the confidence of the ruling PP. But, the un-institutionalised PP has a tendency to becoming a source of threat to the PM occasionally when intra-party conflicts get intensified. Since the PP is

TABLE 5:1
Nature and Quality of Discussion in PP Meetings

Data in Percentage

Content	*Party' policy*				*Government Programme*				*Bills*			
	Total	*NC*	*UML*	*RPP*	*Total*	*NC*	*UML*	*RPP*	*Total*	*NC*	*UML*	*RPP*
	245	123	89	12	245	123	89	12	245	123	89	12
Intensive	20.0	15.4	25.8	16.7	24.1	12.2	39.3	25.0	12.2	9.8	13.5	8.3
General	62.0	69.1	57.3	66.7	54.3	66.7	43.8	58.3	50.6	51.2	50.6	83.3
Not discussed	12.2	13.8	13.5	8.3	14.3	17.1	13.5	9.3	29.0	35.0	31.5	0.0
Others	1.2	0.8	2.2	0.0	2.0	1.6	2.2	0.0	2.9	3.3	3.4	0.0
No Response	4.5	0.8	1.1	8.3	5.3	2.4	1.1	8.3	5.3	0.8	1.1	8.3
Total	100	100	100	100	100	100	100	100	100	100	100	100

Source: NCCS (2002).

not yet institutionalized, the nature of government-PP relations is mainly informal and inter-personal and is guided by a system of patron-client relation. An MP aspires for support from ministers to enhance his/her personal and political interests and ministers use their influence among MPs for consolidation and promotion of their position in the government and the party. The government's control over its PP is considered as natural because, "The principle of parliament is obedience to leaders" (Quoted Walter Bagehot in Prakash, 1995: 297). Three major sources through which the PM commands and controls the PP are: (1) distribution of patronage (2) threat of punishment and (3) authority in party organization.

Patronage Distribution

One of the means with which the PM controls the PP is through the distribution of patronage and resources. To be PM means to become resourceful. He has formal power to select the members of the Council of Ministers from among several MPs of the ruling party. As the leader of parliament, he/she can play a decisive role in posting MPs in privileged positions and or executive posts of Houses, i.e. Speaker and Deputy Speaker of the HOR, Chairman and Vice-Chairman of the National Assembly, Chairman of parliamentary committees. He could offer other incentives, material as well as political, to the MPs. Hopes of MPs to get support from the PM for promotion as ministers or for taking other advantages make them docile to the PM.

The PM generally uses his/her power of patronage distribution keeping in mind the survival of government as the top most priority. Unlike the President in the presidential system who enjoys a fixed term of office and can only be dismissed by impeachment, the PM in the parliamentary system could remain in office so long as he/she commands the confidence of his/her PP and the Lower House of parliament. PM Margaret Thatcher – portrayed as 'elected monarch' and re-elected as the leader in 1989 by 85 percent MPs of the Conservative Party – was forced to resign in 1990 due to challenge posed to her leadership by a marginal number of Conservative back bench MPs (Elgie, 1995). This is one of the several instances to show that a person can be elected to the post of PM by majority MPs of the ruling party but it does not ensure his/her survivability. In retrospect, the PM is expected to use his/her patronage distribution power, particularly in constituting the cabinet, considering internal power equation of the ruling party.

The failure of G.P. Koirala to accommodate his dissidents in the cabinet eventually led to the fall of his government prematurely in 1994. Later, when he came back to power in April 1998, he included dissidents in the cabinet and this contributed to the continuity of his government till the May 1999 general election. K.P. Bhattarai, succeeding Koirala as the PM, followed the same, considering the internal balance of power of the NC in selecting ministers for his government. Such a reconciliationary measure was not respected in subsequent governments of the NC, led by G.P. Koirala (March 2000 – July 2001) and later by S.B. Deuba. Instead, each formed a big cabinet to woo the members. Deuba was a catalyst for introducing a jumbo-sized cabinet – with numbers of ministers extending to 49 during his coalition government, and 41 in the majority NC government under his leadership. There is a lone case in the UK that in 1975 the Labour PM "Harold Wilson had 118 MPs in jobs as ministers, junior ministers, or as parliamentary private secretaries" (Rose, 1980: 55). S. B. Deuba, for the survival of his government, relied much on distribution of patronage in different forms, particularly providing ministerial posts to many MPs. He did not hesitate to say repeatedly that he constituted a jumbo cabinet (in 1995 and 2001) to win the game of head counting of the MPs (*Kantipur*, 17 June 1996; 5 February 2002). But the absence of dissidents in the Deuba government suggested a new trend that appeared from the time of his immediate predecessor G.P. Koirala. Such trends appeared as an impact of three new developments in internal politics of the NC. One, personal interest of the party rank and file replaced the loyalty to the leader as a detrimental factor for alignment and realignment of factional politics in the party. Two, from March 2000, the leader of parliament had been elected by majority votes of the NC MPs against previous records of selection through consensus by a few party executives. Third, after K.P. Bhattarai was humiliated and forced to resign from the post of PM, the factional groups lost flexibility and modesty. Consequently, the NC was formerly split in May 2002.

The UML, whenever it came to power, had always placed few members of the minority factions in the government. So internal squabbles of the UML had never arisen as a factor behind the fall of both its minority government and coalition government. The RPP leaders resorted to a strategy of inclusion of its MPs in the government. It had only 19 members in the HOR in the second parliament (1994-1999) but most of them – sometimes 17 out of 19 – were given ministerial posts in three successive coalition governments (from September 1995 to April 1998), first led by

S.B. Deuba, and then L.B. Chand, and finally S.B. Thapa. But, some RPP ministers played a decisive role behind the fall of all these three coalition governments. These cases and the fall of the NC government led by K.P. Bhattarai did not support the general logic that "the more widely a Prime Minister distributes jobs among groupings within the parliamentary party, the broader the base of support" (Rose 1980: 56). Another factor that needs to highlighted is the PM's power to punish as one of the important instruments to retain his control over the PP.

Punishment

The PM enjoys enormous authority to stick to members of his PP. He has sole authority to sack ministers. In the 1990s, there were only two instances that prompted the PM to fire his colleagues from the cabinet abruptly. First in December 1991 the then PM G. P. Koirala sacked six cabinet ministers for showing greater loyalty to party leaders, Ganesh Man Singh and K. P. Bhattarai, than to the PM. Another case was the removal of C.P. Mainali from the cabinet of the UML's minority government in July 1995 for his violation of the party discipline. There are several other mechanisms and systems through which the PM commands and controls the PP. The most significant is the whip system. The party whip is the key instrument to implement the party's policy and the leader's decision in the House. The party MPs normally vote as a cohesive bloc. Particularly voting on bills, there was no record of defying the party whip in the 1990s, except one bill related to mining and natural resources that failed to pass in 1994 because of absence of the NC dissidents in parliament.

Party MPs normally follow the whip because of the risk being involved it. The constitutional provision of abandonment of MP posts is elaborated by the anti-defection law. Accordingly, an MP will lose his post in parliament if he/she violates the party whips (SP, 1997). By their own respective constitution of PP, the NC listed five points and the UML spelled out eight points to explain the conditions of violation of discipline by MPs (NC, 1994 [b]; UML [b], 1994). Absence in the House without taking permission, violation of PP constitution and code of conduct, disobeying the leader and whip's order, voting against party line, etc. are taken as acts for which the party can take a variety of disciplinary actions against the MP, including expulsion from the party which automatically leads to abandonment of his/her post in parliament. There were several records that each parliamentary party registered demands to evict their own MPs for the violation of party discipline.[3] But none of the cases of expulsion of MPs from their respective parties was translated into action, as none of them was deprived from membership. In the case of the RPP and the UML, it was understood that dissident MPs invoked another provision of the anti-defection act forming separate political party by taking 40 percent MPs from the parent organization. Why the anti-defection act had not been enforced in other cases was not explained. This, however, showed the practical limitation of Nepal's PM to command and control the PP members.

Defection of the party whip by a group of MPs could be detrimental to the survival of the government and the unity of the party. The NC government led by G.P. Koirala fell because of the absence of 35 dissident MPs during voting on the government's annual policy and programme. The case repeated in March 1997 that the NC led coalition government under PM S.B. Deuba collapsed owing to the absence of two NC's MPs in voting on the confidence motion. The defection of party whip by 20 MPs of the UML in August 1993 on elections to the National Assembly and another case of defying the party whip by 27 MPs in voting of the ratification of the Mahakali treaty were a prelude to disintegration of the party in March 1998. In the RPP, defection of the party whip was a normal practice than an exception during the second parliament (1994-1999), which ultimately led to the formal split of the party in January 1998. These cases reveal that the PM's power to punish will become ineffective in two situations, one if the PM's position in the party central apparatus is so weak, and the other, if internal conflicts lead to the disintegration of the party.

Prime Minister, Party Central Committee and Parliamentary Party

Several instances of the defection of party whip and non-implementation of the anti-defection act suggested the limitation of the PM to control the PP by the stick of disciplinary action. This also applied to the leader of opposition parties. This indicated the problems in relations between organizational and elected wings of the party. Party-government relations in the Western and other South Asian countries are less tense because of two main reasons. One, the PM or President generally holds the leadership of both the government and the party. In case of separation of leadership in two fronts, the formal post of party leadership is generally given to a less influential person. For instance, the BJP President Venkaaya

Naidu could hardly challenge the power and position of PM Atal Bihari Bajpai. Two, the Western countries and India have developed a system – through long practice and tradition – in which the party organization usually plays subordinate and supportive roles to the elected leaders.[4] The 1990s experiences of the party system in Nepal revealed that the party-government relationship was not defined and this had an impact in creating problems in relations between the PM and the PP.

TABLE 5:2
Structures Contributing to Cohesion in PP

Percentage Based on Multiple Responses

Content	*Total (245)*	*NC (123)*	*UML (89)*	*RPP (12)*
Party Central Committee (CC)	63.3	74.0	48.3	75.0
Parliamentary Department of Party CC	42.0	27.6	66.3	33.3
Executive Committee of PP	38.0	34.1	47.2	41.7
Leader of PP	46.9	39.8	59.6	58.3
Whip	58.0	75.6	46.1	33.3
Others	3.3	3.3	3.4	0.0
No Response	4.1	0.8	0.0	8.3
Total	255.5	255.3	270.8	250

Source: NCCS (2002).

In response to a question to find out three major structures that play a greater role for the party's cohesive role in parliament, the majority respondents pointed out 'party CC' as the main structure, followed by 'whip', 'leader of PP', "Parliamentary Department of CC', 'Executive Committee of PP' respectively. There were some variations among the NC, the UML and the RPP in this regard. The NC MPs gave almost equal weight to 'Party CC' and 'whip' as the key institutions that instructed and directed MPs. The role of 'Leader of PP' and 'Executive Committee of PP' came next to the party CC and Whip. For the UML MPs, the key structure to regulate their role in parliament was 'Parliamentary Department of party CC'. Next to it, they identified the "leader of PP" as another important person/structure in playing a directive role to MPs. They gave almost the same weight to 'party CC', 'Executive Committee to PP' and 'whip' as structures contributing to cohesive behaviour of the party MPs. The RPP's MPs gave much weight to 'party CC', followed by 'leader of PP', 'Executive Committee of PP', 'Parliamentary Department of party CC' and 'whip' in listing the structures which regulated the behaviour of party MPs.

The primacy of organizational structure, CC in particular, in all parties to maintain cohesion in the PP suggests that the PM's ability to control the PP is largely determined by his position in party organization and his relations with the party executives. The coming sections deal with experiments of triangular relations among the PM, the PP, and the party CC in the 1990s.

NC Experience

While forming the NC government after the 1991 general election, the party top executives selected PM G.P. Koirala and his cabinet members. Koirala was equal to two other senior leaders of the party, G.M. Singh and K.P. Bhattarai, in the NC's troika structure (Hachhethu, 1992). G.M. Singh, one of the front line leaders of the party since its inception and as commander of the successful 1990 mass movement, enjoyed the status of the supreme leader (*Sarbamanya Neta*). K.P. Bhattarai, despite his defeat in the 1991 election, regained the pre-eminent position after his re-election as the NC president unanimously in February 1992. As the president of the party who had formal authority to nominate all members of the party CC, Bhattarai's domination in the party's top organizational structure was obvious. G.P. Koirala was the PM and the most influential leader among the party rank and file. Taking into account the collective leadership of the party and sources of power of each of the troika leaders, two alternatives were available in framing the party-government relations. One was sharing of power by the PM with the party top leaders for which Singh and Bhattarai insisted strongly. The NC's CC took a number of decisions in concurrence with the party leaders' plea for a system of the party's control over government.[5] The party's collective authority was extended to some extent to elected bodies as it was reflected with the presence and sitting of Singh and Bhattarai (despite not being an MP) along with Koirala in the meetings of the NC-PP. Bhattari, instead of Koirala (leader of NC-PP), presided over the meetings of the NC-PP.

Another alternative model for party-government relations was granting of greater autonomy to Koirala to exercise his formal power and authority as the chairman of the cabinet and as the leader of the NC-PP. Koirala's cabinet reshuffle in December 1991 at his own discretion indicated his ambition to emerge as the most powerful leader. This could be possible on two conditions. One is voluntary withdrawal from active politics by the party leader as accepted by Western standards that the incumbent leader, after his defeat or no-contest in election, transfers leadership to the new one having electoral legitimacy. Otherwise, the PM generally uses his position and privilege to curb the influence of the party leader. PM Koirala also proposed to end the troika system and change in the presidential structure of the party organization but did not push it forward effectively as his moves for strengthening the PM's position turned counter-productive for the survival of his government. For another condition propelling the position of the PM against the party heavy weights, the emergence of Indira Gandhi as unchallenged leader of the INC in 1967 showed an example that it could achieve only at the cost of unity of the party. Koirala did not follow in the footsteps of Indira Gandhi despite intra-party conflict intensified to the extent that the party leaders searched the way for displacement of Koirala from the PM's post. K.P. Bhattarai's bid for the February 1994 by-election was a clear manifestation of the strategy of the anti-Koirala faction. Defeat of Bhattarai because of internal sabotage (*antarghat*) further heightened the pressure for Koirala's resignation. The NC's CC minuted for resignation of PM Koirala by majority of 15 out of 27 members. But Koirala refused to abide by the party decision on procedural grounds that he could be removed only by majority members of the NC-PP or by majority of a total of 205 members of the HOR.

As a consequence of such developments in party-government relations, PM Koirala's relations with the NC-PP changed after the February1994 by-election. Previously the NC-PP, including dissident MPs, followed the government line while confronting the opposition parties on several issues, i.e. the strike launched by civil servants, Tanakpur case (a treaty signed with India), Das Dhunga incident (in which UML top leaders Madan Bhandari and Jib Raj Ashrit died), etc. But in the post-February 1994 by-election, dissensions in the NC-PP turned into an internal rebellion prompting 36 dissident MPs of the HOR to carry out the party leaders' agenda of Koirala's resignation. They even went to the extent of refusing to abide by the whip of the NC-PP – instead followed the whip issued by party President Bhattarai – while voting against the no-confidence motion tabled by the UML in February 1994. Koirala failed to manage the situation either through patronage distribution or through punishment to rebellion. His proposal for the accommodation of dissident MPs in the cabinet was rejected outright as the party leaders changed their strategy from their earlier demand of power sharing to resignation of Koirala. The lack of the anti-defection act and constitution of the NC-PP at that time constrained the PM's power to punish. The party constitution of the NC and the constitutional provision of anti-defection, before it was elaborated by a separate act, allocated power to the party authority only for taking disciplinary action against MPs.[6] In such a situation, Koirala became helpless when 35 NC's MPs of the HOR defied the party whip by absenting from voting on the government's annual policy in July 1994. This led to resignation of PM Koirala and announcement of a mid-term poll through the dissolution of the HOR.

G.P. Koirala's relations with the PP was different when he came back to power in April 1998 and again in March 2000. Before he was reappointed as the PM, he was already elected as the party president in May 1996 and re-elected in January 2001. Holding two highest positions of the government as well as the party, he took several of important decisions, including change of coalition partner from the ML (August-December 1998) to the UML (December 1998-May 1999) without much objection from his dissidents in the party. The projection of the Koirala government (April 1998-May 1999) as the interim government to hold elections and his role as the party president in selection of candidates also counted in neutralizing his opponents in the party. Besides, he accommodated his dissident MPs in the cabinet. But later, when Koirala succeeded K.P. Bhattarai in March 2000, dissidents refused to stay in the Koirala government. They even registered a vote of no-confidence against PM Koirala in December 2000. Despite the number of dissident MPs increased from 35 in 1994 to 43 in 2000, Koirala resisted comfortably the pressure to relinquish from one of two posts, party president or PM. His position as the party president helped Koirala to retain his command in the NC-PP and to prevent defection of dissident MPs. PM Koirala resigned in July 2001 partly because of internal compulsions but mainly because of non-cooperation of the king and the army to his plan of military mobilization against the Maoist insurgency. Deuba's succession to Koirala brought back tension in the PM's relations with the PP and the party leaders as had happened before. Holding of two separate posts by two individual leaders seemed to strain relations between the PM and the party president.

Earlier, after the NC regained majority in the 1999 election of the HOR, K.P. Bhattarai became the PM of the country. Bhattarai's position in the internal power equation of the party was much worse than Koirala's influence in 1991-1994. G.P. Koirala succeeded Bhattarai as the party president since May 1996. By reconstituting the party CC in July 1999, Koirala cut the size of the pro-Bhattarai group from its strength of 9 seats in 26 members in May 1996 to 6 in the total of 31 members in the highest body of the party. Worst of all – despite Bhattarai was elected unanimously as the leader of the NC-PP – the pro-Bhattarai group was in minority in a total of 113 MPs of the NC in the HOR. A majority of NC's MPs of the HOR registered no-confidence motion against the leadership of Bhattarai thrice from December 1999 to March 2000 which ultimately forced Bhattarai to resign on March 16, 2001. G. P. Koirala succeeded him as the PM but could not stay in power for long. S.B Deuba replaced Koirala as the PM in July 2001.

Deuba held the PM's post for the second time. Previously, he led a coalition government of the NC, the RPP and the NSP from September 1995 to March 1997. At that time Deuba was neither in top ranking leadership of the party nor had a stronghold in the NC-PP. Being the PM of the coalition government, Deuba had difficulty to maintain the balance between his party and other coalition partners. In order to ensure the internal equation of the RPP for the continuity of the government, Deuba granted a larger share and power to the RPP, i.e. inclusion of all RPP's MPs, except two former PMs Chand and Thapa, in the government and re-entry of renegade ministers in the cabinet. But this issue – which led to discrediting Deuba – provided a ground to play for the dissidents against the government. Party-government relations changed after G. P. Koirala was elected the party president in May 1996. Koirala's ambition to lead the parliamentary front posed a real threat to the survival of the Deuba government. The power game culminated when two NC's MPs abstained in voting on a confidence motion, leading to the fall of the Deuba government on 6 March 1997. Koirala replaced Deuba as the leader of the NC-PP on 9 March 1997.

But, the situation was different when Deuba came back to power in July 2001. He succeeded G.P. Koirala as the PM by a majority of 72 against 40 votes of Shushil Koirala – nephew of G.P. Koirala and mastermind of the Koirala faction – in the election to the leader of the NC-PP on 21 July 2001. Deuba had already projected himself as a rival of G.P. Koirala contesting elections for the leader of the NC-PP in March 2000 and for the party president in January 2001. Deuba was defeated in his earlier attempts but gained later to be elected as the leader of the NC-PP. The Koirala faction dominated the party CC that only 9 out of 31 CC members belonged to the Deuba faction. The party-government relations remained tense. Sushil Koirala, general secretary of the party, publicly disclosed the move of signature campaigns by the NC's MPs to oust Deuba from the post (*Space Time Daily*, 9 April 2002). Parallel to the signature campaign by dissident MPs, the party President G.P. Koirala worked out with leaders of other political parties for a national government.[7] Despite his weak position in the party authority structure, circumstances favoured Deuba in pulling out the party CC in line with the government policy vis-à-vis the Maoist issue, either for peaceful negotiation in August-November 2001 or for the mobilization of the army from November 2001 and extension of emergency in February 2002. Once the party blocked the government's move for further extension of emergency, Deuba opted for dissolution of the HOR in May 2002. Nevertheless, his decision led to the split of the party.

The NC experiences showed that the triangular relations among the PM, PP and the party CC were not operated under any particular system, values and norms. It was the situation that dictated. Their relations appeared more problematic when the post of the PM and the party president was held by two different leaders. It was less problematic when a single leader dominated two fronts as the leader of PP and the party president.

UML Experience

Theoretically, the NC and the UML adopted two different models of party-government relations. The constitution of the NC-PP allowed only a minimal role to the leaders of party organization. The UML formally acknowledged the supremacy of the party organization over its elected bodies. The constitution of the UML-PP placed the Parliamentary Department of its party CC as the super institution that enjoyed many powers and authorities, i.e. convening meetings, setting agendas, nomination of some members for the Parliamentary Board, role allocation to MPs, (UML, 1994) which were, in the NC and other parties, performed by the leader and the Executive Committee of PP.

Taking into account that the UML's top leaders held ministerial responsibility during its minority government led by M.M. Adhikari (November 1994-September 1995), the party created new posts and structures, i.e. Deputy General Secretary (held by Bam Dev Gautam), Central Secretariat, and State Affairs Department. One of the arguments behind these new innovations was to enforce the principle of the party supremacy over the government, adopted by the party constitution and other documents.[8] But the practical limitation in adopting this principle was clearly expressed by Bam Dev Gautam, "In a multiparty system, the party, rather than the government, should be the supreme body.... (But) how can the party intervene in the work of the government when the party chairman, general secretary and majority of the party Standing Committee members (6 out of 9) are in the government ?" (*The Rising Nepal*, 13 February 1995). The contradiction of the party's principle of organizational supremacy and the practice of the government domination over the party led to highlighting intra-party conflicts that manifested in different forms, (Mishra, 2001), one was tension between the government led by PM M.M. Adhikari and Deputy-PM Madhav Nepal and the party run by Bam Dev Gautam. Before manifestation of party-government tensions in parliament between the MPs of these two factions, the government fell in September 1995.

The autonomy to the government team was not granted when the UML attained power in March 1997 as a partner of the coalition government led by RPP leader L.B. Chand. Three factors affected the shaping of relations between the party and the government teams of the UML. One, the party deputed Deputy-PM Bam Dev Gautam as the leader of the UML team in the government to foil an earlier move in February 1997 to oust Madhav Nepal from the post of general secretary by his rival faction in the party led by Gautam. The UML's sixth National Congress was scheduled for January 1997 in which Nepal and Gautam appeared as rival candidates for the party general secretary's post. The party top leaders, i.e. Chairman M.M. Adhikari, General Secretary M. Nepal stayed away from the government. The implication of these three factors for the party-government relation was obvious. The UML's backbencher MPs loyal to the M. Nepal/Khadga Oli faction played an active and decisive role behind Deputy-PM Gautam's withdrawal from his earlier decisions, i.e. appointment of Khagendra Sangroula as chief of the Police Intelligence Office and anti-terrorist bill. Besides, M. Nepal directed five UML ministers to relinquish their posts in the government, but they refused to abide by this instruction.

The UML's experiences also support the logic, as explained above in the NC case, that the PP and party CC become more friendly to the PM when one leader holds two highest positions of the government and the party. This logic, however, was not applicable to the RPP.

RPP Experience

The party-government relations in the RPP – while the party was in power from September 1995 to March 1997 – was full of chaos, disorder and anarchy. The RPP united in 1992 after the merger of two separate parties, one led by L. B. Chand and the other by S.B. Thapa. The party adopted a system of collective leadership of Chand and Thapa, Chand holding the post of the leader of the RPP-PP and Thapa as the president of the party. But their conflicting approach in choice of coalition partner – Chand for the UML and Thapa for the NC – and their own interest to become PM led to a clear division among the RPP's MPs. The frequent change of camp by the party MPs led to a rapid change in the internal equation of power, sometimes in favour of Chand in placing him as the PM (March-October 1997) and other times S.B. Thapa helping him to become PM (October 1997- April 1998). The internal conflicts in the RPP-PP manifested in the most dirty ways, i.e. defying the party whip, floor crossing, issuing two different whips at the same time by Thapa and Chand, seating some party MPs in the treasury and others in the opposition bench at the same time, re-entry as minister just after betraying the government, etc.

Government – Opposition Relations

In the 1990s, the pattern of government-opposition relations changed in three different forms, from street confrontation in the first parliament (1991-1994) to coalition making and unmaking in the second parliament (1994-1999), and finally consensus building in the third parliament (1999-2002). The moot question was to what extent the PM showed his ability to rule over the country taking the opposition into confidence. The constitution – by its provision of the composition of "Constitutional Council" and "Judicial Council" by the leaders of the government, opposition and others and other provisions of ratification by two-thirds member of parliament on important executive actions, i.e. emergency, major foreign policy decisions, constitutional amendment – had made it imperative to have a sort of cooperative and reconciliatory relations between the government and opposition.

The aggregated data show that the majority MPs identified 'lack of parliamentary culture' and 'different ideology and goal' were two major factors that lead to inter-party tensions in parliament. Consideration of 'lack of parliamentary culture' as the main reason contributing to inter-party conflicts indicated two things. One, Nepal had short experience of parliamentary process, started only from 1991. Two, the ideological background of many parties, except NC, was hostile to the principle of the parliamentary system. In the ideological/political spectrum of the

TABLE 5:3
Factors Contributing to Inter-Party Conflicts in Parliament

Percentage Based on Multiple Responses

Content	*Total (245)*	*NC (123)*	*UML (89)*	*RPP (12)*
Different ideology and goal	73.1	74.8	70.8	83.3
Government's irresponsibility	53.1	23.6	86.5	75.0
Opposition obstruction	37.6	65.0	7.9	16.7
Lack of parliamentary culture	81.2	85.4	79.8	83.3
Role of retrogressive forces	14.3	13.8	16.9	0.0
Role of external (foreign) forces	10.2	6.5	12.4	16.7
Others	4.1	3.3	5.6	0.0
No Response	1.2	0.8	0.0	0.0
Total	247.7	273.2	279.8	275.0

Source: NCCS (2002).

country, each major party has a distinct identity, i.e. NC as 'democrat' and 'centrist', UML as 'leftist' and 'progressive', and RPP as 'rightist' and 'conservative'. Divergence in parties' ideology was more evident in the first parliament (1991-1994) since government-opposition relations at that time were more dominated by a high degree of confrontation than cooperation.

Disaggregated data reveal some divergences among MPs in party line while giving weight to a particular component of inter-party conflicts. The party's position in parliament reflected clearly in their opinion. The UML had long been in opposition. So its MPs stressed more the factor of 'government's irresponsibility' for producing tension between the treasury and opposition. But, MPs of the NC – since the party had been in power for long – ranked this factor to fourth position in preferential order. They obviously blamed the opposition's obstructive role as one of the important reasons behind inter-party confrontation. The role of external forces – palace and donor countries – as actors contributing to inter-party conflicts were considered least by MPs of all parties.

Inter-party relations changed from greater confrontation in the early 1990s to more consensuses since the late 1990s. Irrespective of the parties' past position vis-à-vis the political system – NC for multiparty, UML for one party, and RPP for partyless system – major parties consented to four fundamental principles of the constitution: constitutional monarchy, popular sovereignty, multiparty parliamentary democracy, and fundamental rights. Their exposure to and experiences of parliamentary processes paved the way for developing some common programme. With

TABLE 5:4
Factors Contributing to inter-party Reconciliation

	Percentage Based on Multiple Responses			
Content	*Total (245)*	*NC (123)*	*UML (89)*	*RPP (12)*
Convergence on principles of constitution	82.0	90.2	79.8	91.7
Parliamentary experiences	77.1	82.1	74.2	50.0
Common programme	53.5	45.5	59.6	75.0
Fear of regression	22.4	17.9	30.3	0.0
Maoist's threat	35.1	45.5	23.6	33.3
Role of external (foreign) forces	3.3.	1.6	2.2	8.3
Others	3.7	1.6	5.6	0.0
No response	1.6	0.8	1.1	0.0
Total	278.8	285.4	276.4	258.3

Source: NCCS (2002).

a plea for national consensus, the NC brought out its 14-point programme that was followed by the UML with its 22-point programme and by the RPP's 6-point programme. These separate documents, proposed by the three major parties, included some common important agendas for all party consensuses.[9] The consensus politics was developed in response to threats to parliamentary democracy from the Maoist as well as the palace (for details, see Chapter 7 and 8). Nevertheless these factors were considered least by MPs for developing a new pattern of inter-party relations in parliament.

In fact, government-opposition relations would generally be a mix of conflict and cooperation. But the PM should always try to seek the confidence of the opposition. To govern the country with cooperation and confidence of the opposition means to cultivate the idea and strength of opposition parties for executive's governance that would definitely help the PM to enhance his position vis-à-vis other political forces. The coming section focuses on how the post-1990 PMs of Nepal deal with opposition parties.

First Parliament

G.P. Koirala – while sitting in power for the first time in 1991-1994 – was constrained to develop competitive politics in a cooperative manner. The 1991 general election brought the two-party system, placing the NC in power and the UML as the major opposition party. To deal with the communist forces both as an ally of popular movement, and a partner for democratic consolidation, PM Koirala was expected to be reconciliatory to the left parties. But, Koirala's image as a hard-liner against the communists was restated by the government's intolerance vis-à-vis opposition. The government's intransigent attitude and behaviour were manifested in many ways and forms, i.e. it refused the UML's quest for sharing executive posts of parliament except for granting the chairmanship of the Public Accounts Committee; it passed bills while the UML and other communist parties boycotted the House; and it resorted to harsh coercive measures against the violent agitations launched frequently by communist parties. The government-opposition relations in the first tenure of parliament was full of stresses and strains, except for making inter-party understanding and agreement three times – one in April 1992 to create a peaceful environment for the local election, the other in July 1992 on policy related to Bhutanese refugees problem, and the last in July 1993 to restore law and order situation. The ruling Congress and opposition communists confronted each other for a long time on the civil servants' strike in 1991, on the Tankpur issue in 1992, and on the Das Dhunga incident in 1993. Government-opposition conflicts were publicly demonstrated in a way like battle between 'democrat' and 'communist', and 'pro-Indian Congress' and 'anti-Indian communist'. On policy matters, i.e. for harnessing water resources, the government emphasized bilateral cooperation with India, whereas the UML propagated multilateral cooperation; and the government adopted the privatization policy but the UML opposed it. The hangover of the past largely shaped the perception of the NC and the UML treating each other as hostile ideological forces. So both failed to give due respect to the new role – NC as the ruling party and UML as the major opposition party – in the parliamentary system.

PM Koirala had also been constrained by obstructive roles of the major opposition party (UML) and other communist parties. The UML's declared strategy to oppose from *Sadak dekhi Sadan sama* (from street to parliament) embarrassed the government. Call for *bandh*, launch of violent street agitation, boycott of public programmes attended by the PM and ministers, etc. were some of the obvious ways adopted by the UML in alliance with other communist parties. The UML chose non-parliamentary venues to a greater extent to display its oppositional role. This largely led to drive out the oppositional politics from the parliamentary structure and process. It, therefore, searched for other avenues. The UML and other communist leaders felt comfortable in dealing with the NC organizational leaders,

K.P. Bhattarai and G.M. Singh. Understanding made at party level sometimes helped the government to restore normalcy. But PM Koirala's ongoing struggle with Singh and Bhattarai had its own impact on his suspicion of hobnobbing between leaders of the NC and the UML. Their secret understanding to displace PM Koirala – which was exposed publicly (*Gorkhapatra*, 18 August 1993) – manifested in different forms, i.e. contest of by-election by K.P. Bhattarai in February 1994, summon of special session of parliament in March 1994 to table no-confidence motion, etc. The understanding and agreement made at party level ended in a fiasco. But Koirala's inability to be in contact and consultation with the opposition parties, at least to the minimum level, was the worst record in the government-opposition relations in the post-1990 period (Hachhethu, 1995).

Second Parliament

Government-opposition relations remained more conflicting in the early phase of the second parliament (1994-1999). The 1994 mid-term election produced a hung parliament placing the UML to the position as the largest party by marginal seat from the second largest NC in the HOR. The RPP, with its 19 seats, emerged as a party balancing between the first and the second largest parties. Parties' ideological and political rigidity was reflected in their dislike to forge an alliance for government formation. Consequently, the UML formed its minority government. The UML's previous stand on the Tanakpur treaty and the Das Dhunga incident backfired as the opposition parties challenged the government to come up with a definite line on these issues. The NC along with other opposition parties criticized the government bitterly for minister Padma Ratna Tuladahar's public speech on cow slaughter and the executive decision for news bulletins in Sanskrit.

For its survival, the minority government is generally expected to hold minimal power and build a programme-based working alliance with the third largest party in parliament. But the UML minority government took a contrary line, monopolizing and expanding executive power and taking populist measures in social and economic sectors. This led to bring the opposition parties closer against the minority government. One of the ways to prevent the possibility of alliance formation among the opposition parties was to bring the RPP in the government. The UML's CC, by its decision made in May 1995 by a majority of 18 against 13 members, gave a mandate to make a coalition with the RPP (CNAS, 1996: 67) and some leaders made attempts to implement the party decision. But the government's preference and line was to hammer the opposition parties by invoking the PM's power to dissolve the HOR. But the Supreme Court revived the HOR and consequently the UML minority government collapsed in September 1995.

The end of the UML minority government was the beginning of a new trend in government-opposition relations. In each of the three successive coalition governments – first led by the NC-PP Leader S.B. Deuba (September 1995-March 1996) and then RPP leader L. B. Chand (March-October 1997) and finally RPP leader S.B. Thapa (October 1997-March 1998) – power was the key issue in determining inter-party relations in parliament. The main concern of parties in power, the PM in particular, was to survive the government by all nefarious means i.e. bribery, horse trading, blackmailing, abduction of some unreliable ministers and MPs, conspiracy and manipulation of constitutional loopholes. This applied to means used by the opposition aspiring for executive power. Soon after the fall of its minority government in September 1995, the UML's CC decided to return in power forging alliance with the Chand faction of the RPP, and the plan materialized in March 1997 with the formation of the RPP-UML-NSP government led by L. B. Chand. The NC followed the same game offering S.B. Thapa, chairman of the RPP, the PM's post in its proposal of another coalition of the RPP-NC-NSP that turned into reality by October 1997. Since the RPP's MPs divided on the time of government making and unmaking games, the shortage of one to fourth MPs for contending parties to win 103 seats of the HOR placed the small parties, i.e. NWPP and NSP in particular, in the position of "king maker" or breaker. As parliamentary parties concentrated themselves on power game, the executive's policy, plan and programme had largely become immaterial in government-opposition relations. Their confrontation appeared occasionally on immediate issues, i.e. the NC's bitter criticism against the Chand-led coalition government for monopolization of power and excessive abuse of state resources in the 1997 local election by the UML ministers.[10]

The pattern of party-government relations changed when G.P. Koirala assumed power again in March 1998. The situation for PM Koirala was much more congenial than in earlythe 1990s. The UML's democratic credentials increased after it adopted a programme of the People's Multiparty Democracy in January- February 1993. Ideological rigidity had become a gone issue in setting inter-party relations since parties with different ideological backgrounds had already shared power in coalition government under a hung parliament. PM Koirala's position was much more comfortable in the sense that unlike his predecessors he did not have to rely much on an arithmetical equation of parliament for the survival of his government, as disintegration of both UML and RPP maximized his political options. Koirala's image also changed drastically from that of anti-communist to conciliatory leader co-opting the ML and then the UML in his government in August 1998 and December 1998 respectively. The emergence of Koirala as a reconciliatory leader meant the acceptability of his leadership. This leverage could be used for governance and crisis management. So, PM Koirala had advantage of using such a conducive political environment to manage the Maoist crisis had he given proper attention to this problem. But he missed the opportunity.

Third Parliament

Resolution of the Maoist problem remained one of the three top agendas – two others are good governance and reduction of corruption – of G.P. Koirala when he came to power again in March 2000. Against this background, he had put forward the idea of a national consensus to deal with the Maoist and other problems of the country since the NC government was headed by K.P. Bhattarai after the 1999 general election. Bhattarai's tenure (May 1999-March 2000) was eventless except for the opposition parties, the UML in particular, which forced the government to form a high level all party committee for election reform. They opposed some of the government programmes, i.e. "Bishweshwar with Poor" and "Ganesh Man Singh Peace Programme".

In March 2000 G.P. Koirala succeeded Bhattarai as head of the government and followed a non-confrontationist line with the opposition. The escalation of the Maoist violence compelled mainstream parties to make a joint effort against the insurgents. Opposition parties publicly sought to resolve the problem through peaceful negotiation but without obstructing the government's plan to exert coercive measures. Koirala's ability to cultivate opposition parties ended with implication of his name as chairman of the cabinet by the Commission for Investigation of Abuse of Authority in corruption charges in the Lauda air deal. It was a big blow against Koirala that all opposition parties completely boycotted the whole session of parliament (February- April 2001) demanding his resignation. Taking new developments after the royal massacre on 1 June 2001, Koirala tried to find a new life for his government pushing the idea of national consensus with 14 specific points that soon extended into 17 points accommodating the UML's point of view. Despite developing programme-based consensus, the oppositions continuously reasserted their demand of PM Koirala's resignation. This adversely affected Koirala's deal with the new king for his proposal of army mobilization in full swing. Ultimately Koirala was compelled to resign in July 2002.

Succeeding G.P. Koirala, S.B. Deuba brought out action programmes in implementing consensus politics. In concurrence with the agreement made between the NC and the UML before swearing in power, the Deuba government brought out a nine-point package programme of socio-economic reforms, i.e. land reforms, abolition of untouchability, empowerment of Janajati, women's property rights, reduction of corruption, electoral reform, etc. Deuba had a past record of being a good manager to translate consensus politics into action. The Mahakali treaty, signed between Nepal and India, was ratified by the parliament by 220 in a total of 261 MPs of both Houses in September 1996 when Deuba led a coalition government. After coming to power again in July 2001, PM Deuba appeared accommodative considering the opposition's views in legislation. So many important pending bills related to the armed police force, regional governance, anti-terrorism, land ceiling, women's property rights, anti-corruption, etc. were easily passed by the parliament. He called all party meetings successfully before each of the three rounds of talks, held from August-November 2001, between the government and the Maoists. In taking a reverse course too after the Maoists left the negotiation table, PM Deuba succeeded in gaining support of all mainstream parties for the government's decision of declaration of emergency and military mobilization since November 2001.

Circumstances also favoured the government in gaining the oppositions' support for opting suppressive measures, as the mainstream communists, including the UML, changed track from their earlier position of passive neutrality between the NC government and the Maoist insurgency to active offensive against the Maoists'. Escalation of Maoist's violent activities and expansion of their territory led to displace the UML from the grassroots level in many areas. The UML along with other mainstream communist parties rejected the Maoists' proposal – put forth twice in pre- and during the negotiation period – of a broader communist alliance for the constituent assembly and republican system. Despite the party's assessment of the government's failure to resist the increasing Maoist attack under emergency, the UML along with the RPP and the NSP supported the government's proposal for the extension of emergency, as it was passed by 194 against 7 members of the HOR in February 2002.

But the government mainly failed to translate consensus politics into effective governance vis-à-vis the Maoists, leading to raising a question on the ability of Deuba's leadership. The government's one-way track of seeking a military solution differed from the parties' suggestions to keep the possibility of dialogue with the Maoists as an alternative option. Parties' suspicion on PM Deuba's role and action favouring political regression also created a distance between the government and major parties, including the ruling NC party. The search for national government as an alternative to the Deuba government partly explained a fact that the mainstream parties did not want to lose from either front in their twin battle, one against the Maoist insurgency, and the other against the palace. Later, the Deuba government was isolated by all parties following Deuba's decision to dissolve the HOR.

Conclusion

The post-1990 PMs appeared largely incapable of managing parliamentary institution, i.e. parties, PP, oppositions, etc. Despite holding two posts – party president and PM – in 1997-1998 and in 2000-2001, G.P. Koirala could not emerge as a strong and powerful leader of the country. Similarly, PM S.B. Deuba could not translate consensus politics into effective governance in dealing with the Maoist insurgents either through negotiation or military mobilization. Other leaders who were placed in the PM's post in the post-1990 period are/were not exceptional as far as their personal ability and skill of governance were concerned. In sum, the post-1990 PMs lacked leadership quality.

The post-1990 PMs had been constrained by the development of a number of adverse situations. First, the power centric intra-party conflicts in the ruling party continued to weaken the PM's position. The case of party-government relations of the NC in the early 2000s was an evident. After he was compelled to resign from the PM's post because of the palace's non-cooperation, G. P. Koirala pleaded for strengthening the PM's position vis-à-vis monarchy. But his role and action, i.e. on the Maoist issue, emergency, army mobilization, all party consensuses for seeking national government, etc. were most embarrassing and discrediting to PM Deuba. Two, the position of PM was devalued considerably in the second parliament, featured by hung parliament and coalition politics. Both M. M. Adhikari was *de jure* leader and S. B. Deuba was junior leader in their own respective parties when the former held the PM post of the UML minority government and the latter led a coalition government of NC, RPP and NSP. The personality of the post-1994 PMs was further overshadowed by a system of high command (constituted by top leaders of coalition parties) and/or by the dominant personality of the second man in the cabinet: Deputy-PMs Madhav Nepal and Bam Dev Gautam in governments led by M.M. Adhikari and L.B. Chand respectively. The leadership of RPP in two successive coalition governments from March 1997-April 1998 and its proximity with the palace had its own implications for weakening the PM's role vis-à-vis the monarchy. Third, the post-1999 PMs' dependency on the king increased as a consequence of the intensification of the Maoist violent activities for which the government was compelled to resort suppressive measure, through the mobilization of army. The constitutional provision of keeping the military away from the jurisdiction of the cabinet and the army's loyalty to the monarchy limited the PM's power in a crisis situation. Fourth, both the NC and the UML – while sitting in opposition – formally requested the king to disarm the PM from his prerogative to dissolve the parliament. Recently, PM Deuba and political parties put the ball in the court of the palace to escape from the constitutional stalemate arising from their realizations that election could not be held as scheduled for November 2002. Deuba recommended for the extension of his government for one more year but the NC and some other parties requested the king to reinstate the dissolved HOR. All the above-mentioned factors had an accumulative effect in weakening the PM's power and position and in expanding the space for the monarchy to intervene in realpolitik.

NOTES

1. G.P. Koirala had repeatedly refereed this statement while explaining the reasons behind weakening democracy in Nepal.
2. The NCCS conducted a survey with 245 members of parliament in April-May 2002.
3. The first case of demanding eviction of MPs was against Amik Serchan, put forward in 1992 by his party, the UPF. The NWPP moved similar actions twice, one against its MP Bharat Kumar Saha in September 1995 and the other against Bhakta Bahadur Roka in December 1996 as they changed the party, Saha with the UML Roka with the NC. In September 1995, The NSP also demanded to abandon the MP post of Hridiyesh Tripathi and Rameshwar Yadev because they formed a separate party in June 1995, but returned to the parent party later. The NC also expelled its two MPs Chakra Bahadur Sahi and Dipak Jung Saha

and demanded to evict their post as MP for their absence in voting on confidence motion tabled by the then PM S.B. Deuba. The RPP took similar actions against its 10 MPs, including L.B. Chand, in December 1997. The UML also expelled 10 leading dissident leaders, including Bam Dev Gautam and C.P. Mainali, and asked the parliament to remove them from MP posts in March 1998. The latest case is the NC's decision of expelling Minister J.P. Gupta from the party in April 2002 that notified to the NC-PP and the Speaker for abandonment of his post in the government and in the parliament.

4. For party-government relations in the Western countries, see Katz (1994); for Indian experiences, see Morris-Jones (1957); Maner (1994).
5. Two instances are refereed here for instances. One, in September 1991 the NC's CC took a decision, "Decisions should be taken by consensus among the leaders of the troika on all major issues, including appointment to high ranking posts such as secretaries, general managers, ambassadors, etc." See *Bimarsa Weekly*, 20 September 1991. Another decision made by the party CC in December 1992, "The government is responsible to the parliament as well as to the party. The party Central Committee is the main apparatus which coordinates all the said bodies." See NC (1992).
6. Article 49 (1:f) of the constitution stated "if the party of which he was a member when elected provides notification in the manner set forth by law that he has abandoned the party" as one of the provisions for the removal of MP. See MLJ (1990).
7. Once G.P. Koirala pleaded for national government to the extent saying that "Forget about your majority (in parliament), forget your 113 seats, 113 is nothing when weighted against the interest of the nation. Major issues are the nation and democracy." *The Himalayan*, 21 December 2001.
8. For formal and legal provisions of a system of the party's supremacy adopted by the UML[a}(1993); UML (b) (1993); UML (1994).
9. Some common agendas found in separate proposals presented by NC, UML, and RPP for all party consensuses are: amendment of constitution, reformation in election, constitute of all or non-party election governments, mainstreaming excluded groups, and socio-economic transformation, etc.
10. For details about coalition politics in Nepal, see Kumar (2000).

CHAPTER 6

PROBLEM OF GOVERNANCE

Nepali politics has long been in a state of transitional flux. The initial transition phase, backed by the spirit of the 1990 popular movement and restoration of multiparty system in April 1990, promulgation of a new constitution in November 1990, general elections 1991 and local elections 1992, was smooth in demolishing partyless panchayat structures and setting up democratic institutions. The constitution ensured to stabilize the system with a provision of making popular sovereignty, constitutional monarchy, multiparty parliamentary system, and fundamental rights of citizens as unamendable. The avowed commitment to the fundamental principles of the constitution by both the rightist Rashtriya Prajatantra Party (RPP) and several leftist splinter groups, irrespective of their different ideological stands in the past, showed how the first phase of transition was successful in setting up democratic structures and in assimilating major ideological and political forces into the mainstream of the parliamentary process. But, the first phase of transition came to an abrupt end with the defeat of the ruling Nepali Congress (NC) in the 1994 mid-term elections (Kumar, 1995).

Nepali politics entered into another phase of transition. Contrary to expectations, democracy in its functional attributes, overwhelmed by power centric intra-party and inter-party conflicts, was widely perceived as eroding. It was manifested in the instability of the government since the emergence of a hung parliament after the 1994 mid-term elections. In the second tenure of parliament (November 1994- May 1999), Nepal had experienced 8 governments of different types and nature.[1] The frequent change in the government was an evident of the degenerating nature of Nepali politics into a naked power struggle. In recurring plots of government making and unmaking, the power contenders spared no foul tricks, i.e. bribes, horse trading, blackmail, abduction of some unreliable incumbent ministers and law makers, conspiracy, manipulation of constitutional loopholes, etc. The use of such nefarious means in power politics led to a political and constitutional crisis that surfaced in more than one ways: the court's political intervention to curtail executive power and prerogative in favour of constitutional monarchy; confrontation between executive and judiciary and also between executive and legislature; blatant violation of parliamentary norms and values by parliamentarians themselves; flouting the spirit of the party system with several records of defiance of the party's whip in parliament leading to a split among some major political parties(Communist Party of Nepal, Unified Marxist-Leninist or UML and RPP); decline in moral standard of the power elite because of excessive manipulation of state resources for personal benefit (Sharma, 2000); and widespread public apathy and disillusionment regarding politics, government, political parties and leadership. In sum, democracy in Nepal suffered from the weakening of norms and value-based politics, erosion in leadership quality, power-centric intra-party conflicts, unhealthy inter-party competition, cynical manipulation of constitutional provisions, instability of the government, incompetent governance, excessive political intervention particularly in the bureaucracy and educational institutions, pervasive corruption, and mismanagement, irresponsibility and unaccountability in the public sphere.

The crisis emerging with hung parliament was expected to end by the result of the 1999 general elections since it brought back a two-party system – similar to the post-1991 elections – with NC's majority government and UML as the main opposition in parliament. The contesting parties, NC and UML in particular, during their election campaigns, projected "a system of majority government" as panacea to all problems facing the country. Besides, they stressed for majority government considering it as indispensable for political stability, good governance and development (Khanal and Hachhethu, 1999). But, the NC government led by Krishna Prashad Bhattarai was accused as incompetent to govern the country and on this ground he was compelled to resign after holding the post of Prime Minister (PM) for ten months. Girija. P. Koirala succeeded Bhattarai as the PM of the Congress government in March 2000. But the return of

Koirala to the highest post of the government made no substantial difference in the style of governance. The national crisis emerging since the time of the hung parliament remained at a standstill and even escalated over time.

This chapter tries to explore the problems of transitional politics in Nepal with the perspective of party politics prevailing since the restoration of democracy in 1990. Beside the fact that political parties are like steersmen in the multiparty system, party politics has been considered as the main instrument of analysis with the assumption that "One of the most difficult obstacles facing the new democracies in their efforts at democratic consolidation is the weakly institutionalized party system" (Mainwaring, 1998). The first section of this chapter deals with the nature and character of Nepali political parties after they transformed from the movement parties into competitive parliamentary parties. The second section tries to establish a certain correlation between the problems of party building and the emergence of political and constitutional crisis impeding a smooth and healthy democratic transition. The third section briefly assesses the problems of governance.

Transformation of Political Parties

The restoration of democracy through the 1990 popular movement was a landmark for party transformation. Previously, parties existed as symbols of opposition since they originated in the 1930s and 1940s on the eve of the 1950-51 armed revolution against the century-old Rana oligarchy, and these evolved as movement organizations against the partyless panchayat system for the last three decades between 1960 and 1990. With the reinstatement of the multiparty system, the role and functions of political parties changed from that of illegal organizations to legitimate power contenders. Theorists of party change stipulate that the development of the party from birth to maturity appeared with marked change in the party's goal and activities (Michel, 1968; Kirchheimer, 1966 and Panabinaco, 1988). The transformation of Nepali political parties from the phase of movement organizations into competitive parliamentary parties appeared to be characterized by 4-Ds: Development, De-ideologization, Disintegration and De-linking.

Development: Nepali political parties during their movement phase had a weak organizational base. In the post-1990 period, the NC and the UML appeared successful in expanding their support bases among different sections of society. NC's "active members" increased from approximately 30,000-32,000 in the early 1990s (Khatri, 1992) to around 121,000 at the end of 1999. The UML's "organized members" recorded 85,000 in February 2000 (Luintal, 2000). Both parties have developed their organizational strength intensively and extensively, constituting the party's formal units on spatial lines down to the grass-roots level all over the country and creating several affiliated organizations from most caste, community, class, occupation and professional groups. Besides, with the realization of organizational growth and role multiplication, each of them has diversified their own organizational structures based on division of labour and functional specialization. In addition to the party's main structure and affiliated organizations, both NC and UML have a variety of sub-structures, i.e. party in public office composed of the party's elected representatives only, coordination committee constituted by a mixture of the party office bearers and the party's elected representatives, several area based departments/committees, each dealing with areas of their own jurisdiction, i.e. party organization, research, training, publicity, foreign affairs, etc.

Unlike in advanced democratic countries where parties tend to attract the people through the formulation of attractive policies and programmes, Nepali political parties seemed to rely more on maximization of party members and supporters and thereby naming it organizational development. This idea of party building had temporary appeal, however, reverse trends started over time. The people's enthusiasm for seeking party affiliation and association – that appeared immediately in the aftermath of the successful people's movement – soon turned into people's apathy towards and disillusionment of the parties and their leaders. The parties' rank and file leaders showed no interest in party building. One of the major reasons behind the apathy of the people and the party-men's lack of motivation to involved actively in party politics is the erosion of ideology.

De-ideologization: Most Nepali political parties originated along ideological lines. A party's ideology is a composite frame of its faith in a certain kind of political system, its goal, its policy and programme, and norms and values it sets up for collective behaviour. Looking back to the principle doctrine enunciated by each party at the time of their formation, the major parties represent three different ideological groups: the NC symbolizes the multiparty system; the UML professed one-party communist system; and the RPP is popularly considered as a party of former panchas with their political background of being ardent advocates of a partyless panchayat system. A major ideological breakthrough was made by the UML and the RPP giving up their initial faith in the one-party system and partyless system respectively in the changed context after they emerged as power contenders under parliamentary democracy. It is understood that a party aspiring for power cannot continue as doctrinal party. But the change of the party's goal from ideological persuasion to power quest has primarily worked as a catalyst for the de-ideologiation process in the parties. The case of the UML could be cited here. As much as its prospect of gaining power under the existing system brightened, particularly after its emergence as the major opposition party after the 1991 parliamentary elections, its tactical and qualified support to the newly achieved multiparty democracy have been transformed to its commitment to the fundamental principles of liberal democracy since the party's Fifth National Congress, held in January-February 1993, passed the resolution of People's Multiparty Democracy. Nevertheless the ideological ambiguity is characteristic of the UML vis-à-vis monarchy and anti-India and anti-West coloured nationalism. The UML party document called for a republic. Such an official stand had no doubt been abandoned later by a pronouncement of its General Secretary Madhav Nepal in early 1996 when the party was looking for the palace's backing and neutralization of external factors in its strategy to regain power through making a coalition with a faction of the RPP against the then incumbent Centre-Right government led by NC leader Sher Bahadur Deuba. Despite change of political equation from a hung parliament to the majority government of the NC after the 1999 elections, the UML somehow maintained their political alliance with the palace and former panchas. It was manifested by the UML's backing to Ramesh Nath Pandey (King's nominee)'s unsuccessful bid for the Chairman of the National Council (Upper House) in 1999. Later, the UML's members of the National Council voted for Mohammad Mohshin (a leader of RPP) who was elected as the chairman of the National Council, Upper House of the parliament.

Despite the abandonment of their original doctrines, each party's separate identity remains alive in the minds of the people: the NC as liberal and centrist; the UML as leftist and progressive; and the RPP as rightist and conservative. Such identities remain unchanged in the way they present themselves before the people. With its pet slogan "peace, stability, democracy and development" the NC built up its separate identity different from that of other parties. The UML retained its revolutionary image with the communist jargon, "bread for hungry, work for the unemployed, land for the landless, and shelter for the homeless." The RPP projected itself with its leaders' past experiences of governance, its faith in monarchy and its nationalist propaganda against India. But such differences had not been backed up in terms of policy and programmes, particularly while they were/are in power. Rather, the distinct identity of each of the given parties' eroded constantly in different ways after the restoration of democracy in 1990. The NC no longer remains as a political forum of the social democrats since its open door policy for party recruitment had been defended with its quest for new credentials, defining the party as "an ocean where all rivers can mingle" (NC [a], 1991). The NC thrust for its expansion to become a "broader political platform" instead of an "ideological family" had been rationalized with its quest for vote maximization. The UML too, for its electoral interest, initiated its alliance with the RPP a number of times, more distinctly at the time of local elections in 1992 and in 1997; nevertheless it officially treated the RPP as "reactionary". The politics of hung parliament gave further impetus to de-ideologization considerably as politics of compromise dominated the political scene. Thus a critic observes, "What was left in the "Left" party was easily diluted when the undivided CPN (UML) accepted the leadership of a former panchayat Prime Minister (Lokendra Bahadur Chand) and other compromises made for grabbing power at the cost of its identity" (Baral, 2000). Almost all parliamentary parties had, time and again, abruptly disregarded their own distinct political identity for the sake of power. The quest for power cut ideology and identity of these parties, as witnessed in coalition building of parties with distinct identities during the second parliament (1994-1999). One could therefore conclude that Nepali political parties, from the onset of transformation from movement into parliamentary parties, appeared as power seeking organizations whose primary goal is to attain and retain power even at the cost of party ideology and identity.

Disintegration: De-ideologization of Nepali political parties, in the course of their transformation form movement to parliamentary parties, meant the emergence of power as the single most determining factor in party politics. The potential of a party to be in power not only helps in expanding its support base beyond its ideological clientele it also sometimes served for integration. The power element is one of the factors which saved the NC from major breakdown, once helped the UML to expedite its development as the mainstream of left forces, and paved the way for the unity of two separate RPPs in 1992. However, power is, after all, a source of conflict and ideology the source of unity. In this context as power replaced ideology as the predominant factor in party politics after the restoration of democracy, the political parties turned into conflict-ridden organizations and each of them suffered from major or minor splits. Thus, a scholar has rightly observed, "In the period of transformation, there is an inevitable process of disintegration" of political parties (Brass, 1965).

In late 1994 when the unity, cohesion and discipline in the NC party was completely disrupted, a small group of people left the party and formed a separate political platform in the name of *Jana Jagaran Abhiyan* under the inspiration and patronage of Ganesh Man Singh, one of the founding leaders of the NC. This split was a culmination of a series of internal power conflicts among the party troika leaders (the then PM Girija P. Koirala, party president Krishna P. Bhattarai and party supremo Ganesh Man Singh) and factions led by each leader. The internal crisis of the NC was a prelude to differences that arose among its top leaders with regard to political appointments in the early phase of the NC government. It was later aggravated one after another by subsequent developments, i.e. cabinet reshuffle in December 1991 by PM Koirala solely on his own discretion, candidacy of the then party president Bhattarai in the February 1994 by-elections aiming to dislodge Koirala from his position as PM, defeat of Bhattarai as a consequence of *antarghat* (sabotaging) by the Koirala faction, the absence of NC's 35 members of House of Representatives (HOR) at the time of voting on the government's annual policy and programmes leading to the collapse of the Koirala government, dissolution of the HOR abruptly and the call for mid-term poll by PM Koirala completely ignoring party leaders, and the contest in mid-term polls by rebel Congress candidates in several numbers against the party's official candidates.

After the defeat of the party in the 1994 mid-term poll, the NC gradually regained some unity in the party. But the unity in an organization without strong backing of ideology or competent leadership will always be fragile. NC's top leaders Krishna P. Bhattarai and Girija P. Koirala were no longer unchallenged and undisputed in the party. In consideration of the massive erosion in the quality of their leadership, their positions appeared to have degenerated from one of leaders into that of bosses who commanded the organizations by virtue of their control of the party resources, particularly in patronage and ticket distribution. The reacquisition of party unity in a different sort was exposed time and again. A serious problem arose when a coalition government led by Sher Bahadur Deuba collapsed in March 1997 due to the betrayal by NC's two members of the HOR by their abstaining in a vote of confidence, in which the government received only 101 votes, short of 2 votes for the required number of 103 in the total 205 members of the HOR. The party unity was once again jeopardized in December 1997 when the former president Krishna P. Bhattarai threatened to split the party (*Deshantar*, 7 December 1997) on the ground that he felt he had been ignored by president Girija P. Koirala in taking a number of important decisions. The NC, however, managed the problems preventing the party from a split through maintaining a balance among the influential leaders and major factional groups.

Soon after Krishna P. Bhattarai became the PM, power-centric internal conflicts resurfaced in the NC. Reacting to the question of the Bhattarai government's performance, Girija P. Koirala responded, "No work is good work" (*Nepal Press Digest*, 13 September 1999). This was supplementary to his observation, "Despite its majority in the parliament, the government has created an environment of ominous silence instead of infusing enthusiasm among the people" (*Nepal Press Digest*, 20 September 1999). Accusing the Bhattari government of its incompetence, Girija P. Koirala cultivated his influence among the majority of the NC' MPs which ultimately forced Bhattarai for his resignation from the post of PM on 16 March 1999. With a majority of 69 against 43 votes of Sher Bahadur Deuba among the NC members of the HOR, Girija P.Koirala became the leader of the NC's Parliamentary Party (PP). But from the day Koirala took oath as new PM many speculated that he would soon have to face the same fate of Krishna P. Bhattarai. This speculation was likely to turn into reality since the power equation in the NC-PP was, reportedly, changing in favour of the anti-Koirala faction. These events suggested the lack of strong and cohesive leadership in the NC. So, the party unity and cohesion largely hung on a weak device, its ability in maintaining balance in sharing of power among the party's influential persons and factions. The situation in other political parties was no different.

As a consequence of the failure of the UML to maintain a balance among its heavyweight leaders, it suffered from a major split in March 1998 with the formation of ML. Had not the party undergone de-ideologization, perhaps it could have prevented the split as it had successfully resolved a number of serious internal crises in the past. In aftermath of the restoration democracy, internal factions based on differences on the party's ideology (People's Multiparty Democracy versus Refined People's Democracy), on its official stand on the Integrated Mahakali River Treaty with India (1996), on the question of making coalition with the RPP, and on several other issues had surfaced. But as much as the UML veered towards the direction of becoming a "catch all party" to capture power, ideology and issues had become peripheral and instrumental in the power-centric personality clash among its top leaders. Nevertheless, for public consumption and rationalization of the party split, the newly split ML tended to raise the strident communist rhetoric of achieving *Janatako Janabadi Ganatantratmak Vyabastha* [People's Republic](*Kantipur*, 20 March 1998), a republican utopia and ultra-nationalist stand against India and the West. The roots behind the disintegration of the UML went back to the time of the formation of its minority government when a demand for resignation of the then deputy-PM Madhav Nepal from the post of general secretary of the party was put up unsuccessfully. The internal conflict deepened irreparably since the post of deputy general secretary, held by the party strongman Bam Dev Gautam, was scrapped.

Thus, due to the lack of a consensus leader in the UML, it could not prevent the increasing divisive tendency in the party. The succession of the late Madan Bhandari by Madhav Nepal as general secretary of the party in May 1993 did not help bringing change in his image as a second fiddler in the minds of other leaders of the UML. The inconsistency in the behaviour of party president Man Mohan Adhikari and some other junior leaders of the party Central Committee regarding their relations with the party's factional leaders further aggravated the ambitions of other top leaders, particularly Bam Dev Gautam and Khadga Oli, aspiring for the post of general secretary. With no consensus leader, a tendency of minority tyranny appeared defying party whips in parliament and disrupting the unity, cohesion and discipline in the party. The party's sixth National Congress, held at Nepalgunj in January 1998, proved a battleground in which the political and strategic programmes presented by the minority faction was defeated with its 242-244 votes against the majority faction's strength of 598-605 (*Pratipachiya*, 31 January 1998). Instead of observing the general democratic principle of the rule of the majority, the minority faction led by Bam Dev Gautam formally split the party in March 1998, invoking provision of the Anti-Defection Act that a separate parliamentary party could be formed if 40 percent MPs agreed to disassociate themselves from their parent party.

A similar development had already occurred in January 1998 in splitting the RPP. After the defeat of Rajeshwor Devkota by Surya Bahadur Thapa, 391 against 818 votes, in the contest of the party president's post in the party's National Convention, held at Birgunj in November 1997, the minority faction led by Lokendra Bahadur Chand and Devkota constituted a separate party. The RPP – initially appeared as two separated parties, each led by former panchayat PMs Thapa and Chand but united in 1992 – was a most disorganized party. The weakest point of this party is that it was not formed on the basis of ideology, but on the ground of common political background and identity of its ranks and files as the erstwhile panchas. Nor did the RPP have a consensus leader. The party was clearly heading towards disintegration since the day it received the opportunity to stay in power as a key balancing force between the two largest parties, NC and UML, under the politics of a hung parliament. The revival of factional politics, one led by Thapa and the other by Chand, appeared over their differences in choosing a coalition partner. Thapa's preference of NC against Chand's choice of UML was linked with their personal ambition to become PM and thereby control the party apparatus. Both Thapa and Chand succeeded to manoeuvre the most opportunist characters in the party to attain the post of PM. Thapa succeeded Chand as PM of the country through sabotage. The party, which had long suffered from mutual distrust and a complete disruption in organizational unity, discipline and cohesion, and *anterghat* (sabotage), came to its logical conclusion after a clear split.

The cost of party split was very high. The RPP's strength in the HOR reduced from 20 in the second parliament to 11 in the third parliament. The split in the UML prevented it to reach in power. The split had directly affected in losing 43 seats for the UML (Khanal and Hachhethu, 1999). If the votes received by the candidates of the break a way group, the ML, add to the candidates of the UML, it would have received a comfortable majority of 112 seats instead of the 69 seats in the HOR. The split proved counter-productive to newly a break-way groups as well. Both ML and RPP (Chand) failed to obtain even a single seat in the 1999 parliamentary election. This, in turn, contributed to the re-strengthening of the parent parties. The RPP (Chand) merged with its parent party in late 1999 and several ranks and files of ML re-joined the UML. But the unity of these parties along with NC remained fragile because of the erosion of ideology and leadership in party politics.

Delinking: Nepali politics had long been overwhelmed by in-party fighting, and making and breaking of the inter-party coalition. In such a power-centric politics, the need and interest of the people had been grossly ignored. Though the party is conceived as a linkage institution between the state and society (Lawson, 1980), the Nepali parties appeared to have largely failed to observe their basic duty of linking citizens preference with public policy. One obvious reason why parties were moving closer to becoming a part of the state rather than consolidating themselves as 'people's organization' could be found in the parties' rank and file's preference to accumulate property and pursue a luxurious life by all means, particularly through the manipulation of state machinery and resources. Besides, as a consequence of their failure to deliver "public goods" (collective incentive of identity, solidarity and ideology) to the masses, their mindset seemed to be preoccupied with a new way of party building, though granting "selective incentive" (power, status, money, jobs, and other material rewards) to party clients. This idea led the political parties to revolve around the circle of the vested interest groups. Since the party functionaries work for certain lobbies, particularly the business community and others, the parties' advocacy of general people's problems had been noticed through its absence.

The UML, during its minority government, tended to propel the party as an active and powerful state organization through party-run clientelism under the purview of the party's State Affairs Department. Its splinter group, the ML had carried out this scheme, while becoming a junior partner of the NC-led coalition government, believing that it could expedite organizational building activities by being in power and thereby being able to mobilize state resources and machinery. But it soon broke the coalition with the NC since it differed with PM Koirala's plan for early election to parliament. The UML and NSP joined the government in response to Koirala's call for an all-party government to conduct the 1999 general election.

Other parties, like the NC and RPP, were not exceptions in using their position, while they were in power, for party building through granting patronage to the persons of their favour and their own party fellows in executive posts of state apparatus at all levels. One important reason behind the parties becoming increasingly state-oriented was the likelihood of another snap poll since the 1994 election produced a hung parliament. Holding the polls while in power had been the prime target of all major political parties in the country. It means that the party in power will have advantage to use/misuse the state resources for election purposes. The local elections of 1997 could be cited as an extreme example that one of the ruling partners of that time, the UML, was accused for its excessive manipulation of the state machinery for its landslide victory in the election. It beat all previous records of manipulating the state mechanism for election purposes. All parliamentary parties, big or small, wanted to be in power at the time of elections which obviously means that they wanted to manipulate state power and resources to bring the election result in their favour. The 1999 general election, held by the NC-led coalition government with UML and NSP, was not an exception. But, the more the party relies on state machinery and resources for party building the more the party is driven away from the masses.

Political Crisis

The possession of 4-Ds characteristics by Nepali political parties in the course of their transformation from the movement into competitive parliamentary parties had a positive effect for the stability of democratic structures but a more negative impact on transition of democracy at the functional level. The consensus building on the fundamental principles of the constitution, the spread of the notion of political pluralism down to the grass-roots level, and political flexibility against the past ideological rigidity, etc. were some remarkable developments that came up as the impact of party transformation. Each of 4-Ds had, however, separate and compound negative effects in generating political crisis in the country. Political crisis in Nepal could be depicted as BLEAK bewilderment, leadership crisis, erosion, anarchy, and knavery.

Bewilderment: Democracy in Nepal suffered from bewilderment of political parties. In the context of de-ideologization and decline of leadership popularity, major parties suffered from their inability to innovate new ways and thinking with regard to party building. In the advanced democratic countries, a party formed on ideological lines was later transformed into a "policy-seeking party" which tends to appeal to the masses by innovating new principles, setting new goals and formulating realistic and effective policies and programmes. But the parties of extra-parliamentary origin as in the case of Nepali political parties – whose only one target in the past was to overthrow the partyless panchayat system – lacked policies and programmes to resolve the long-standing social and economic problems of the country. A party potential to be successful has, sooner or later, to advance itself as a people-oriented and policy-seeking party. This character was not found in Nepali political parties. Of course, the advent of democracy has in its wake brought into focus a number of pervasive socio-economic problems of the country in different forms and shape, i.e. gender issues, minority problems, grievances of the disadvantaged groups, unemployment, corruption, etc. But political parties appeared largely insincere in addressing such emerging social and economic problems and to give realistic and pragmatic policy incentives. Power seemed to be the single most important target of all parties. They failed even to rationalize their quest for power through appropriate policy commitment and implementation. The party in power, whichever that might be, tended to justify their position with the recurring rhetoric of "political instability" and "democracy in danger."

The lack of vision to reorient parties in the changed context could be found among them in their pursuit of party reformation. Though each major party – NC, UML and RPP – has developed and diversified its organizational structures, the responsibility of most of the party structures and sub-structures is exclusively confined to the parties' internal affairs to look after the business of the elected wing of the party. They lacked in such structures which would be directly responsible for public policy formulation functions. Such an "inward looking" approach of party reformation also reflected on the much vociferous demands for the norms and value-based politics in each party's internal affairs. The demands obvious target was to overcome the problems of in-fighting, division, indiscipline, and against the increasing tendency of individualism, selfishness and opportunistic characters of the party's rank and file. Such "inward looking" approach of party reform could be said to be renovation rather than innovation. The approach of party reformation should also have "outward looking" content relating to general people's concern. The changing time and situation demand that the party should advance with new perspectives, new vision, new outlook, with setting new objectives. The formulation of realistic and effective policies and programmes rather than ideological rhetoric and leadership cult could be a new source of strength for the parties in competitive politics. But, Nepali political parties hardly appeared moving towards a new way of party building. So the nation and democracy – governed by parties which lacked clear principles, vision, goals, policies and programmes – suffered from directionless drift.

Leadership Crisis:The directionless drift or transitional flux might also be seen as a by-product of the leadership crisis. The image of the leaders of Nepali political parties, except those of RPP, was built on the ground of their long struggle and sacrifice for the cause and principle. Their contribution in the early phase of democratic transition – notably in the restoration of the multiparty system and transformation of sovereign power from the palace to the people – was highly appreciable. So the popularity of some parties' leaders, particularly NC's top leaders, the late Ganesh Man Singh (commander of the 1990 mass movement) and Krishna P. Bhattarai (PM of interim government), and also UML's late General Secretary Madan Bhandari, attained a peak. In the changed context of the second phase of transition towards democratic consolidation, the party and the leaders had to prove their worth by their ability to lead and govern the nation effectively.

But the outstanding quality of the leaders was not reflected in their performance, in management of intra-party affairs as well as in administration of the state and government's machinery. Rather their increasing tendency to seek the price of their past struggle and sacrifice in terms of power and position had tended to impede a healthy development of the party system and democracy. Consequently most of the parties turned into conflict-ridden organizations, overwhelmed by power and ego-centric tussles among their respective party leaders, which would ultimately lead them towards disintegration. Judging from the spillover effects of intra-party conflicts and stagnation of national development, instability of government, degeneration of political morale and standards, compromise of democratic norms and values, economic recession and stagnation of national development, one could say that the leadership power appeared to be used more for destructive purposes than for constructive purposes. The incumbent leaders of most of the parties had become obsolete in their performance. But, the prevalence of an obsession that "once a leader would be the leader at all times," disregards the fact that different leadership needs to exist in different stages of party development (Harmel and Svasand, 1993).

The leadership of the PM, though the highest post in the parliamentary system, seemed weak and circumscribed by the politics of the hung parliament and power equation within the ruling party/parties. All governments under the hung parliament was obsessed with survival crisis and the priority of all PMs was to retain the post as long as possible rather than consolidation of one's own leadership position through providing effective and strong government. This trend continued to exist despite the changed political situation after the 1999 elections. The authority of both former PM Krishna P. Bhattarai and incumbent PM Girija P. Koirala was eroded considerably by intra-party factionalism in the NC. Moreover, the leadership of the PM had further been weakened by disarming the PM's prerogative to dissolve the HOR. Thus, parliamentary democracy as a prime ministeral system no longer existed in Nepal.

Erosion: The curtailing of the PM's power and prerogative was one among several instances of erosion in the spirit of the 1990 mass movement and the constitution. The 1990 mass movement brought out one crucial dimension of Nepali politics, i.e. palace versus people. The 1990 Constitution limited the role of the king as constitutional monarch in contrast to his active and assertive roles as sovereign ruler in the past. But as much as the popular forces were weakened by intense intra-party and inter-party rivalries, the expansion of the palace's role in realpolitik was felt continuously, i.e. in nomination of members of National Council, in appointment of ambassadors and other high ranking posts in particular (Hachhethu, 1995). It was in fact the parties and their leaders who laid the ground for the palace's intervention in power politics. There were records of major parties – NC, UML and RPP – defending the PM's prerogative to dissolve the HOR when they were the ruling party, but the same parties had actively solicited the constitutional monarch not abide by the decisions of the cabinet whenever they were in opposition. As the parties spared nothing to manipulate the constitutional provision for their short-term interest the palace had gradually regained its eminence and influence.

It was widely speculated that the palace had revised its role as "king maker" but from the back door. An ex-pancha, "who is believed by many to be a hard-core, pro-palace, rightist ex-pancha" had become instrumental behind the coalition formation between the rightist Chand faction of the RPP and the leftist UML (Sharma, 1995). As this coalition came into being, NC leader Girija P. Koirala had attacked the palace by implication when he repeatedly said that the problem of the country lay in the force which had worked as a catalyst to join the extreme rightist Chand and the extreme leftist Bamdev Gautam. But, Koirala himself admitted that he had successfully replaced the Chand government by a coalition of the Thapa faction of the RPP and the NC only after the king gave a green signal to his (Koirala) repeated attempts to convince the king on its viability (*Punarjagaran*, 17 February 1998). The irony was that once Koirala himself led a coalition government with ML, led by Bamdev Gautam, and maintained an alliance with the splinter RPP, led by Chand, in the parliament whom he previously blamed as stooges of the palace. The above instances suggested to what extent the parties and their leaders tended to violate the norms of constitutional monarchy and to what extent the palace influenced the realpolitik. Such development encouraged the palace for direct and visible intervention in politics, as suggested by the king's refusal to abide by the decision taken by the then Thapa government to dissolve the HOR. Manipulating an ambiguous constitutional provision of Article 54 (in which the word "may" mentions instead of "shall") with regard to the king's role in the dissolution of parliament, King Birendra had already indicated that he had the right to prevent the cabinet's decision on this matter despite his affirmative response to the cabinet's decision of dissolving the HOR by the NC government in July 1994 and by the UML government in July 1995. The Supreme Court, however, gave two contrasting verdicts on the cases of dissolution of the HOR, affirmative to the decision taken by the NC majority government in 1994 but negative to the UML minority government in 1995. This further widened the ground for manipulation. King Birendra followed the advice submitted by the Supreme Court in February 1998 that the PM's power to dissolve the HOR was "limited and conditional" (Text of *Advice Submitted by the majority of 6 against 3 Supreme Court judges to the King on the subject of Constitutional provisions of Article 53 (3)"*, February 1998). The palace, in fact, manoeured the constitutional loopholes skilfully and took the legitimacy from the Supreme Court directly and from all parliamentary parties indirectly to equip the king with preventative power against the PM's prerogative to dissolve the HOR. The palace's intervention had been felt in another serious issues, i.e. refusal to consent to the cabinet decision to appoint Bishownath Upadhaya as Chairman of the Human Rights Commission. Moreover, PM Girija P. Koirala was compelled to change his strategy, in dealing with Maoist "terrorist" activities, from his earlier stand for invoking constitutional provision of Security Council to negotiation with the Maoist party. The role of the Security Council was exclusively confined to the use of the army and by making a separate constitutional provision in this regard; the army was kept away from the executive power of the cabinet. Taking these several instances as references, Bishownath Upadhaya (former Chief Justice and Chairman of the Constitution Recommendation Commission) rightly remarked that "there is duel rule in Nepal" (*Nepal*, 30 July-16 August 2000). In fact, the article 35 (2) of the constitution which bound the king to follow "the advice and consent of the Council of Ministers" was being constantly eroded visibly and invisibly. Minus effective enforcement of this provision, the 1990 Constitution could possibly be relegated to the status of the 1959 Constitution. The implication of constitutional monarchy in the sense of the "king can do no wrong" was not applicable in Nepal.

Anarchy: Had there been any positive impact of diluting the PM's executive authority, the regaining of the palace's eminence could be considered as a blessing in disguise. But the Supreme Court's verdict of August 1995 against the then PM Man Mohan Adhikari's dissolution of the HOR was a prelude to invite political uncertainty, instability and anarchy. The politics after this verdict had been relegated into a number game of 205 members of the HOR, between the parties in the government and parties in opposition. In such a game of winning by a majority of 103, nothing was sacred to the contending parties. All means, i.e. horse-trading, *anterghat*, floor crossing, defiance of the party whip, paralysis of constitutional and legal provision of anti-defection, etc. were adopted by completely violating parliamentary norms and behaviour. In fact, the morale and standard of Nepali politics was degenerated to the lowest ebb.

Sher Bahadur Deuba relied more on his appeasement policy and political manoeuvrability through horse-trading when he was the PM of a coalition government of NC, RPP and NSP. His political manoeuvres were wide open: formed a jumbo cabinet of 48 ministers; increased the perks and privileges of parliamentarians including the facility to import duty free vehicles; provided the state's resources to a number of power holders and power brokers (in the name of medical treatment and other relief measures, etc.) and sent five incumbent but unreliable ministers representing the RPP and one opposition member of the HOR abroad on the eve of voting on the no-confidence motion against his government in December 1996. The UML concealed its aberrations through its strong and effective propaganda. But, once it was exposed it was known that this party played the dirtiest game of power politics. It did not hesitate to indulge in horse trading and inviting the business mafia into politics and bribing other parties' MPs – Rs. 20 million in September 1995 for its unsuccessful attempt to keep intact its minority government, Rs. 5 million in June 1996 and Rs. 2.6 million in December 1996 for its desperate efforts to regain power. Besides, the supply of prostitutes to some MPs to bring them in track in the party's plot to capture power was also revealed. Moreover, during the UML's minority government, it was alleged that the party had a close affinity with smugglers, commission agents, deflectors of letters of credit and others involved in the black market (*Jana Astha*, 4 March 1997).

Even in the changed context after the 1999 elections the politics of the number game continued to exist in other forms. Krishna P. Bhattarai resigned from the post of PM only after a majority of NC's MPs submitted a petition for his resignation. Girija P. Koirala succeeded Bhattarai but through voting among the NC's members of the HOR. Such a number game was seen as revival of *ghat-pratighat* (sabotage and counter sabotage) in the NC, said by outgoing PM Bhattarai (*Text of Speech by PM Krishna P. Bhattarai to the House of Representatives,* 16 March 2000).The power contenders were active in search of space for the use of their evil designs in a recycling game of government making and felling. A unique game prevailed in the political spectrum of the country in which the guilty were not punished but rewarded with posts, position and power. The general drift of Nepali politics, particularly from 1995 onwards was characterized by chaos and anarchy.

Knavery: In the given situation of political turmoil, the power elites had taken personal benefits even at the cost of people, democracy and nation. In a country where nearly half the population live below the poverty line it is ridiculous that the perks and privileges of the people's representatives had increased constantly. Even though, they devoted hardly any time to the job for which they were elected as it was witnessed by the record of absentees in parliamentary business. The time they saved by absenting themselves in parliament was hardly used for constructive thinking or work. Most of the ministers, parliamentarians and other influential politicians seemed busy either to enhance their own personal benefits or to give patronage to the persons of their favour. Guided by their personal interest to be re-elected next time, they strove more for providing services to the power brokers in their own electoral constituency. The way of granting and receiving favours brought to mind the tradition of the *Chakari* system and patron-client relations which now appeared to have received a new lease of life in an altered format in the new constituency-oriented culture. The revival of patron-client relationship obviously meant the narrowing down of politics among the power holders and power brokers only. The very notion of democracy as people's participation in the government through organized parties was absent in Nepal. Some major ingredients of democracy, i.e. people's representation, responsibility and accountability to the people hardly existed in essence.

Problems of Governance

In a country where sovereignty lies in the people, the notion of governance should be equated with the goal of people's empowerment. "If sovereignty is understood as the source from where all state power emanates, citizens need to feel empowered beyond the role they play as voters in periodic elections" (NESAC, 1998). But the people component is the most neglected part in the politics and government of Nepal. Viewed from another perspective of governance as the capacity of the government to "sustain legitimacy, promote socio-economic development, and maintain order without coercion" (Kohli, 1992), the finding was more disappointing. The non-existence of governance in the broader sense, "a process of political management, aims at maintaining order, ensuring popular legitimacy, responding to problems through appropriate mechanisms and strategies, remaining neutral in providing basic human rights to people and developing both effectiveness and accountability in all activities undertaken at the state level" (Baral, 1993) was all too obvious. Nepal Development Partners also pin-pointed the lack of essential ingredients of good governance – efficiency, accountability, transparency and the rule of law – in the country (Text of *Memorandum Presented to PM G.P. Koirala by a Group of Donors Representing an Overwhelming Majority of Donor Agencies Working in Nepal, Nepal's Development Partners*, 15 May 1988). Here the problems of governance in Nepal could be said in essence to be LOST-lack of political will, over politicization, spoil of professionalism and threat to democracy.

Lack of Political Will: Preoccupied by the party's plan to opt for snap polls, the UML's minority government – the first government after the 1994 mid-term election – fostered populism and propaganda instead of pursuing a sustainable policy and programme. Subsequent governments led by Sher Bahadur Deuba, Lokendra Bahadur Chand and Surya Bahadur Thapa respectively concentrated mainly on survival of their own beleaguered coalitions. One former PM told the author during a personal conversation that the governance, administration and management had become peripheral since he foresaw a serious threat to the survival of his government. Other PMs under the hung parliament were not exceptions since they opted for all sorts of compromises which impeded the smooth sailing of the government and administration. The return of Girija P. Koirala as the PM under the hung parliament did not make any difference in the prevailing conditions in the country. Though the Koirala government had to its credit the withholding of much publicly criticized MP's facility to import duty-free vehicle, conducting local elections in some districts of the Maoist's strongholds, and passing the newly amended Civil Service Act (which supposedly limits political intervention in bureaucracy) yet the general impression was that Koirala had come to power again just to hold the 1999 general election and to manipulate state resources to serve the interest of his own party rather than to provide an effective and strong government. This impression could be substantiated by referring to the qualitative difference of his working style from that of the past. As the first elected PM after the restoration of democracy, Koirala appeared eager to rule the country effectively and so he used to consult experts frequently on all important issues and subjects. But this part was completely missing during his second tenure of premiership, as it was evident by the resignation of his hand-picked official adviser Prof. Krishna P. Khanal on the ground that he could not find space in the PM's scheme of things. Citing the gap between the words and deeds in dealing with the Maoist problem as one of the solid instances, Khanal had come to the conclusion that the government was there only in the leaders' words, speeches and promises and also in the so-called structure of the Central Secretariat but not in functional mechanisms and in will power (*Deshantar*, 1 November 1998).

The end of the hung parliament after the 1999 general election did not bring a substantial change in the style of governance. The lack of vision of leaders was clearly manifested when Krishna Prasad Bhattarai, just before taking the chair of PM, said that cleaning of Kathmandu city and initiating the Melamchi Water Project for the supply of drinking water to Kathmandu valley were priority areas of his government. The failure of PM Bhattarai to give a clear direction to the nation was expressed by a minister of his own cabinet in these words, " The need of reform and radical change in social, economic and political sectors of the country is obvious but these things are hardly discussed in the cabinet" (Dahal, 1999). A new team of the Congress government, under the leadership of Girija P. Koirala, had come with its three-point agenda: good governance, resolution of the Maoist problem, and reduction of corruption. But no substantial change had come to avert the deteriorating situations in the country except some decisions taken against political intervention in administration. Koirala, like his immediate predecessor Bhattarai, was preoccupied by internal problems of his own party that was aggravating to the extent of a threat against the survival of his government. Good governance did not seem a priority of the Koirala government.

Over Politicization: It was widely felt that the state and government machinery was heading towards collapse as a consequence of over politicization of such institutions. The frequent change of the government was always followed by change in the executive posts at all levels not only in the bureaucracy but also in other public institutions, i.e.

corporations, hospitals, educational institutions, etc. This led to instability in public institutions which are generally considered as stable organs. The annual report of the Public Service Commission clearly showed that a situation of disorder, indiscipline, aberration and anarchy was increasingly being felt in administration of the country as the impact of excessive political intervention and by a tendency of undermining the laws, rules and regulations from the persons holding executive power (*Kathmandu Post*, 17 October 1998). The impact of over politicization was most glaring in policy inconsistency and paralyzing state organs and functionaries.

One widely noticeable omission of the rule of law was the granting of political protection to those who overstepped their authority. The several reports of the Public Accounts Committee of the HOR, the Auditor General and Abuse of Authority Investigation Commission showed that the government hardly ever followed their recommendations to punish the guilty persons. The Regmi Report found that the police and others representing different departments of the government who were assigned to check smuggling and other crimes at the Tribhuvan International Airport had served as number one ally of smugglers (*Deshantar*, 27 September 1998). Further, the Auditor General's report exposed the magnitude of economic irregularity, mismanagement, corruption found in all sectors and levels, from that of the three branches (executive, legislative and judiciary) of the government to the public corporations (*Bimarsa*, 11 September 1998). These were the indications how corruption, irregularities, mismanagement, irresponsibility and unaccountability were increasingly rampant in public sector. Under the prevailing situation, governance in the country became a chimera.

Spoils of Professionalism: One glaring effect of over politicization could be found in the workplaces of the intelligentsia and other professionals. The bureaucracy, corporations, universities, schools, hospitals, etc.– which are places where the largest number of Nepali educated people are involved – seemed defunct. Most of the educated people were divided along party lines. The alliance between the party and intelligentsia, which was built during the struggle for democracy in the past, expedited in euphoric phase of the post-1990 mass movement through the formation of the party's ancillary organizations in all types of occupational and professional groups, was sustained by a strong system of party run clientele. As a consequence of excessive politicization and division of intelligentsia and other educated persons along party lines, most of them were unable to maintain their professional ethics and honesty. De-professionlization obviously affected the quality of service they provided to the people, nation and democracy. It should be remembered that the effectivity of the state and government machinery will largely depends on the ability and quality of professionals working in such institutions. It was widely felt that professional ethics and integrity were losing ground considerably among the intelligentsia of the country which could have far more enduring and far-reaching negative consequences to the country.

Threat to Democracy:As much as the parties, leaders, people's representatives, professionals and others involved in state power apparatus in different capacities failed to provide governance in terms of delivery of service to the people, the loss of people's faith and confidence was inevitable. A pre-1999 election survey, therefore, found "the activities of political parties and leaders" as the main source of threat to democracy in Nepal (Sharma and Sen, 1999). One should not overlook the fact that the authoritarian nostalgia was gradually taking place in different forms and shapes. Be its manifestation concretely with the regaining of the palace's eminence, or symbolically with rewarding people like Chand and Thapa, PMs of the popularly disavowed panchayat system, to the same post (from March 1997 to April 1998) under the democratic polity, or in open rallies demanding the restoration of active and assertive monarchy with the partyless system, the old force was trying to show its presence. On the other hand, the violent activities of the Maoists were spreading. The perceived or the real threat to democracy from the extreme rightist and the extreme leftist was being increasingly realized since the people were losing confidence in the parties and the leaders. One could not deny the fact that the people's euphoria and enthusiasm awakened by the successful mass movement in 1990 was turned into indifference, frustration and disillusionment towards the political parties, the political leaders and the government in general. In the light of non-performance of the party and the government, one could just hope that democracy in Nepal would survive just because "Democracy is the worst system of government but is the best among the prevailing ones."

The exclusion of people component in the party politics was the root cause of problematic politics prevailing in the country. This was seen in the parliament, in the government and in other state institutions and among state functionaries, as reflected by their non-performance in regard to delivery of services to the people. Moreover the governments and the parliament had been preoccupied by a mindset tuned to the politics of making and unmaking of the government. Individuals and parties contesting for power tended to expand their manoeuvring capability by the use of money power generated through the manipulation of state resources or making alliances with political mafia. By its very nature the mafia usually works underground, uses the state and government tools for its interest and, at the same time, it paralyzes the state and the government machinery's potential to serve the people. Deeply affected by the complex factors of mafia politics, political corruption, leadership crisis, excessive use of aberrant means in the game of government making and unmaking, de-professionalization, the whole state and governmental machinery suffered from indiscipline, disorder, aberration and anarchy. The condition prevailing was "dysfunctional anarchy" (Baral, 1998). In the absence of any indication of corrective measures being actively pursued in any quarter one might not be dismissed as being cynical while summing up the above discussion about the situation in the country in the words of a scholar, Prayag Raj Sharma who said, "We are inviting a catastrophe" (*Deshantar*, 24 May 1998).

Conclusion

Political parties of Nepal, since their inception in the 1940s, have been perceived as instruments of change in the social, economic and political spheres of the country. Their credentials as change agents was re-established by their catalyst role in the 1990 mass movement and in framing the 1990 Constitution. But, they largely failed to consolidate newly achieved democracy. Erosion of ideology, exclusion of people's interest and internal factionalism remained the dominant trends of party politics in Nepal in the 1990s. So the 4-Ds characteristics that they acquired after their transformation from movement organizations to competitive parties produced a political crisis in the country, what was explained above in the phrase of BLEAK. While emerging political parties, NC and UML in particular, as contenders of power politics, they suffered from the lack of clear vision, policy and programmes which were essential to expedite their declared objectives, i.e. good governance, political stability and economic development. These stated goals were sidelined since parties' leaders and workers indulged in self-aggrandizement by all possible means. They were, therefore, more interested in the game of government making and unmaking, irrespective of the nature of government (minority, coalition or majority government) by all foul tricks, violating all norms and processes in this regard. The intervention from the palace in party politics complicated the situation further, leading to political instability and anarchy. This showed a leaderless situation prevailing in Nepal. Along with erosion of ideology and intra-party factionalism, the lack of performance legitimacy caused the erosion in the leaders' authority.

Transformation of parties with 4-Ds characteristics and BLEAK political crisis had accumulative effects in creating problems of governability, explained above with the LOST word. Obsessed by insecurity filling, the leaders of the government and party paid the least attention to national problems. Politicization in bureaucracy, educational institutions and other areas killed the professional ethics, impeding democracy, governance and development. The lack of good governance paved the way for escalation of armed activities by the Maoist party. The threat from the extreme rightists increased as well. Leaders were aware of the increasing crisis but instead of looking for remedy of the national crisis they constantly indulged in the power game. So the people and nation would continue to suffer from the situation of non-governance in the days ahead.

NOTE

1. Governments formed in the second tenure of parliament (1994-1999) were in chronological order: (1) UML's minority government (November 1994-September 1995), (2) NC-led Centre-Right coalition government with RPP and NSP (September 1995-March 1997), (3) RPP-led Right-Left government with UML and NSP (March 1997- October 1997), (4) RPP-led Right-Centre government with NC and NSP (October 1997-April 1998), (5) NC's minority government (April-August 1998), (6) NC-led Centre-Left government with ML and NSP (August-December 1998), (7) NC's minority government (December 1998) and (8) NC-led Centre-Left government with UML and NSP (December 1998- May 1999).

CHAPTER 7

MAOIST INSURGENCY

> This plan of initiation of the people's war would be based on the principle that everything is an illusion except state power. While remaining firm on the principal aim of the armed struggle as to capture political power for the people, the party expresses its firm commitment to wage a relentless struggle against all forms of deviationist thoughts and trends including economism, reformism and anarchism (CPN[Maoist] [b],September 1995).

> Universal democratic and civil rights including multiparty competition, periodic elections, universal suffrage, rule of law, freedom of speech and press, fundamental and human rights, etc. should be guaranteed (CPN [Maoist], April 2003).

Introduction

On 13 February 2005, the Communist Party of Nepal (Maoist) celebrated the ninth anniversary of the 'people's war'. Within this short span of time, the insurgency, according to the Maoists, reached the stage of 'strategic offensive'. The advance of insurgency passing through 'strategic defensive' and 'strategic balance' followed an increase in its military capacity and war economy. Its People's Liberation Army (PLA) consisted of 3 Divisions, 9 Brigades, and 29 Battalions. There was no way to verify whether the Maoists' armed construction (Division, Brigade and Battalion) was according to international standards or not and estimation, therefore, varied on the actual number of the Maoists' armed force. An expert, however, assumed the Maoists' armed strength as 'one of the largest non-state military formation in the world' (Kumar, 2004: 12). The Maoists collected money through forced donations, bank looting and taxation. Reportedly, it was one of the richest 'terrorist' organizations having accumulated between US $ 64 million and 124 million (Kumar, 2003: 184). Parallel to the increase of the military strength was the formation and expansion of the Maoist's own administrative areas. The insurgency spread all over the country, except two (Manang and Mustang) out of 75 districts of the country that remained untouched from the direct armed confrontation between the state security forces and the Maoist guerrillas. In line with the party's policy of protracted people's war and to suit best with its pursuance of base areas, the Maoists had started forming its own government at village level by late 1998. The Maoists had its four tiers of governments: central (United Revolutionary People's Council led by Babu Ram Bhattarai), regional (nine autonomous regional governments), district, and village/city.[1] The Maoists' claimed capturing rural parts of the country cutting the space of the 'old regime' (state) into the capital and headquarters of districts.[2]

The Maoist insurgency progressed rapidly and many factors contributed to the escalation of violent conflicts and expansion of its influence all over the country. The blueprint of the insurgency (CPN [Maoist) [a], March 1995) that designed a year before its implementation showed the Maoists' confidence in the following accounts:

- "The geographical situation (of Nepal) is the most favourable for waging guerrilla war with direct links with the people.
- A good mass base for guerrilla war can be created from the struggle against the national oppression on the majority of nationalities (ethnic groups).
- There is no condition of direct military collision among the enemies for political power, from which the armed forces of the people could take advantage to seize a definite area.
- There is possibility of initiating and developing guerrilla wars in different parts of the country by taking the peasant revolution as the backbone, by centralizing activities in the rural areas and by relying on and uniting with the poor peasants.
- The people's support will keep increasing if the right revisionists are thoroughly exposed and the tactics of armed struggle are pursued carefully.
- The pace of development of armed struggle to establish people's

alternative revolutionary power would be faster and inspires us to undertake bold tactics to achieve the same.

- Nepalis working in foreign countries – mainly those working in India – would be mobilized by conducting political work amongst them and using the area for supply of various logistics for success of the armed struggle in Nepal".

Such a well-thought and well-planned blueprint of the Maoist insurgency indicated the possibility of the advancement of the armed struggles by careful utilization of Nepal's topographical location, its geographical proximity with India, mobilization of the peasant and the excluded ethnic groups, and guerrilla tactics. Besides, analysts found several factors, i.e. social injustice, unemployment, underdevelopment, problems of exclusion, lack of good governance, etc. contributing to the escalation of the Maoists' armed activities.[3] Of course, the Maoist insurgency had its own multi-dynamics, but analysts differed in identification of the major and minor factors that led to successful intensification of insurgency. Divergence of views followed mainly in line with disciplinary background of analysts.

Developmentalists shared an argument that the Maoist movement "is basically a social and economic issue and is produced and sustained by failed development" (Pandey, 1999: 12). "The Maoist insurgency is mainly fuelled by poverty" (Gurung, 2003: 4). It is worthwhile to mention that the Maoist armed activity was started from the Mid-West hills – the heartland of insurgency – and hill districts of this region (i.e. Rolpa, Rukum, Salyan, Dailekh, Jajgarkot and Dailekh) fall into the category of the 18 lowest rank districts in the human development index of Nepal (NESAC, 1998: 264-65). The influence of the Maoists was the strongest in the economically and socially deprived northern and western parts of the country.

Sociologists and ethnic activists saw the Maoist insurgency mainly from the ethnic angle. The hill high caste Hindus, Brahmin and Chhetri, and Newar (an urban ethnic group) – with their combined strength of 35 percent in the total population of the country – have long been in a dominant position in the power structure of the country. Others, i.e. hill ethnic groups, tarai caste and tribal groups, and Dalits are generally considered as the excluded and marginalized groups. The restoration of democracy in 1990 witnessed the emergence of ethnic activism. About the link between ethnic rising and the Maoist insurgency, one argues that

"People's war ... has blended class-based and caste/ethnic-based insurgency in the country" (Bhattachan, 2000: 159). The hill ethnic groups had always been in the forefront in battle grounds irrespective of ideological content, be it in the time of the unification of Nepal in 1768 or in the 1950-51 anti-Rana revolution or in several small-scale armed protest movements in the post-1960 period. An additional part was the involvement of some other marginalized groups, i.e. Tharus of tarai, Dalits and women in the insurgency of the Maoist party.

Political scientists analysed the failed governance as the main reason behind the constant weakening of the state and strengthening of the Maoists. The post-1990 politics had been characterized by ambiguity of the constitution, the king's assertion for power against the spirit of constitutional monarchy, lack of effective leadership, power-centric intra-party and inter-party factions and conflicts, political instability, lack of institutionalization of party and parliament, pervasive corruption, etc. All these factors had impeded the task of democratic consolidation in Nepal.[4]

The Maoist insurgency had its own dynamics and factors such as poverty, unemployment, underdevelopment, exclusion, corruption, bad governance, etc. contributed to enlarge the canvas of the insurgency. These were, however, supplementary factors that were not sufficient to explain why the Maoists opted for the course of armed struggle, not other options, despite the advent of democracy in 1990 broadened the space for expression of discontent and non-violent protest. The political and ideological aspects could give a convincing answer to the question about why the Maoists took the path of armed struggle. Class struggle in the form of armed revolution is the core of communist philosophy. The primacy of the political and ideological factor was evident by an avowed goal of the Maoist insurgency: overthrow of the polity based on multiparty parliamentary democracy and constitutional monarchy through armed revolution and its replacement with a new political system known as new people's democracy. The Maoists' key agendas – round table conference, interim government, and constituent assembly – put forth during the last two negotiations with the government in August-November 2001 and April-August 2003 – further showed the crux of the issue. Of course, the Maoist insurgency had its own multi-dynamics, including social, ethnic and economic, it was basically an ideological and political offence against the prevailing political system of the country.

In retrospect, the Maoist insurgency had been expanding and

escalating on three major grounds. First, the left or progressive ideology and identity – monopolized by the communist parties of Nepal – is popular among the people of Nepal. To be left or communist, in Nepali understanding, means to speak for "*gans, bas, kapas*" (food, shelter and cloth) for the poor, to advocate for radical and revolutionary change, and above all to stand for absolute economic equality even at the cost of political liberty. Second, restoration of multiparty democracy in 1990 synchronized with the ethnic revival and among the competing forces running to cash on the post-1990 ethnic uprising, the Maoists seemed more successful both in mobilizing the ethnic capital and in giving a political framework for ethnic demands – autonomy and federalism. Third, the internal conflicts and contradictions among the state actors had reduced the state's power and capacity which obviously placed the Maoists in an advantageous position.

Primacy of Ideology

The primacy of ideology of the Maoist insurgency could be seen in the origin and evolution of the communist movement in Nepal in general and the CPN (Maoist) in particular. Three different timeframes could be traced to the origin of ideology, strategy and organization of the Maoist party (Rawal, 1988; K.C, 1999). The Maoist party's proclaimed goal was to establish a 'new people's democracy', a prototype of Mao's China model. This conformed to the objective of the Communist Party of Nepal (CPN) – a parent organization of all communist parties of Nepal – set at the time of its formation in 1949. In addition to the adaptation of core components of communist ideology i.e. class struggle, armed revolution, dictatorship of proletariat etc., the communist movement of Nepal has its own native contents, i.e. republican, nationalism based on anti-India and anti-West, and non-conformist against the Westminster system. The Maoist party upheld both theoretical and native contents of communism in Nepal.

On adoption of strategy suitable to the proclaimed goal, differences among the Nepali communists had glaringly appeared since the early 1960s which led to splits in the party one after another and consequently the emergence of several splinter communist parties. Each of the splinter groups at the time of its inception appeared radical vis-à-vis monarchy, liberal democracy and India. But overtime most of them turned into moderate groups, including the CPN (Unified Marxist-Leninist or UML) which originated in the early 1970s as a Naxalite group professing the line "annihilation of class enemy" but later in the post-1990 period, it turned into a defender of the system of constitutional monarchy and parliamentary democracy. To be moderate left meant to be involved in a broader democratic movement and process in alliance with the NC. Opposing this line of thinking, the CPN (Fourth Convention) came into existence since the early 1970s and most of the senior leaders of the present Maoist party had started their careers from this party. The United National People's Movement (UNPM, a joint front of five Maoist splinter groups) kept itself at a distance with other left parties despite its participation in the 1990 mass movement, launched jointly by the NC and the United Left Front (ULF, consisted of seven communist splinter groups). The UNPM differed from the ULF's approach of considering the multiparty system at least as an interim arrangement between dismantled partyless panchayat system and the proposed system of new people's democracy. Realignment among leftist forces in the post-1990 period led to the formation of the CPN (Unity Centre) – consisting of several splinter groups of the parent organization, the CPN (Fourth Convention). The CPN (Unity Centre) – through its political wing, United People's Front (UPF) – contested the 1991 parliamentary election and the 1992 local election as a strategy to 'expose the sham of parliamentary democracy'. The newly formed CPN (Unity Centre) under the leadership of General Secretary Pushpa Kamal Dahal (popularly known as Prachanda) upheld the faith in armed revolution against the prevailing system of monarchy and democracy.

The question of translating the idea of armed struggle into action led to formation of the organization of the Maoist party as a separate group. Only in February 1995, the CPN (Maoist) was established formally, as a consequence of a split of the leaders and workers of the CPN (Unity Centre). Those who stood for continuous involvement in the parliamentary process inherited the name of the party CPN (Unity Centre) and others advocating for the implementation of the armed revolution gained a new name, the CPN (Maoist).

The Prachanda- led Maoist faction's non-conformist stand to the post-1990 political set up and its contentious adherence to ideology of class war was evident by its stands taken in recent political developments from the 1990s.

- The UNPM – the Prachanda faction, which functioned under the formal name of Masal– pleaded for advancing the 1990 mass movement to the point of achieving a new people's democracy unlike the ULF's stand for the restoration of the multiparty system.

- The Masal (Prachanda) demanded the election of the constituent assembly against the drafting of a new constitution by the Constitution Drafting Commission in 1990.
- The CPN (Unity Centre) with the Prachanda faction as a partner condemned the 1990 Constitution – which provided a system based on parliamentary democracy and constitutional monarchy – as 'a reactionary constitution'.
- The political report adopted by the Unity Congress of the CPN (Unity Centre) in December 1991 stated, "Our political strategy is to establish a new democratic republic of Nepal with a people's democratic dictatorship against feudalism and imperialism and on the basis of an alliance of peasants and workers under the leadership of the proletariat.... For this, it is a must to adopt the line of protracted people's war with a strategy of encirclement of the city from the countryside". This Unity Congress elected Prachanda as the General Secretary of the CPN (Unity Centre).
- The Prachanda faction of the CPN (Unity Centre) boycotted the 1994 parliamentary elections and it adopted a new name the CPN (Maoist) in February 1995. The third expanded meeting of the central committee of the party held in March 1995 decided to launch the protracted people's war.
- Since February 1996, the Maoist party had formally taken the actions of protracted people's war and it gained rapidly in expanding territories under its control.

The increase of popularity of left and progressive ideology in Nepali is clearly evident by a fact that the CPN gained only 4 out of 109 seats in parliament in 1959, whereas the combined strength of different communist parties in the post-1990 period was 82-95 out of 205 members of the House of Representatives (HOR). The popular vote of communist parties was around 40 percent in all the three parliamentary elections held after the restoration of democracy. Among those competing for the increase of left popularity, three different courses had taken place. One was the adaptation to the parliamentary system. The UML made considerable strength placing itself as the major communist party of the country through this course. The second course was involvement in the electoral process but retaining a non-conformist ideology vis-à-vis bourgeois democracy. The CPN (Unity Centre-Mashal) and the Nepal Workers and Peasant Party (NWPP) took this line. The third course was armed insurgency resorted to by the CPN (Maoist) since February 1996.

In a situation marred by a combination of political/constitutional impasse in the mainstream politics and intensification of the Maoists' insurgency, it was generally believed that the balance sheet of political power and influence was changing at a faster pace. The following paragraph illustrates a case to explain how the situation was heading towards in favour of the Maoists.

From one perspective, the Maoist insurgency in its mid-western stronghold areas could be seen as a renewal of an old confrontation between the Thakuri Raj and the radical left. The Thakuris (descendants of the rulers of the old principalities) and their clients had long since dominated this area, and the nature of their rule at the local level was repressive. This was in accord with the authoritarian regime at the centre during the partyless Panchayat system (1960-1990). Even after the restoration of democracy in 1990, the former Panchas survived, reviving their power base with a new political trademark by responding to the Nepali Congress's policy of incorporating the traditional social and political elites in its scheme of party building during the early 1990s. However, the sense of popular empowerment that spread after the successful 1990 mass movement introduced a new power equation against the traditional forces. Both the UML and the CPN (Maoist, formerly the UPF) emerged as the most influential left forces in the people's fight against various forms of the Thakuri Raj in this region. The equation among the left forces changed in favour of the CPN (Maoist) as a consequence of the UML's move from the left to the centre, while the Congress party was constantly heading towards the right from the centre in the political spectrum of the country. The local Thakuri-centrist alliance in the mainstream parties had never been strong under the democratic set-up, and it deteriorated during the period of the hung parliament (November 1994-May 1999). Because politics was concentrated at the centre in the game of government making and unmaking, the parliamentary parties grossly ignored the need for party building at the local level. This was the most appropriate time for the CPN (Maoist) to create its own space and territory for a long 'People's War'.

Of several concerted efforts made for creating and expanding its own territory, cleansing opponents was one of the main strategies exerted by the Maoists. They killed the civilians considered to be 'enemies of the people', such as party workers, elected persons, landlords, businessmen, moneylenders, exploiters, and police informants. Looking at it from the class perspective, one foreign anthropologist observed, "People with large houses, guns, money and gold are more at risk than poorer less well-resourced people" (Pettigrew, 2002: 308). While launching the people's war in the most organized way, the Maoists adopted a uniform plan of action in different places: first disarm the local people by seizing their weapons and then kill some persons (whom they accused as 'anti-people') in an inhuman and cruel way in daylight. As one explained the brutality of actions, "People have been killed while eating, dragged out of their houses into the courtyard and killed in the presence of the family members, thrown off, tied to trees, hacked and shot in various parts of their bodies to let them die of utmost pain" (Kattel, 2003: 60). The strategy seemed to create a fear and terror situation rather than to take lives of many people. Consequently, people's representatives at local elected bodies and parties' local cadres fled to district headquarters for their security. The eviction of parties' cadres was synchronized with withdrawal of other state machineries.[5]

The Maoists' monopoly in several parts of the country would have a definite impact on the popular bases of other parties and it surfaced when competitive politics would be tracked back in the future.

For the leadership of the CPN (Maoist), the armed struggle was their conscious choice and motivated to achieve the ideological goal. Baburam Bhattarai stated clearly that "People's war was initiated with a proclaimed aim of establishing a new democratic socio-economic system and state by overthrowing the present socio-economic structure and state .... The people's war is the inevitable instrument for overcoming the oppressive situation in the process of the historic new democratic revolutionary transformation" (1998). What would be its meaning to the supporters and cadres of the CPN (Maoists)? The party invariably contextualized the ideology of class struggle with poverty, injustice and exploitation. One foreign anthropologist observed in Dhorpatan of Baglung district, "People hear that communism is about the redistribution of wealth, and as most people in the area are extremely poor, this notion is very appealing, especially to disillusioned youth who turn to Maoism because it promises to improve their living conditions (Millard, 2002: 293). The ICG report could be a good reference of contextualizing the class ideology in the local milieu.

> The Maoists have quite successfully appealed to what are widely viewed as deep injustice within Nepal, including abuses by the security services. Much of their attraction has stemmed not from the resonance of Maoist theory among

> poor and often illiterate villagers, but from the frequently inescapable logic of a general population that feels at best poorly served by their government and at worst preyed on by officials. Early Maoist attacks were effective in capturing the public's imagination because they targeted some of the most obvious signs of inequality in the form of local upper caste politicians, police posts, the judiciary, rural banks and land revenue offices (April 2003: 13).

Besides, prompt delivery of justice, though at gunpoint, against all sorts of exploitation and social aberrations (i.e. gambling, alcohol, sexual assault, etc.) by the Maoists' 'people's court' was widely appreciated.

Ethnicization of Insurgency

The CPN (Maois) made concerted efforts in taking advantage of the post-1990 ethnic upsurge in Nepal. The ethnic groups along with Madheshi (original inhabitants of tarai) and Dalit has been marginalized as a consequence of the historical process of the state's designed nation-building scheme.

Since the time of unification of the Nepal in 1768, the rulers – Shahs, Ranas and Panchas – had tried to develop Nepal as a homogeneous, monolithic and unitary state providing protection to one language (Nepali), one caste group (hill Bahun-Chhetri), and one religion (Hindu), ignoring the reality of diversified and pluralistic character of the Nepali society.[6] Besides, the state-designed 'Nepalization' process – through Hinduization, spread of the *parbatiya*'s culture, institutionalization of the caste system converting separate identity of ethnic groups into caste structures, and centralization of politics and administration – had led to increased disparity among different social groups. The hill high caste Brahmin-Chhetri and Newar have long been in a privileged position. Other groups, i.e. Janajati, Madheshi and Dalit are generally marginalized. The legacy of history is well-reflected in unequal distribution of socio-economic resources and in representation of the political power structure of the country (Bista, 1991; Gellner et al., 1997; Lecomate-tilouine and Dollfus, 2003).

Discontent against the domination of the hill high caste is the central issue of the emerging minority movements in Nepal. The unequal power distribution among the caste/ethnic groups could not be changed in the prevailing structures of the Nepali state: monarchical rule, Hindu state, unitary form of government, primacy of one language (Nepali), domination of hill Brahmin, Chhetri and Newar, centrality of Kathmandu, centralized administration, feudalism and patron-client based authoritarian culture. With a project of state restructuring, the minority groups have asserted their inclusion. The agenda of state restructuring has several interrelated components: i.e. secular state, republican system, federal form of government, regional and ethnic autonomy, proportional electoral system, devolution of power to local government, equal treatment for all languages, equitable sharing of state resources, positive discrimination/ reservation for minorities, and representation of different groups in the public positions.

The ethnic concerns are well addressed by the CPN (Maoist). One famous sentence that had been used since the inception of insurgency is, "To maintain the hegemony of one religion (Hinduism), one language (Nepali), and one nationality (Khas), this state has for centuries exercised discrimination, exploitation and oppression against other religions, languages and nationalities and has conspired to fragment the forces of national unity that are vital for proper development and security of the country" (Quoted in Sharma, 2002: 16). The Maoist proposal of state restructuring converged the ethnic demands. Some key points of the Maoists' scheme of state restructuring that have direct bearing with ethnic and minority rights are:

- Declaration of Nepal as a secular state,
- Equal treatment to all languages of Nepal.
- Ethnic and regional-based autonomy and right to self-determination,
- End of caste, ethnic, regional and gender-based discrimination, and
- Special policy for the promotion of interest of Dalits and women

The CPN (Maoists') concerted efforts to blending ethnic rights and class war was evident by the formation of ethnic and regional-based frontier organizations. Between 1998 and 2000, the Maoists formed seven ethnic-based and two regional- based front organizations.[7] The Maoists could penetrate in and expand their armed activities in the eastern hills and tarai region only after the party's ethnic and regional-based front organizations began to work. Furthermore, based on ethnicity and regionalism, the CPN (Maoist) adopted a federal structure with its nine autonomous regional governments.[8]

The ethnicization of class ideology rendered help tremendously in strengthening the insurgency. The Maoists acclaimed that "New and young party members from poor peasants, women, depressed communities, oppressed nations and nationalities and backward regions rapidly came out of the crucible of the people's war in an unimaginable number" (CPN [Maoist], February 2001). To see it in another perspective, the CPN (Maoist) had internal imperatives in ethnicizing the insurgency since the people from ethnic groups had considerable influence in the party organization. They were indeed dominant in the armed wing of the party. By appointing the party leaders from different ethnic groups as head of the related regional government, the CPN (Maoist) maintained a caste-ethnic balance in the internal power equation of the party and this could be considered as preventive measures against the possibility of internal rebellion by a certain group of people within the party. Strategically speaking, the inserting ethnic contents in insurgency served the party's interest in appealing and mobilizing the people of the excluded groups. Though the Maoists' 'people's war' was political, the insurgency had a greater ethnic content in terms of composition of its PLA and militias.

Internal Contradiction of State

The institution of monarchy had always been in a central position throughout the history of Nepal. But the survival of such a central institution was in question. Gyanendra reached the throne in the background of the royal massacre of June 2001 in which King Birendra along with all his family members and five other royalties were killed. The report of the probe committee found the then Crown Prince Dipendra as the culprit of the royal massacre; it was not bought about by the masses and they, rather, suspected a conspiracy behind this great tragedy. This event had brought a change in relations between the monarchy and the people. The parliamentary parties consciously ignored the mass psychology but the CPN (Maoist) which was championing for the republic capitalized a it for obvious reason. Unlike his predecessors, the new King Gyanendra had some sort of legitimacy problem. His popularity further declined by his ambition to become a 'constructive monarch'. The royal takeover of power that started since October 2002 invited a confrontation with the major political parties, like the NC and the UML, which were faithful to the principle of constitutional monarchy. The palace's move of taking power back was backed by the international regime which thought that it would help to integrate the state's political and military power under the command of the king. The Royal Nepal Army (RNA), which did not feel comfortable in working with parties leaders – was traditionally loyal to the institution of monarchy. But unlike the anticipation of international communities, the distance between the king and parties increased. This limited the palace's manoeuvrability that was manifested during the second negotiation between the king's nominated government and the Maoists in April-August 2003. The major parliamentary parties, NC and UML, took a non-cooperative line resemble to the palace and the military's position in the first negotiation between the elected government and the Maoists in August-November 2001. The division between military power commanded by the monarchy and the popular force represented by the parties had always been the advantage of the Maoists for both the pre- and the post-October 2002 times.

The Maoists had constantly gained strength exploiting the weakness of its opponent, the state. The post-1990 politics was characterized by anarchy reflected in the major events that occurred in the past twelve years, such as parliamentary elections called four times; recommendations for dissolution of the HOR made six times; special sessions of the HOR summoned seven times; and the government changed thirteen times. All these events happened because politics was excessively concentrated on the power game. Besides, the political instability, frequent change of government, politicization and division in police, erosion of ideology, decline in the credibility of political parties and their leaders, all these counted for weakening the state's crisis management capacity vis-à-vis the Maoists. Since politics concentrated at the centre in the game of government making and unmaking, parliamentary parties grossly ignored the need of party building at the local level. This helped the Maoists in creating its own space and territory for its 'long protracted people's war'. The Maoist insurgency started at the time when the state was heading towards instability, anarchy and crisis owing to the unholy alliances, both in nature and purposes, among the parliamentary parties.

The state's capacity to deal with the crisis had been severely constrained by a division of the mainstream parties in their perception and strategy vis-à-vis the Maoists in the initial phase of the insurgency. Two different reports, prepared by members of parliament (MP) after their visit to Rolpa district during the Romio operation period, had clearly indicated such a division. The NC MPs interpreted the Rolpa incident as "terrorist activities", whereas the left MPs called it "political confrontation between the NC and the UPF" (political wing of the Maoist party). Worst of all, the mainstream parties wanted to use the Maoist insurgency for their own petty interests against other parliamentary parties. For the NC, the rise of the Maoists could become emergence of a countervailing force against the dominant position of another communist party, UML. The

UML also tried to cultivate the Maoist issue to cut the size of its immediate electoral rival, the NC, as the Maoists made the NC workers the main target of its *safaya* (cleansing) actions.[9] Such a misunderstanding and wrong strategy naturally misled them unless they realized a common threat perception, particularly after the UML's interest was directly affected by the formation of the Maoist people's government at different levels. Of 25 districts where the Maoists formed their district level government, 21 districts were the UML's stronghold areas in terms of the result of the 1997 local election and the composition of the District Development Committees (DDC) (Hachhethu, 2004: 77). The change of the UML's role was clearly reflected in its (and also by other parliamentary communist parties) rejection of the Maoist proposal – put forth on the eve of the first truce and during negotiation with the state in August-November, 2001 – to have a loose left coalition on agendas of the republic system and election of constituent assembly. The UML indeed endorsed the policy of armed mobilization for counter insurgency and the declaration of emergency (in November 2001) and its extension (February, 2002). The changing role of the UML and other left parties contributed to building a common approach and action plan againsts the Maoist. But, it was too late and by that time the Maoists gained great strength, which demanded the use of the state armed capacity to resist insurgency.

The consensus among the parliamentary parties vis-à-vis the Maoist insurgency was, however, overshadowed by their division in relations to the monarchy after King Gyanendra took over power since October 2002. Four parties including the UML were in the king's nominated government led by Prime Minister (PM) Sher Bahadur Deuba. Other four parties led by the NC had continuously taken street in opposing the royal 'regressive' steps. The UML changed the camp from five parties' alliance opposing the regression to the palace camp in reacting to non-cooperation of allies on its ambition to lead the proposed all party government. For the leadership of the NC, the ongoing protest movement was a pressure tactics to reach in power. Pointing out the root cause of conflicts among the leadership of parliamentary parties, the then US Ambassador Michael Malinowski stated, "Nepal's house is on fire and the politicians are arguing about who gets to sleep in the master bedroom" (ICG, April 2003). Contrary to the leadership's quest for the king's favour for power, the leaders of many political parties, including the NC and the UML, were under tremendous pressure by the workers of their respective parties to go for the republic and constituent assembly. This was another contradiction facing most parliamentary parties.

The state's capacity to use armed forces was/is limited by the fact that the army was not under the control of civilian government. The party-military hostility was compounded by the factors of historical legacy[10], constitutional ambiguity[11], and non-cooperation.[12] Exchange of heated words between civilian leaders and military officials accusing one another for the escalation of the Maoist crisis surfaced publicly several times. The government-military relation was further complicated by the palace's separate dealing with the Maoist. Maoist leaders, Prachanda and Baburam Bhattarai claimed of having their *aghosit karyagat yaketa* (undeclared tactical alliance) with late King Birendra and they said that Birendra was not in favour of the government's plan to mobilize the army against the people's war (*Kathmandu Post,* 4 June 2001). The army had deliberately and consciously kept itself at a distance from the elected government and multiparty parliamentary democracy as if its primary duty was only to protect the palace.

The Maoists cultivated internal contradictions and crisis among the state actors – particularly conflicts among political parties, and confrontation between the palace/army and political parties – to enhancing its strength and capacity. The possibility of takeover by the Maoists through armed insurgency was, however, least likely.

Concluding Remarks

People's war started from the remote areas of the mid-west hills in February 1996 by a few dozen ideologically motivated hard-core Maoists was in headway expanding its impact all over the country. It was through contextualizing the ideology of class war with poverty, injustice and exploitation and through ethnicizing the insurgency, the CPN (Maoist) strengthened its capacity of popular mobilization and ability of armed fighting.

Moreover, the CPN (Maoist) acquired power more through taking advantages of weakness and internal contradictions of its opponent, the state, than the strength it gained through its own concerted efforts. Taking back the executive power by King Gyanendra on 4 October 2002 heightened the conflict between the palace and the parliamentary parties. The failure of the post-1990 democratic governments to address the long-standing socio-economic problems of the country, i.e. poverty, unemployment, deprivation and discrimination against the minorities (Dalit, ethnic groups, and women in particular) etc. helped to enhancing the Maoist's strength, power and influence. People's apathy towards the leadership of mainstream parties and internal crisis, conflict and contradiction among the state actors and institutions (i.e. palace, parties, parliament, etc.) paved the way for escalating the Maoists' insurgency.

Negotiations held between the Maoist insurgents and the state twice in the past failed to bring about a peaceful solution of armed conflict. Its resumption, however, could not be ruled out. Despite the CPN (Maoist)'s claims of advancing the insurgency to the stage of strategic offensive, the state backed by the international regime was still heavyweight in military strength in terms of arms, ammunition and manpower. The state's military supremacy was confronting with the Maoists' talent and motivation to rebelling. The hope of negotiation was based on a fact that, "This war (between the Maoist and state) is militarily unwinnable" (Philipson, 2002: 19) for either side.

Another pertinent question related to explore the possible way out of the problems of insurgency was the ideological goal of the CPN (Maoist). Would the Maoists stick to its ideological goal or was it willing to be flexible for an amicable solution of the problem? With a declared objective to achieve new people's democracy, the CPN (Maoist) started 'people's war from 13 February 1996. It was distinct from other left parties of Nepal mainly because of its rejection of the system of monarchy and parliamentary democracy. It was indeed different from other parties because it applied Mao's dictum "power grows out of the barrel of a gun" into action. If the CPN (Maoist) stuck to its ideological goal, the possibility of peaceful settlement was unlikely. As one argues, "The case of Nepal is intrastate in which the stakes of both warring parties are high that relates to the survival of the insurgency and its success, on the one hand, and the survival of the monarchical regime on the other. If the Maoists win, monarchy will be eliminated, republicanism established; if the state wins, the revolutionaries would be eliminated" (Kumar, 2005: 3).

The CPN (Maoist) had repeatedly shown a green signal for ideological flexibility. Its threefold demand – round table conference, interim government and constituent assembly – did not include the republic. It postponed its republican agenda though its demand for the election of constituent assembly might pave the way to achieve it in future.The election of the constituent assembly was the bottom line of the Maoist party which itself was a reconciliatory agenda, taking into consideration of its ideological position for the republican state that was not included in agendas of negotiation. Furthermore, the party reaffirmed to accept the multiparty system if the problem could be settled at the negotiation table. The CPN (Maoist) position was well reflected in Baburam Bhattarai's response to ICG's question –Would the CPN(Maoist) leadership be willing to accept a constituent assembly with the precondition that multiparty democracy and constitutional monarchy be guaranteed ? – "... if the particular historical condition and the prevailing balance of forces so demand, there can be a common understanding on certain issues during and after the election, but not certainly in the very beginning or right now and on fundamental questions of democracy. On our part, we are committed to multiparty democracy and other prerequisites of basic political, economic, social and cultural transformation, which we have outlined in the political agenda submitted during the recent peace negotiations" (ICG, September 2003). It seemed that the questions whether the CPN (Maoist) would stick to its original stand for republican and one party communist system or would it pursue a revision for the continuity of multiparty system and 'tactical understanding' for the retention of monarchy depended on how the issue would be settled, through war or through negotiation.

To see the case from the other side of the coin, the minimum condition for the peaceful settlement of the insurgency problem was that the king should give up his ambition to become a powerful monarchy. Of several factors that led to the failure of the recent past negotiation between the state and the CPN (Maoist), three major factors included: the king's unwillingness to give up power, vested interest of army generals, and exclusion of parliamentary parties in negotiation.

Resumption of negotiation could not be ruled out. One should not ignore the fact that there were three contending parties that needed to be involved. The essential rule of negotiation is to make a compromise based on give and take among the contending parties. To be seen from an optimistic point of view, the problems of the old armed conflicts could be settled in making an agreement on the following three points.

1. Revival of the pre-October 2002 constitutional position, for a temporary period, to form an interim government of all parties (including Maoist), separation of military from the palace, absorption of the Maoist's armed guerrillas in employment and the job market before the election of the constituent assembly.
2. A tacit understanding among the political forces for the retention of kingship in the form of full-fledged constitutional monarchy by

the new constitution.

3. A provision of amendment in the constitution providing options to change anything of the constitution through referendum.

NOTES

1. About the way how the Maoists run the parallel administration, one stated, "Outside the Kathmandu Valley and district headquarters, they have maintained a tight control over the movement of people, transport of goods and delivery of services. Through a short electronic message, they can bring the nation to a complete standstill, because of the fear they have been able to create over years". (Katel, 2004: 38). Another elaborated, "They have also started practice of governance by establishing rules and regulations as well as developing textbooks for teaching at schools by banning the bourgeois subjects and Sanskrit teaching. By issuing a separate budget, introducing a visa system for visitors to the Maoist-infested areas, taxing the inhabitants, charging levies on commercial tourists, or trekking transactions and extracting commissions from sale of timber and herbs like *yarshagumba,* the Maoists have registered the semblance of independence by creating a state within the state. (Kumar, 2004: 14).
2. Such a claim had ground to believe in the case of the hill districts of the mid-west region – the epicentre of insurgency. But in other parts of the country, the vast areas were buffer zones between the Maoist-controlled area in remote parts and the state-controlled area in district headquarters. The presence of both forces was felt in such buffer zones by patrolling of the police and army in daytime and by the Maoist guerrillas at night. (This statement was based on observation of 79 investigators who made a month long field work in August 2004 as enumerators of a survey on the State of Democracy in Nepal).
3. For details see, Karki and Seddon (2003); Hutt (2004); Thapa and Sijapati (2003); Thapa (2003): Muni (2003); Karki and Bhattarai (n.d).
4. To understand Nepali politics in the post-1990 period, see Baral (1993; 2000); Baral, Hachhethu and Sharma (2001); Hutt (1994) Hoftun, Raeper and Whelpton (1999); POLSAN (1992); Borre, Pandey and Tiwari (1994); Kumar (1995; 2000); Brown (1996); Hachhethu (2002).
5. Some reports indicating the state withdrawal in 1999-2000 were: Among the 43 VDCs in Rukum, only six had chairpersons residing in their respective village. (*Kathmandu Post,* March 10, 2000). Among the 26 police posts in Rukum, only 11 had been retained. (*Kathmandu Post,* March 11, 2000). The number of cases registered in the Rolpa District Court for nine months (from July 1998 to April 1999) was only 28 against its previous record of having court cases at least 30-35 per month. (*Himal Khabar Patrika,* April 15-30, 1999).
6. The 2001 census of Nepal recorded 101 caste and ethnic groups and 91 languages and dialects. Based on caste, ethnic, regional, cultural and linguistic cleavages, Nepali population can be broadly classified into three major groups: *Parbatiya* (hill people) and *Madheshi* (plain people); *jat* (caste groups) and *janjati*(ethnic/tribal groups); and high caste and low caste Hindus.
7. Names of the Maoist ethnic and regional organizations are:(1) Magarat National

Liberation Front (2) Tamang National Liberation Front (3)Tamuwan National Liberation Front (4)Limbuwan National Liberation Front (5) Nepal Dalit Liberation Front (6)Tharuwan National Liberation Front (7) Thami Liberation Front (8) Majhi National Liberation Front (9) Newa Khala (10) Madheshi National Liberation Front and (11) Karnali Regional Liberation Front.

8. Name of autonomous regions that the Maoists formed are: (1) Kirat Autonomous Region (2) Tamang Salling Autonomous Region (3) Tamuwan Autonomous Region (4) Newar Autonomous Region (5) Magarat Autonomous Region (6) Tharuwan Autonomous Region (7) Madhesh Autonomous Region (8) Bheri-Karnali Autonomous Region and (9) Seti-Mahakali Autonomous Region.
9. Among the party cadres killed by the Maoist guerrillas till July 2000, the number of NC workers was 136, followed by 22 of the UML, 19 of the RPP and 1 of Mashal (Maharjan, 2000: 172).
10. The army was used by the late King Mahendra to stage a coup in 1960 against the NC government and multiparty system. The army had also been used time and again to suppress movements against the partyless panchayat system (1960-90).
11. The 1990 constitution had a separate provision for military mobilization, the Security Council (consisting of the Prime Minister, Defence Minister and Chief of the Army Staff) which could only recommend it and the king had the right to take the final decision.
12. Non-cooperation by the army was felt widely, particularly during the Maoists' capture of Dunai, headquarter of Dolpa district, in September 2000. The then PM Girija Prasad Koirala resigned obviously because of the army's betrayal on the Holeri incident. The army disobeyed the government's decision to counter the Maoist guerrillas after they kept 76 police in hostage on 12 July 2001 at Holeri in Rolpa district.

Chapter 8

MONARCHY AND ITS LEGITIMACY CRISIS

Following the royal takeover of October 2002 and February 2005, Nepal returned to its old form of monarchical state. King Gyanendra's ambition to become an active monarch was fuelled by the bad record of the multiparty regime (1990-2002) in governance as well as in dealing with the armed insurgency, carried out by the Communist Party of Nepal, Maoist or CPN (Maoist) since February 1996. But contrary to general expectation of improvement in the political and security situation, the Maoists consolidated its position further under the monarchical rule from October 2002 onwards. Shift of political alignment of political parties with the palace in the past into the CPN (Maoist) in post February 2005 was also detrimental for eroding the legitimacy of the monarchy.

This chapter tries to explore the legitimacy crisis of the Nepali monarchy on the following accounts: (a) sources of monarchical power and erosion of royal legitimacy (b) revival of confrontation between the palace and parties and (c) change in role of international community from support against the Maoists' 'terrorism' to oppose against the king's act of derailing the democratic process.

Challenge against Divine Rights

While taking power on 1 February 2005, King Gyanendra asserted his inherent rights to rule over the state. He stated, "The Kingdom of

Nepal was built on the foundation of unification process initiated by King Prithivi Narayan Shah the great" (*Text of King Gyandendra's Royal Proclamation*, February 2005)

Prithvi Narayan Shah, the unifier of Nepal, established the Shah regime based on the right of the sword. The Shah monarch, as a hereditary institution, was reinforced by the traditional Hindu view of the nobility of birth as it was an accepted tradition all through the ancient and the medieval times. His successors were weak, so post-Prithvi Narayan Shah Nepal was marked by struggle among *bhardars* to capture power. The instability and chaos created by the power struggle among the *bhardars* culminated in the Kot massacre of 1846, which led to the emergence of Jung Bahadur Rana as a strong Prime Minister (PM), more powerful than the king. Hence, the Shah King reduced to the position of *de jure* head and the Rana family as *de facto* ruler. For both the Shah and the Rana rulers their political authority was derived from the traditional authority system. Both regimes were based on the patrimonial system and the military and the administration were instruments of their rule.

The traditional authority system in Nepal was challenged by the 1951 revolution leading to the end of the century-old Rana regime, and following the assurance of the then King Tribhuvan to establish a polity based on popular legitimacy. But in due course of time, the 1959 Constitution provided a mixed system in that it respected the inherited idea of sovereign right of the monarch and the political process based on democratic procedure. But, through a coup in 1960, King Mahendra dismantled the multiparty system and he introduced the panchayat system with its two basic characteristics: active monarchy and partyless polity.The panchayat constitution stated, "The sovereignty is vested in His Majesty and all powers – executive, legislative and judiciary – emanate from him". The late King Birendra himself defended the traditional authority of monarchy derived from divine right. Once he said,"In Nepal, the monarchy and his subjects have been governed by Dharma, a system drawn from the Hindu religion. The King cannot change this value system" (quoted in Shaha, 1975: 7). However, he was forced to put the panchayat system on trial in the 1980 referendum. The panchayat acquired plebiscite legitimacy by a margin of ten percent against the multiparty system. Some procedures of liberal democracy were introduced. But in essence, the panchayat regime was an authoritarian system.

The Nepali Congress (NC) and communist parties called for a joint popular movement in 1990 that succeeded in bringing the end of the panchayat system along with the traditional authority system based on divine right of the king. The constitution drafted by the commission, approved by the interim government and accepted by the then King Birendra, was promulgated on 9 November 1990. The constitution provided a polity based on constitutional monarchy and parliamentary democracy. It made the people ultimate sources of power and vested sovereignty in the people.

To ensure the stability of the parliamentary system introduced after the 1990 mass movement, the king's sincere commitment to the letter and spirit of the 1990 Constitution was required mainly for four major reasons. One, King Birendra's consent to the 1990 Constitution – which reduced his position from absolute ruler to constitutional monarchy – did not come up with his conviction. Instead he was forced to promulgate it by the post-1990 mass movement situation (for details see Chapter 2). Two, despite formal reduction of the king's position, the 1990 changes were limited in political and legal structures. The popular forces were able to capture elected bodies, i.e. local government, parliament and government, but the domination of royal trustees in leadership of other state organs, i.e. court, bureaucracy, police, army, constitutional bodies, etc. remained unchanged. Three, the history, culture and tradition of the country had also influenced the mindset of Nepali elites, including parties' leaders, while considering the palace as one of the power centres of Nepal despite formal transformation of sovereignty from the king to the people by the 1990 Constitution. Fourth, the constitution itself allocated the position of monarchy beyond just a figurehead vesting with him some discretionary, prerogative, and preventive powers, though ambiguously, that the king could play a crucial role at crisis time, i.e. dissolution of the House of Representatives (HOR), emergency, and mobilization of army. It was widely felt that the palace had manoeuvred such loopholes of the constitution to expand its space in realpolitik. Taking into account constitutional provisions and practices of political system in the 1990s and the early 2000s, one could say that Nepal had, in fact, a "semi-constitutional monarchy".

The transition to democracy in the post-1990 period did not have a good record (for details see Chapter 6). People's discontent against parties had its own implications in the growth of the Maoist insurgency that was started from February 1996. The state's capacity under the democratic regime (1990-2002) was limited by the fact that the army was not under the control of the civilian government. Instead, the army's loyalty to the monarchy had been used to derail the democratic process and the 1990 Constitution by King Gyanendra.

Unlike the people's initial hope to improve the situation with a revival of monarchical rule, the royal regime failed to gain a support base within and outside the country. Instead, the CPN (Maoist)'s violent 'people's war' was rapidly intensified and spread all over the country. The CPN (Maoist) further consolidated its position under the monarchical rule from October 2002 onwards. The king's limitation of political manoeuvrability was exposed by the political parties' constant opposition against the royal regression since October 2002 and opposition forces had gradually acquired strength. The 12-point understanding made between the mainstream Seven Parties Alliance (SPA) and the CPN (Maoist) in November 2005 proved a landmark event for mass mobilization that reached the point of grand success on 23 April 2006 when King Gyanendra was forced to reinstate the parliament which was dissolved in October 2002.

In retrospect, since the unification of the country, the Shah dynasty had made concerted efforts to blend inherent rights with divine authority promoting Hinduism as a symbol of Nepali nationalism. The 1990 Constitution, upholding all previous constitutions, respected the historical and traditional legitimacy of the monarchy with the following provisions:

- His Majesty is a descendant of the Great King Prithivi Narayan Shah and an adherent of Aryan culture and the Hindu religion.
- Nepal is a Hindu, Monarchical Kingdom.
- His Majesty is the symbol of Nepalese nationality and the unity of the Nepalese people.

These provisions were reflective of the traditional legitimacy of monarchy in Nepal. After the unification of Nepal in 1768, the unifier King Prithivi Narayan Shah attributed Nepal to *asali Hindustan* (pure land of Hindus) which indicated the state's roadmap of national integration under the Shah regime (1768-1846). The Hindu polity – in which monarchy and religion have a decisive role – was further enforced during the Rana period (1846-1951). The Rana PMs were also monarchs by title (*Shree Tin Maharaj*) and by the power they enjoyed. Jung Bahadur Rana, founder of the Rana regime, promulgated a Civil Code in 1854 providing the legal framework to the Vedic prescription of social order in a hierarchical society. In fact, the Hinduization process in Nepal followed casteism and the Civil Code 1854 integrated originally non-Hindu ethnic groups into the Hindu fold giving them a *matwali* status below Brahmin and Chhetri in descending order. In the post-Rana period, the Hinduization process continued albeit in a lesser degree and in a reformed manner. The decade of the 1950s under the first experiment with democracy noticed a relaxation but the reinstatement of absolute monarchy under the partyless panchayat system (1960-1990) revived the Hinduization process. But integration through Hinduization during the panchayat period was somehow different from orthodoxy under the Rana regime. The new Civil Code of 1963, in contrast to the old one, formally withdrew the state's support to the caste system. Though reformed, the panchayat regime continued the state's policy of promoting Hinduism in various forms. For instance, national symbols set by panchayat are associated with monarchy and Hinduism (Gurung, 1997: 505).

The promotion of Hindu nationalism by P.N. Shah and his successors, including the Rana rulers, was taken into consideration of two major factors/interests: legitimacy and nationalism vis-à-vis India. The Hindu polity places the king as a sovereign lord, a protector of territory and subjects, a guardian of moral order, an upholder of traditions, and the source of all spiritual and temporal power (Sharma, 1997: 4475). Another factor propelling Hindu nationalism was to give Nepal a distinct identity different from secular India. Projection of Nepal as the only Hindu state of the world had a two-pronged strategy: to put itself at a distance from the Indian state and, at the same time, to associate with the Hindu population of India for the interest of the Hindu king of Nepal. Nepal's Hindu monarchs had tried their best to use their leverage among the Hindus of India to counter the possible alliance between the secular forces of India and Nepal against his interest (Dangol, 1999). King Gyanendra's visits in India twice within a year in 2002 and his visits to a number of religious places of India demonstrated a continuity of Nepal's Hindu king's strategy to cultivate Hindus of the world, those of India in particular, at crisis time. The 7th World Hindu Conference, held in Gorakhpur (India) in February 2003, passed a resolution to protect the Hindu state and monarchy of Nepal by declaring the king of Nepal as emperor of the Hindus of the world.

Among the rulers of the post-unification period – from P. N. Shah to Gyanendra– those who had a greater legitimacy problem pursued further for Hinduization. P.N. Shah conquered Nepal by the sword. The authority acquired through the sword was not sufficient to establish legitimacy among the people of vanquished lands. So his project of making Nepal an *asli Hindustan* was guided by his interest to gain legitimacy in newly conquered land. The need for the establishment of new legitimacy also explained the reason behind the initiation for active and rigid Hinduization by Jang Bahadur Rana, the founder of hereditary Rana oligarchy in which the PM's position was a *de facto* ruler while the king had *de jure* power. He also introduced the Rana regime by sword and his quest for religious legitimacy was well reflected in what he said, "In this age of *Kali* this is the only country where Hindus rule"(Quoted in Sharma, 2002: 25). Revival of Hinduization by King Mahendra was another example of invoking traditional legitimacy by a ruler who did not have a popular base. By staging a coup in December 1960, King Mahendra ended the multiparty system and instead introduced a partyless panchyat under his leadership. The panchayat constitution of 1962, unlike the previous constitutions of 1951 and 1959, made Nepal formally a Hindu state.

King Gyanendra succeeded to the throne against the background of 1 June 2001 royal massacre in which King Birendra along with all family members and five other royalties were killed. The report of the probe committee found the then Crown Prince Dipendra as a culprit of the royal massacre, though the people in general did not buy the findings of a two-member committee headed by the Chief Justice. Wrapping up the committee in a hurry and suspicious manner, the Committee's finding was taken by the people as an eye wash of the conspiracy in the palace. The massacre had however brought a change in relations between the monarchy and the people. Gyanendra's succession was in a horizontal line and so unnatural and against tradition, if not illegal. He tried his best to project kingship as the core of the Hindu ethos and also cultivating leverage of Hindu monarchy for obvious reasons. In sum, the promotion of Hindu nationalism was closely linked with the legitimacy of Nepali rulers. Following the line of the late King Birendra to defend divine right, King Gyanendra, in replying to a question of *Time*'s correspondent said that he was glad to see his role as the preserver of all things, a role that has been spelled out for a king in Hindu mythology as the personification of God Vishnu (Quoted in Khanal, 2005: 40).

Nepal's identity of the Hindu state was challenged in the post-1990 period by surging ethnic awareness as well as by others. It had obvious implication to a long-standing political struggle against the validity of divine authority of the Hindu monarch. The revival of ethnic movements in the post-1990 period along with ethnic assertion by the Janajatis for their distinct identity as non-Hindus gave strength to the ideology of secularism. The emerging trend of identity movement demanded the change of national identity from a Hindu state to a secular state. Discontents against some signs and symbols – associated with the Hindu state and Hindu monarchy – i.e. national symbols, national anthem (phrased in a way that equates patriotism with worship to king), use of Sanskrit language in education and media, etc. were agendas of oppositional politics and minority movements.

Along with the demand of a secular state, the ethnic movements stand for restructuring the Nepali state. The agenda of state restructuring is a clear rejection to some historically inherent characteristics – built in from the time of unification of the country in 1768 – of the Nepali state, i.e. monarchical rule, Hindu state, unitary form of government, primacy of one language (Nepali), domination of hill Brahmin and Chhetri, centrality of Kathmandu, centralized administration, feudalism and patron-client based authoritarian culture. The monarch had long been the protector and promoter of these features of Nepal state which are now rejected. Those engaged in the mission of state restructuring are civil society, ethnic organizations, political parties and the CPN (Maoist), and there is a broad consensus among them in seeking alternative structures, i.e. secular state, federal form of government, etc.

The ethnic demand for a secular state and restructuring of the Nepali state is now well received by political parties. All communist parties stand for secularism. The NC – the oldest and influential centrist party – recently changed its stand from neutral position to secular state. Moreover, the insurgent Maoist group – whose presence was felt all over the country – is the catalyst in bringing about a new political and ideological equation with clear republican and secular agendas. It had succeeded in stopping singing of the national anthem and teaching of Sanskrit language – symbolized with monarchy and Hindu religion – in its controlled areas.

The foreseeable change in the cultural domain of the country – that is obviously against supremacy of the Hindu religion – would have natural repercussions on the legitimacy of the Hindu monarch. The ethnic rise in the past, particularly during the 1980 referendum, was capitalized for the survival of the then panchayat regime (Gurung, 1997: 526; Shah, 1982: 160). But the monarchy's clout among the ethnic groups had been changed by parliamentary parties in the post-1990 mass movement period and recently by the Maoist party in hostility. In conformity with general speculation about successful ethnicization of the Maoist insurgency, the Maoists acclaimed that "New and young party members from poor peasant, women, depressed communities, oppressed nations and nationalities and backward regions rapidly came out of the crucible of the people's war in an unimaginable number"(CPN [Maoist], 2001). So, anti-monarchical forces, rather than the palace, were far ahead in capitalizing on the emerging ethnicity for political purposes.

There was/is a broad consensus among the ethnic organizations, civil society, political parties and the CPN (Maoist) on the agenda of restructuring the Nepali state. In the proposed state restructuring project, there was/is no space to accommodate the monarchy, at least to the active and executive king. This was a clear indication of erosion of the legitimacy of the Nepali monarchy. The recent declaration of Nepal as a secular state was a conscious attempt to hammer against the claim of divine right by the monarchy of Nepal.

King Gyanendra's Ambition

A monarch confronting the social legitimacy problem had put its future at stake seizing political power by royal takeovers of October 2002 and February 2005. On 4 October 2002, King Gyanendra dismissed an elected government led by PM Sher Bahadur Deuba accusing him as being 'incompetent'. Hence, he began to form the government through nomination. The king's acts of taking over power reached the climax on 1st February 2005 while dissolving his own nominated government and then grabbing the post of chairman of Council of Ministers. He tried his best to justify his acts of taking over power on the grounds of failures of multiparty governments both in countering the insurgency and tackling the Maoists. The 1stFebruary 2005 proclamation was all about accusations against political parties and leadership. For instance, he said:

> Today, we have once again reached a juncture where, in keeping with popular aspirations, a historic decision must be taken to defend multiparty democracy by restoring peace for the nation and people. Even when bloodshed, violence and devastation have pushed the country on the brink of destruction, those engaged in politics in the name of the country and people continue to shut their eyes to their welfare. Tussle for power, abuse of authority on gaining power and unhealthy competition in fulfilling personal and communal interests at the expense of the nation and citizenry contributed to the further deterioration in the situation. There were attempts to flout the universally accepted rule of law in the name of politics. Our desire to ensure social, political and economic justice for our beloved people through the meaningful exercise of multiparty democracy could not be materialized. There was a steady rise in crimes against the nation and people, including destruction of development infrastructures constructed for the people's benefit. Whereas all democratic forces should have adopted an unified approach against terrorism, leaders instead continued their

> tussle for power, encouraging simple political workers to vandalize public utilities in the name of politics. Faced with this steadily declining situation, it is now time to bring to an end the ongoing acts of terrorist violence and pledge, in earnest, to fulfil the people's aspirations with the restoration of peace and security in the country (*Text of His Majesty King Gyanendra's Royal Proclamation*, 1 February 2005).

The king's accusation against political parties was not baseless. The post-1990 politics was characterized by anarchy. So, the people were dissatisfied with the way democracy worked and this was clearly manifested in a nationwide survey conducted with 3,249 respondents in August-September 2004 (Hachhethu, 2004). The same survey revealed that parties and parliament were the least trusted among the state's political, constitutional and administrative organizations. The people's apathy towards parties was manifested in the other form that the masses did not join anti-regression movements launched by political parties since October 2002.

Besides ill handling of democracy, the state's capacity to deal with the Maoist insurgency was constrained by internal contradictions among the state actors. In the initial phase of the insurgency, political parties failed to take a common stand vis-à-vis the CPN (Maoist). Later, all mainstream parties felt a threat from the CPN (Maoist) as well as the monarchy so agreed to work together against King Gyanendra. The hard earning consensus among the political parties was however disrupted by the palace's successful intervention. Four parties including the UML were in the king's nominated government before the royal takeover of 1st February 2005. The other four parties led by the NC took to the streets in opposing the royal 'regressive' step of October 2002. The king's act of seizing all state power by 1st February 2005 compelled all political parties to be united once again.

The state's capacity under the democratic regime (1990-2002) was limited by the fact that the army was not under the control of the civilian government. The relations between the government and military reached the worst situation that the then PM G.P. Koirala was eventually forced to resign on 18 July 2001 after the army betrayed him by disobeying the government's decision to act against the Maoist guerrillas who took about 70 policemen hostage on 12 July 2001 at Holeri in Rolpa district. The separation of military power commanded by the monarchy and the popular forces represented by the parties had always been the advantage of the Maoists for both the pre- and the post-February 2005 times. Moreover, the CPN (Maoist) acquired power more through taking advantages of weakness and internal contradictions of its opponent, the state, than the strength it gained through its own concerted efforts.

In retrospect, the palace's dismay with a new position of constitutional monarchy was manifested since the day of inauguration of the 1990 constitution. Even King Birendra – attributed as a low profile king – had slowly but steadily taken back power.The monarch had therefore gradually taken power back manoeuvring troublesome politics of intense intra-party and inter-party rivalries. There were several records of the palace's offensive against words and spirit of the Article 35 (2) of the constitution which bound the king to follow "the advice and consent of the Council of Ministers". The expansion of the palace's role in realpolitik had been continuously felt in nomination of members of the National Assembly, in appointment of ambassadors and other high ranking posts. Moreover, there were instances that the palace went against the decision of elected government, i.e. in dissolution of parliament, in appointment of chairman of the Human Rights Commission, and of a bill related to distribution of citizenship were too few to mention here. The palace had taken double advantage of the Maoist insurgency limiting the elected government's capacity of counter insurgency by not allowing the use of the army and thereby discrediting the popular forces for their inability to tackle the Maoist insurgency. Nevertheless, the late King Birendra confined himself in manoeuvring the troublesome politics in favour of the palace.

The palace's high handedness was increased to a great extent since Gyanendra, brother of the late king Birendra, ascended the throne. Unlike the late King Birendra, his brother King Gyanendra was more aggressive, assertive and ambitious. From the day of ascendance to the throne he had given enough indication of his ambition to become executive monarch. He said, "The days of monarchy being seen but not heard, watching the people's difficulties but not addressing them and being a silent spectator to their tear-stained faces are over". The palace had increasingly appeared as the most influential player in realpolitik of the country, particularly after the intensification of the political crisis following the declaration of emergency and mobilization of the army against the Maoists' armed insurgency since November 2001, and dissolution of the HOR and split of the ruling NC in May 2002. The sequence of events reached a point on 4 October 2002 with King Gyanendra sacking PM S.B. Deuba on the charge of "incompetence". This was a beginning that logically reached the climax in February 2005 seizing all power by King Gyanendra.

Unlike King Gyanendra's claim "in accordance with popular will and aspiration" of taking power back, a nationwide survey conducted in 2004 revealed that people rejected a system of executive monarchy. Eighty-four percent among the respondents said that the situation after 4 October 2002 was bad and the worst. Against the king's project of militarization to deal with the Maoist insurgency, the majority of respondents wanted a peaceful solution of the problem. The overall finding of the survey is summarized:

> Nepali citizens retain their trust in democracy as the best form of government despite disappointment with the working of democracy and the behaviour of politicians. The people clearly reject non-democratic alternatives. They don't want the king to be executive head. People strongly disapprove of the previous instance of dismissal of popular government and the takeover of executive powers by the king. Nepali citizens would like the current deadlock to be resolved through a round table discussion involving the Maoists and the political parties. These views belie the claims of the palace justifying the recent 'temporary' measures as essential for democracy, governance, peace and security of the nation (Hachhethu, 2005: 62-68).

Royal Takeover and International Community

A monarch facing the legitimacy problem on the domestic front was isolated further by the international regime. The role of external forces was a contrast before and after February 2005. Though the practice of executive monarch had started from October 2002 it was well received by external players as they took the post-October 2002 political project as a scheme to combine monarchy and democracy against the Maoist 'terrorist'. The external support on the post-October 2002 project could be seen in three interrelated factors. One, the Maoist insurgency in Nepal had been treated as a part of the post-9/11 global war against terrorism. This obviously meant that international forces wanted to suppress the Maoist insurgency through military means. India and the USA gave the Maoists the a label of 'terrorist'. The second factor was linked with their preference of military means to deal with the CPN (Maoist). The army, which did not feel comfortable in working with party leaders – was traditionally loyal to the institution of monarchy. Three, they assessed that parties were incompetent to deal with the Maoist insurgency.

In sum, the international regime took the post-October 2002 project in a way that it would help to integrate the state's political and military power under the command of the king. Nepal acquired more sophisticated weapons and other military gadgets from the USA, UK, India and other countries at that time (Kumar and Sharma,n.d.). Manoeuvring international support to the post-October 2002 project, King Gyanendra seized all power by a proclamation on 1st February 2005. This proved that the international community's calculation of bringing king and parties together – what they considered as 'twin pillars of Nepal' – against the Maoists was wrong. ICG rightly pointed out:

> International policy on Nepal has failed. Quiet diplomacy and support for the king have not worked. Since 2002, the main players – India, the US and the UK – have been urging the king to work with the political parties to develop a common political strategy towards the Maoists. The EU has taken a similar stance. ... despite repeated warning from all sides, the king has seized power, and the situation has worsened significantly. Acceptance of the present course would lead to further instability and hasten a possible takeover by the Maoists (February, 2005).

With a realization that King Gyanendra outmanoeuvred external support, international communities disapproved the king's act of seizing power on 1st February 2005 and they spoke with one voice that it was a 'setback to democracy'. The principal suppliers of military aid, e.g. India, USA and UK postponed security aid. Many donors withdrew or cut their earlier commitment to development aid as well. For instance, Norway withheld its earlier commitment of financial aid to the Melamchi Water Supply project. The problem of external legitimacy of King Gyanendra was well reflected in India's successful move of postponing the SAARC summit. The king was compelled to cancel his plan to attend the meeting of UN General Assembly because international dignitaries, including the US president and UN General Secretary reportedly rejected the government's request for the king's meeting with them. India, which was assigned to play a lead and coordinating role by the international community, took a tough stand asserting the reinstatement of democracy as a precondition for foreign aid and support. Taking into consideration King Gyandendra's rigidity and uncompromising temperament, the international community backed the 'anti-regression' struggle, launched by political parties. India played a role in bringing the mainstream parties and the Maoists together for the democracy resurgence movement. After 1st February 2005, King Gyanendra was isolated, humiliated, and de-recognized by the international community. International communities, including diplomatic missions to Nepal, bilateral and multilateral donors, and international organizations, i.e. UN, collaborated with political parties for the restoration of democracy and peace.

Political Realignment

Change of the role of the international community paralleled the change in parties' relations vis-à-vis the monarchy. Political polarization in the post-February 2005 posed a real threat to the survival of the monarchy in Nepal. Of the three mega actors – monarchy, political parties and the Maoists – the first two were put in a basket of 'constitutional forces' vis-à-vis the third one. The 1990 Constitution guaranteed the perpetuity of constitutional monarchy and multiparty parliamentary democracy. While defending the constitution, parliamentary parties strongly countered the Maoists' agenda of republicans asserting that there could not be a compromise on constitutional monarchy and multiparty democracy. Parties' ideological position vis-à-vis the monarchy changed in reverse gear as their hope of reconciliation with the monarchy was dashed by the royal takeover of 1st February 2005. The UML passed a resolution making *loktnatrik ganatantra* (democratic republic) as the declared goal of the anti-regression movement. Similarly the NC, by its latest national convention, deleted the word 'constitutional monarchy' (its faith carried out from the time of party formation in 1947) from its own party constitution. Parties made a review of their own position vis-à-vis the monarchy in reacting to the king's act of seizing power.

Demand for the republic system was not merely confined to reaction to King Gyanendra's act of taking power back. It was linked with a long-standing dismay to what his predecessors also did. The four kings of three generations – Tribhuvan, Mahendra, Birendra and Gyandendra in sequence – all showed their discomfort with democracy and constitutional monarchy. And all of them imposed executive monarchy as an alternative to democracy. King Gyanendra's takeover of power in February 2005 was a reincarnation of the 1960 royal coup by King Mahendra. Parties had their own historical and ideological imperatives that they could not offer the king more than a position of constitutional monarchy. As the king rejected what the parties offered, a new generation of party workers and civil society members exerted pressures on the parties for a revision of their position on monarchy. A leading political scientist, Lok Raj Baral, observed sharp polarization of Nepali politics – monarchy versus republic – in the post-February 2005 situation that there was now no meaning of carrying out the middle path (Baral, 2005).

The February 2005 event opened up a possibility of a new political equation. In a new foreseeable power equation, parties and the Maoists were likely to be together against the royal rule despite parties reluctantance to make a common front with the Maoists because of its declared objective: overthrow of the present polity based on multiparty parliamentary democracy and constitutional monarchy through armed revolution and its replacement with a new political system known as new people's democracy. Both sides gave enough signals to come together, provided one respect the basic stand of the other. Once the CPN (Maoist) leader Baburam Bhattarai proposed the parties, "you accept republicanism, we will accept multipartyism" (Bhattarai, 2002). In conformity to this line and against its ideological stand for one-party people democracy, the Maoists now inserted the component of competitive party politics in its recent proposal of the 'new model of democracy'.

Political parties and many others suspected whether the CPN (Maoist)s' revised ideological position was its tactic or commitment. But they showed considerable flexibility. For instance, they realized the need of the election of the constituent assembly which was the bottom line of the CPN (Maoist) for negotiated settlement of insurgency. A reversal change in parties – Maoist relations manifested in other ways as well. In November 2001, the UML and other left parties rejected the Maoist proposal to form a loose left coalition on agendas of the republic system and election of the constituent assembly. Later all communist parties and the NC worked to bring the Maoists in a struggle against the royal regime. The 12-point understanding made between the SPA and the CPN (Maoist) in November 2005 was a landmark event to unite popular forces to fight against 'absolute monarchy'. The mainstream parties endorsed the Maoists demand of election of the constituent assembly and the Maoists reciprocated with its assurance to accept the multiparty competitive system. The 12-point understanding between the SPA and the Maoists gave strength for a successful popular mobilization in the April 2006 mass movement.

Conclusion

Republican sentiment was rising in Nepal since the day Gyanendra became king. As he was put on throne against the backdrop of the tragic event of the royal massacre, the monarchy in Nepal was now not respected as it was before. The masses of Nepali people, who didn't believe the report of the probe committee of the royal massacre, suspected the credibility of King Gyanendra. Ethnic assertion for a secular state and popularity of restructuring the Nepali state project had negative consequences for the traditional legitimacy of the monarchy.

The CPN (Maoist), an emerging and dominant political force, had a clear republican agenda. Moreover, by taking executive power back since 4 October 2002, King Gyanendra opened up another battleground with parliamentary parties, in addition to fighting against the insurgent Maoist group since February 1996, which naturally aggravated the vulnerable position of the monarchy. King Gyanendra's ambition to becoming active monarchy brought a change in the role of political parties in the reverse direction, from an ally championing for the cause of constitutional monarchy in the past into promoter of the republican project. After February 2005, political parties fuelled republican design in political landscape. As the royal takeover of 1st February 2005 derailed the democratic process, the international community made a U turn in its role towards the monarchy, from active supporter to serious opposition. The implication of overall developments in the post-February 2005 was rightly assessed by the Jansakti Party (a splinter group of the Rashtriya Prajatantra Party) that "the space for pro-constitutional monarchy is dangerously shrinking"(JSP, 2005).

Since King Gyanendra was alienated by emerging social forces (ethnic rise and civil society movement), rising political organization (Maoists), established political forces (mainstream parties) and external power (international community), it would be ridiculous to believe that the royal regime could give an effective counter to the Maoist insurgency.

Epilogue

Jan Andolan II – an unprecedented event of mass uprising of April 2006 participated in by 3-4 million people in a country of total 23 million population – led to achieve the twin goal, end of monarchical rule and the end of a decade long Maoist insurgency. The reinstated parliament, by its political declaration of May 2006 known as the *Magna Carta* of Nepal, formally cut down two arms of monarchy by making Nepal a secular state and by deleting the title 'royal' from the military and all other state organizations. This could be taken as a prelude to the path of republic Nepal. Hence, Nepal exercised republic as the king had been kept away even from symbolic activities to be done by head of the state all over the world and these were exercised by the PM. Besides, surveys reveal that public opinion favouring a republic increased substantially from that of only 15% in 2004 to 59% in 2007 (Hachhethu et al., 2008).

The post April 2006 transition was a reversal to the previous one undertaken in the aftermath of mass movement I (1990) as the monarchy was 'in' and the Maoists 'out' in the past. In transition following the *Jana Andolan* II, exit of monarchy from the state affairs coincided with entry of an insurgent group. The CPN (Maoist), championing for a republican system, has been one of the dominant actors in making decisions on the future of Nepal. Despite the idea of retaining kingship in the form of 'cultural monarchy' or 'baby king' was aired, the mainstream parties eventually submitted to the CPN-Maoist's uncompromising stand for republic system. So, the survival of a two and half century long Shah dynastic rule in Nepal was in the stake.

The Interim Constitution, promulgated in January 2007, also opened up a possibility of transformation of the Nepali state into republic through ballot. It provides a provision that a decision on future of monarchy would be made by a simple majority of constituent assembly members in its first meeting. This provision was invoked in May 2008 while formally declaring Nepal a republic country by the constituent assembly.

CHAPTER 9

LOCAL GOVERNMENT
Bhaktapur Municipality

Located just 13 km east from the capital (Kathmandu), Bhaktapur is a puzzle city for many people in many respects. Inhabited by Hindu Newar with more social stratification than Vedic's prescription of four *verna* (Brahmin, Chhetri, Baishya and Sudra), caste is central to the lives of city dwellers. Some anthropologists (Levy, 1990; Parish, 1997) have taken an interest in exploring the hierarchical caste-based society of Bhaktapu's Newar and complementary relations among the Newar communities of different strata. Bhaktapur is much more than caste. Its inclusion in the World Heritage list shows the status of the city as "living heritage" or "living museum" representing the medieval characteristics such as cultural events, festivals, *bhajan* (hymns), *dafas* (prayer groups) dramas, folk dances and *guthis*. Cultural historians (Slusser, 1998; Anderson, 1998; Berrier, 1970) in their research of Kathmandu valley find Bhaktapur as a unique city for its historical monuments (temples, palace, and *mathas*), rich architectural heritage, and retention of centuries-old tradition of art,

* This chapter includes information collected from interview – conducted in December 2001 – with Narayan Man Bijukchhe (Chair, NWPP), Prem Suwal (Mayor of BM), Gyan Bahadur Nyanchyan (former Mayor of BM), Ash Kumar Koju (Member of BM), Rabindra Kharbuja (Member of BM), Dhruba Libi (Member of BM), Tilak Kayastha (NC local leader), Babu Raja Joshi (Chair, NC's Bhaktapur City Committee), Raja Ram Ranjit (UML local leader), and Uttam Bati (RPP local leader).

culture and craftsmanship. For economists and developmentalist (Gutschow and Kolver, 1975; Haaland, 1982; Acharya and Ansari, 1980), renovation of historical monuments such as temples, shrines, buildings, etc. and preservation and conservation of medieval art, culture and tradition have become their priority for making Bhaktapur a true cultural capital of Nepal. The city's infrastructure building seems to bc the second priority area. Bhaktapur's economy featured by agrarian society and pre-industrial position, and lack of migration from outside are some of the uncommon characteristics of general urban life. The most striking thing is that Bhaktapur city has not yet been studied from the political perspective.

Politics in Bhaktapur has its own distinct character. Nepal Workers and Peasants Party (NWPP), a communist party, had constantly dominated in bringing the elections result of Bhaktapur Municipality (BM) in its favour for the last twenty years. This was uncommon to general pattern as the Nepali Congress (NC), which captured more than 50 percent seats of the local government all over the country in 1992 local elections, was reduced to the size of 30 percent in 1997 local elections. The strength of the Communist Party of Nepal (Unified Marxist-Leninist or UML) in local government increased from 29 percent in 1992 to over 50 percent after the 1997 local elections. Unlike the change of power equation and parties' position in local governments in corresponding periods, the NWPP had continued to retain its predominant position in BM. What were the reasons behind this success: leadership and or governance?

This chapter deals with the urban politics of Bhaktapur from two major perspectives: leadership and governance. For the last twenty years, leaders of BM had mostly been constituted by *Jyapu*– a low caste group and previously excluded community – suggesting the emergence of a new group in political leadership of Bhaktapur city. Why was it so? Was it mainly because of the NWPP's conscious effort in bringing the downtrodden section of society to the helm of city affairs? How far did socio-economic changes contribute to caste and class consciousness of the *Jyapu* community? To what extent did the introduction of plebiscite system of representation and restoration of multiparty democracy open and expand political opportunities to citizens in general and disadvantaged groups in particular irrespective of their position in the social and economic set up? Under the leadership section, the paper covers many contents such as social setting, elections, parties and candidate selection, social, economic and political backgrounds of BM leaders. Another aspect is leadership capacity in providing good governance to Bhaktapur city.

Governance in essence is delivery of state services to the society and citizens. Many questions related to local governance of BM such as leadership's vision, decentralization and devolution, generation of financial resources, mobilization of capital and human resources, people's participation, development plan and projects need to be addressed to assess the performance of elected representatives of Bhaktapur.

Leadership

Bhaktapur district is divided into two parliamentary constituencies, sixteen Village Development Committees (VDC) and two municipalities. BM, one of the two municipalities of Bhaktapur district, consists of 17 wards. One ward chairperson and four ward members, including one woman ward member, were elected from each ward in addition to the election of Mayor and Deputy Mayor. Bhaktapur Municipal Council had, therefore, 87 elected representatives and 18 nominated members. BM Board consisted of 19 elected members (Mayor, Deputy Mayor and ward chairperson from each of 17 wards) and two nominated members. The major contesting parties in Bhaktapur were the NWPP, the NC, the UML and the Rashtriya Prajatantra Party (RPP).

Bhaktapur is a stronghold of the NWPP. From the time of its participation in electoral politics since 1981 during the partyless panchayat period, the NWPP had constantly gained the legislative seat except for the loss of one from two parliamentary constituencies of Bhaktapur district in 1991 and 1999 general elections. It had limited influence in rural areas but had managed to gain the top post (Chairman) of DDC through electoral alliance with other parties. Numerically, the NC and the RPP had greater representation, four from each party, in 13 members DDC. The NWPP and the UML had two seats each in the DDC. But the NWPP's dominance in Bhaktapur city could not yet be challenged by other parties despite an alliance made among the NC, the UML and the RPP against the NWPP in the 1997 elections for BM. The NC appeared once as the most popular party in rural areas of Bhaktapur and had gained many seats including the Mayor and Deputy Mayor posts of the newly formed Thimi-Madhepur Municipality in the 1997 local elections. The party won one of the two parliamentary constituencies in the 1991 and the 1999 general elections but lost in the 1994 mid-term elections. The RPP was the third force in Bhaktapur district but gained more seats than its size in both the 1992 and the 1997 DDC elections through alliance with other parties. Relatively, the UML was less influential, though it won half of the

TABLE 9:1
Parties' Position in Local and General Elections, Bhaktapur District

Parties	*House of Representatives*			*DDC*		*Municipality*			*VDC**	
						Bhaktapur		*Thimi*		
	1991	*1994*	*1999*	*1992*	*1997*	*1992*	*1997*	*1997*	*1992*	*1997*
NWPP	1	2	1	3	2	18	17	2	5	2
NC	1	-	1	4	4	1	1	10	12	3
UML	-	-	-	2	2	-	-	3	2	8
RPP	-	-	-	4	4	-	1	2	2	3
Others	-	-	-	-	1	-	-	2	-	-
Total	2	2	2	13	13	19	19	19	21	16

* The figure counts only the Chairman of VDC. The number of VDCs was reduced from 21 to 16 because of the establishment of a new municipality (Thimi-Bhaktapur municipality) consisting of the previous 5 VDCs.
Source: ECN (1991, 1992, 1994, 1997, 1999).

total 16 VDCs of Bhaktapur district in the 1997 local elections.

Social Cleavages and Leadership Building

Before entering into the main subject— leadership structure of BM— it makes an overview on the general pattern of leadership structure in Nepal in order to trace the picture of Bhaktapur city in comparative perspective. Nepal shares the experience of other South Asian countries that leaders are generally drawn disproportionately from the people of a higher socio-economic background. Education, wealth and social status are 'political resources' behind the formation of leadership (Putnam, 1976). Nepal and other South Asian countries have common patterns with high caste groups and big land holding class dominating political leadership.

The hill high caste Brahmins and Chhetris have dominated social, economic, administrative and political structure of Nepal. The reason behind it goes back to social stratification of the people of the Hindu Kingdom of Nepal into four groups – Brahmin, Chhetri, Vaishya and Sudra – as prescribed by the Hindu Vedic ethos. In the descending order, Brahmin and Chhetri are placed at the top with their high ritual position: Chhetri was the ruling class and Brahmins worked as priests and advisors to the ruler. Such a hierarchical social structure was legally reinforced and strictly practiced as the state protested ideology with the enactment of the Civil Code 1854 that further classified several caste and ethnic groups into three broader categories- *Tagadhari* (sacred-thread wearing caste) at the top, *Matwalis* (alcohol drinking ethnic groups) in the middle, and *Asuddha* and *Achhut* (impure and untouchables) at the lowest layer. Though the New Civil Code of 1963 legally abolished the system of caste domination and discrimination, the hill high castes have continued to retain their domination over political power structure even today.

The domination of hill high castes in Nepali politics is witnessed by a previous study. Brahmin and Chhetri— with their size of 30 percent (Brahmins 13 percent and Chhetris 17 percent) in the total population of Nepal— constituted 70.5 percent among the central leaders of three major parties: the NC, the UML and the RPP. And they constituted nearly two thirds of total 205 members of the House of Representatives (Baral et al., 2001: 48-49). This shows a correlation between social status and political power. But other groups that considered as "unprivileged communities" such as hill ethnic groups, the plain caste and tribal groups have relatively greater representation in constituting political leadership at the local level (Hachhethu, 2002: 81-92). Because political parties usually recruit their local leaders from the locally dominated caste/ethnic population irrespective of their social status vis-a-vis- Brahmins and Chhetris. The general picture of political leadership at the central and local levels reveals that the leadership at the apex level is more elitist, and, the leadership at the bottom is relatively accommodative to the unprivileged groups. It needs to stress again — to observe the political leadership of Bhaktapur city in comparative perspective with the micro level leadership structure of Nepal — that local leadership are relatively more mass-based, because parties generally recruit local leaders from the locally dominated population.

Bhaktapur is almost entirely a Newar city and 92 percent of them are Hindu (Levy, 1990: 59) where social life is shaped by the values of the caste system such as hierarchy and inequality. The main source of their livelihood is farming. Two distinct socio-economic characteristics of Bhaktapur city are: it is an agrarian society, and its social order is based on the caste system.

Let me first deal with caste-based social characteristics and its implications for the politics of Bhaktapur city. "A caste system is one that divides society into a large number of hereditary groups, distinguished from one another and connected together by three characteristics: *separation* in matters of marriage and contact; *division* of labour; and *hierarchy*, which ranks the groups as relatively superior or inferior to one another" (Levy, 1990: 73). The division of Newars to several social rankings dates back to the medieval period when King Jayasthiti Malla divided his *Praja* into 64 castes on the basis of their occupations. Before the unification of Nepal in 1769 by King Prithvi Narayan Shah, the Malla dynasty ruled over the small principalities of Kathmandu valley including Bhaktapur. Levy finds 350 *thars* (last name of city' Newar population) and arranged them in twenty distinct levels (ranked from Brahmin to untouchable) in Bhaktapur's urban macrostatus system (1990:72). For convenience of this paper, Bhaktapur Newars are regrouped into five categories in hierarchical order: upper caste (Brahmin, *chha-thari* and *panch-thari*) at the top, Buddhist Newars (without ranking in Hindu hierarchical order), *Jyapu* in the middle, low caste groups in the lower middle, and untouchable at the lowest position.

Two dominant groups are upper caste Newars enjoying superior status in social ranking, and *Jyapu*, a majority community comprising around 60 percent of Bhaktapur city's population (Gutschow and Kolver, 1975: 40). The upper caste Newar has a collective identity— *syasya* (superior), *sahu* (merchant shopkeeper), *madhyambarga* (middle class)— that distinguishes them from other groups. It refers to their caste status, class position and occupation. They include the descendants of the Malla kings and families of their advisors and administrators. They were traditionally landowners. They are involved in trade, business, bureaucracy, teaching and other learned professions. *Jyapu*, a Newari word, means peasant. Peasant in Nepal refers to the occupation of farming across the caste hierarchy. Peasant as an occupational group includes Brahmin as well as untouchables. However, the meaning of *Jyapu* in Bhaktapur is not only confined to the agricultural occupational group. A person to be *Jyapu* refers to his/her social and economic position in the society. *Jyapu*'s social status is lower than that of the upper caste Newars and also conveys the state of poor economy. Narayan Man Bijukchhe or Rohit, a local inhabitant and Chairman of NWPP, interprets the caste based society of Bhaktapur through the angle of class ideology that *Jyapus* are working class, and others, particularly upper caste Newars, belong to the bourgeoisie (Interview, 26 December 2001). But the caste system dominates the city life. An anthropologist observes "Bhaktapur, even today, is a city of castes, of culturally valued inequalities, the social and symbolic life of the city is organized in terms of these inequalities" (Parish, 1997: 5). The system of hierarchy and inequalities can be observed in social practices, settlement pattern and cultural symbols of Bhaktapur city. Some instances are:

- High caste Newars do not accept boiled rice and certain other food items from individuals of any caste lower than them. Low caste people are barred from entering the upper floors of a high caste house.

- The high castes live in the centre of town and bazzar areas, along the main tourist and trade route, and around the three major squares. Towards the edge of town, status decreases and poverty increases. The *Jyapus* live in *galis*(lanes), between the centre and the outer fringes. The people considered impure and untouchable live outside the traditional boundaries of the city.
- In a chariot during the Bisket festival, the Brahmin representing the king and royal priest take a seat on the right and left of the god Bhairab. Astrologers and non-Brahmin priests (high-ranking Newar) are seated behind the Brahmin. A *Jyapu* takes a seat behind the high-ranking Newar. Four carpenters stand at the four corners of the chariot.

The division of Bhaktapur city's society into superior and inferior groups places the upper caste Newars in an advantageous position. The political history of Bhaktapur shows a correlation between social status and political power. In the social setting of Bhaktapur, the upper castes Newars enjoy the same status as the hill high caste Brahmin and Chhetri in the national context. Being the vanquished to the Shah ruler they lost political power after the unification of Nepal in 1769, but the social customs of Newar, set from the medieval period, remained unchanged and has placed the upper caste Newars in elite positions. In the post-unification period, they were accommodated in the court of Shah and Rana palace. One way or other, they had always been in proximity to political power. Their proximity to the power centre complemented retaining their dominant position in the social and economic life of Bhaktapur city.

The change of political regime from Rana oligarchy to democratic set up in 1951 did not impact much on the privileged position of the upper caste Newars. Instead, they worked as instruments in bringing popular politics under the new political dispensation. Popular politics in Nepal appeared first in the form of opposition to the Rana regime. Parallel to the national context that the hill high caste group and educated middle class were the backbone of the democratic movement in Nepal, the local upper caste Newars led anti-Rana movements in Bhaktapur. Most Congress and Communist parties' leaders of Bhaktapur city in those days belonged to the upper caste Newars. The new values of liberty and equality accompanied by the democratic set up affected less to the traditional caste society of Bhaktapur. The prevalence of the caste system over the modern value of democracy and party was revealed by the result of the 1957 elections of BM. Parties' candidates were defeated from all seven wards except for one candidate of the Communist Party of Nepal (CPN). The elected municipality members were independents and from the upper caste Newars. One candidate from the hill high caste group, not from the *Jyapu* community despite this group being the majority population of Bhaktapur, won the election.

The change of political system from multiparty democracy to partyless panchayat system in 1960 also favoured the upper caste Newar in local politics of Bhaktapur. The selection of political leaders under panchayat system could be divided into the pre-1980 and the post-1980 referendum periods. Before the 1980 referendum, panchayat leaders were largely co-opted by the centre. Out of five persons, who held the post of National Panchayat (NP) member from Bhaktapur district in different periods (1960-1980), two were Chhetris and three came from the upper caste Newars. Of five persons holding the post of *Pradhan Pancha* of Bhaktapur Nagar Panchayat in the same period, three belonged to the upper caste Newars and two from *Jyapu* community. The political history of Bhaktapur has shown that the upper castes Newars had long been in proximity to power in the Shah and Rana court, in parties' local leadership during 1950-1960, and in panchyat's local leadership after 1960.

But the domination of the upper caste Newars in local politics of Bhaktapur ended suddenly in the post-1980 referendum. The introduction of plebiscite for the selection of leadership made a breakthrough for the emergence of new leadership from the majority community of Bhaktapur city. The prevalence of the *Jyapu* community in local politics of Bhaktapur was further ensured after the restoration of democracy in 1990. For the last twenty years the leadership of BM had been mostly constituted by the activists of the NWPP and from the members of the *Jyapu* community.

The overwhelming representation of the *Jyapu* community in elected bodies of BM shows the transformation of leadership from the traditional elite to the previously excluded group. It could be an exceptional case since the hill high caste Brahmins and Chhetris have retained their dominant positions in the elite structure of Nepal irrespective of change of the electoral and political system. It is indeed amazing that the caste-based social customs and practices of Bhaktapur city, in which the upper caste Newars place themselves in the high ranking status, remain unchanged, but the political leadership is transferred to the unprivileged

TABLE 9:2
Caste Composition of Bhaktapur Municipality Leaders

Castes	*1982*	*1987*	*1992*	*1997*	*% in Total Population**
Upper Castes	15.78	15.78	15.78	15.78	27.2
Jyapu	68.42	68.42	73.68	78.94	59.3
Low Castes	10.52	10.52	5.26	-	7.7
Untouchable	-	-	-	-	3.2
Buddhist Newar	5.26	5.26	5.26	5.26	2.2
Non-Newar	-	-	-	-	0.4
Total No.	19	19	19	19	100

* Bhaktapur Development Project, 1977.Source: ECN (1982, 1987, 1992, 1997).

community, *Jyapu*. Of several factors contributing to the transformation of political leadership in Bhaktapur city, the peasant movement is at the top.

Peasant Movements and Land Reforms

Inter-caste relations among the Bhaktapur Newars, traditionally shaped by a system of hierarchical interdependence, got a new content of class conflict owing to the land reform question. Most upper caste Newars were landowners while the *Jyapus* were tenants. They came into direct conflict on several contents of the land reform programme as the interest of one group clashed with the interest of the other.

Since the majority community is *Jyapu*, Bhaktapur city is a peasant society. Till 1980, the *Jyapus'* livelihood was entirely dependent on subsistence farming without any other source of income except for some artisan farmers who were involved in crafts and construction works in agriculture off-seasons. The miserable position of *Jyapu* in land-based economy of Bhaktapur had been observed by an author, "The Newar peasant, who had been exploited also under the Mallas, became even worse off under the new rule (post-unification period). Heavy taxes forced him to sell his harvest at low prices. Later in the year, when he had to buy grains, he became dependent on the moneylenders who gradually took over his land and became big landowners. Many peasants lost all their land and became tenants, a situation that remained until the Land Reform Act of 1964 granted the tenants' rights to the land they were cultivating, as long as they paid the rent prescribed by the state" (Haaland, 1982: 16)

In Nepal, land reform policy had not come as a push factor from the peasant movement. It is rather state's initiated progressive programme resulting in class-consciousness among the peasants. In Bhaktapur as in other parts of the country, the land reform measures taken in the post-Rana period created peasants' awareness to their rights and interest. Abolition of some state's imposed exploitation systems, i.e. *bethbeghari* and *jhara* (compulsory unpaid labour service to the rulers) in the 1950s led to reducing tension between the state and peasant. But the key issues of land reform, which brought out conflict between the *Sahus* and the *Jypaus* of Bhaktapur city were tenancy rights and land rents. About land-peasant relations in Bhaktapur city, one study found that only 2.3 percent farming households owned all the land they cultivated; 58 percent owned some of the land they worked and supplemented it with additional rented lands; and the remainder were non-land owning tenant farmers (Wachi,1980). This shows the significance of tenancy rights and land rent as two vital issues for Bhaktapur city's peasants. Previously before the enactment of the Land Reform Act 1964, tenants had no legal rights to the land they cultivated, and the land rent was fixed by unwritten compromise made between landowners and tenants, which were generally in the interest of landowners rather than tenants. The Land Reform Act 1964 was a big achievement in ensuring legal registration of tenancy rights and fixing land rent. But the main problem was implementation of this Act since "the landlords are not cooperative and the administrative rules and procedures are difficult" (Pandey, 1985: 145).

But the land reform was a crucial question for city dwellers of Bhaktapur because most of them belonged to the peasantry and had no other alternative sources of income. To link this vital issue with local politics of Bhaktapur, it would be appropriate to recall the victory of independent candidates in the 1957 elections of BM suggesting a political vacuum that any organized political force could fill if that served the interest of the majority population of Bhaktapur city. Presumably, the potential forces were the NC, the communist and the panchayat establishment.

The NC gained credit for its initiation of abolishing *bethbeghari* and *jhara* system in the 1950s. Another remarkable way the party penetrated into the *Jyapu* community of Bhaktapur city was volunteer and informal teaching to them by the NC local leaders. But the NC has never been considered as a pro-peasant party in Bhaktapur, partly because of the upper caste background of its front local leaders and partly because of their role against the land reform programme. The NC leaders of Bhaktapur city welcomed the decision of abolishing *bethbeghari* and *jhara* system because it did not hurt their personal interest. They, however, played an opposite role on the question of granting tenancy rights and fixing the land rate by law because of its negative impact on their personal interest as landowners. At organizational level the NC was indifferent to King Mahendra's land reform policy but at the individual level, a number of persons known as Congress sympathizers in Bhaktapur were involved actively against this policy. A local NC leader said, "The relations between the NC local leaders and the city people cut off after the 1960 royal coup against democracy since the party leaders were either in jail or in exile when the land reform programme was announced and implemented" (Interview with Tilak Kayastha, 25 December 2001).

Despite the land reform being a progressive step taken by King Mahendra who propounded the partyless panchayat system, the establishment largely failed to get credit for it in the Bhaktapur context. "At a general level, though directly not visible, there does seem an intra-class alliance between the landlords and the state" (Pandey, 1985: 161) Such a general situation corresponded to Bhaktapur that there was a broad informal alliance among the landowners irrespective of their political and ideological backgrounds, vested interest group, and the state' local authorities to avert the spirit of the Land Reform Act 1964. The domination of landowning class in state apparatus led to rendering the state machineries ineffective for the implementation of land reform policy. For instance, a study on impact of land reform in Bhaktapur found that the official Peasant Organization was irrelevant to the cause of the peasant movement or peasant interests (Pandey, 1985: 72).

The local leaders/workers of the CPN in Bhaktapur, who later turned into a splinter group with a new name, NWPP in 1975, capitalized the land reform issues for the interest of the party. Despite the party centre's ambivalence on this issue and its instruction to the party activists to limit their role according to the law of the country, the local communists of Bhaktapur took both legal and illegal methods to use the land reform issue for the interest of peasants. Some leading party's peasant activists of Bhaktapur city were involved actively and assertively in launching a series of peasant movements. A leading peasant activist said that the party instigated peasant movements of Bhaktapur were launched in three phases by contents and times. The *Napi* (survey) movement: the implementation of land reform act started with *Napi*, quantification of land and registration of names of landowner and tenant. The activists of CPN-Bhaktapur took assertive role in inserting the name of tenants during the *Napi* time.

Balikatne (forcible capture of crops) movement: the CPN-Bhaktapur organized peasants against landowners who evicted tenants through manipulation in *Napi*. Several numbers of peasants were involved in capturing crops forcibly in favour of tenants who had been legally deprived from tenancy rights by landowners. *Bharpai* (receipt) movement: the CPN-Bhaktapur launched a movement for written receipt of land rent given by tenants to landowners. This campaign was launched in retaliating landowners' refusal to give written documents of receiving land rent and taking it as an excuse for deprivation of tenancy (Interview with Gyan Bahadur Nyanchain). Because of the party's contribution for the protection of tenancy rights at critical times the NWPP has been considered as the *Jyapu* party. In fact, the NWPP intensified social cleavages between the upper caste and the *Jyapu* of Bhaktapur Newars through inserting the content of class struggle in their relationship. Such socio-economic cleavages have deeply impacted in creating caste and class-based political equation of Bhaktapur city – a majority community, *Jyapu* is with the NWPP and other caste groups favour other parties.

Socio-Economic Change and its Impact on Caste Consciousness

The success of implementing land reform programme in Bhaktapur had wider implications in bringing marked improvements to social and economic conditions of *Jyapu*. Narayna Man Bijukchhe observes "The position of *Jyapus* of Bhaktapur city changed from slave before 1951 to serf following the abolition of *bethbeghar* and *jhara*sy stems and finally to peasants after the 1964 land reform" (Interview, 26 December 2001). Some visible changes of the land reform programme were: use of *bikashe* seeds and machines in farming and boosting of agricultural economy which naturally helped to improve the financial position of *Jyapus*; repair of houses; increased market activities against the tradition of the barter system; and above all rapid increase of students from peasant families. Ash Kumar Koju, Chairman of ward 10, said that Bhaktapur *Jyapus* have become financially able to bear the cost of education only after the Land Reform Act 1964 was implemented (Interview, 24 December 2001). This view could be substantiated by a record of a school in Bhaktapur city, Vidyarthi Niketan Secondary School, about the number of its students who passed SLC. Among the students who completed SLC from this school, those belonging to *Jyapu* families were only 2 in the 1950s but their number increased to 10 in the 1960s, 82 in the 1970s, and 250 in the 1980s (VNSS, 1998). The exposure to the education has contributed to widen

Jyapus' horizon and in bringing about change in their thinking and behaviour vis-à-vis the upper caste Newars.

Bhaktapur Development Project (BDP), a long run project (1974-1985) under financial aid of the German government, helped in improving the living conditions of Bhaktapur city dwellers, particularly the *Jyapus*. The BDP's contribution was not limited to providing temporary jobs for larger number of people but also produced several trained manpower in construction works. The upper caste Newars failed to cope with the job and skilled development opportunities provided by the BDP because their status consciousness debarred from involving inferior works, i.e. art, craft and construction. The *Jyapu* is temperamentally a hard laborious community and therefore provided labour force to the BDP. The finding of a previous study shows the difference between these two caste groups that the persons 'not in labour force' constituted only 4.8 percent among *Jyapus* but this figure heightened up to 39.1 percent for the upper caste Newars (Acharya et al, 1980: 111). Taking into consideration of its impact, the BDP could be largely taken a pro-*Jyapu* project, which created consciousness and enhanced confidence among the *Jyapus* for second source of income. Hence, a large number of Bhaktapur *Jyapus* have involved in increasing demands of skilled and unskilled labour for booming industries of construction in neighbouring cities, Kathmandu and Lalitpur.

For the upper caste Newars of Bhaktapur, the land reform programme was the third blow against their interest. The reduction of land rent – 23 *pathi* per *ropani* –turned several upper caste Newars into the poor class. Such newly turned poor class has been described as a group of *"kalcha sin wa manacha jaki"* or the people facing the problems of hand to mouth. They failed to make up their economic position since their caste consciousness and arrogance debarred them from involving in the market of wage labour. Two other developments having negative impacts on the economy of the upper caste Newars were closer to the Tibetan border in 1959 and the construction of the Araniko Highway linking Kathmandu with the Chinese border. Bhaktapur lost its vitality as trade centre between the North and South and between Kathmandu and eastern hills. So they had adversely affected the economy of Bhaktapur, particularly to the upper caste Newars. The general perception that Newars are traders and business group is not valid so far concerned the occupation of the *Jyapu* community. Because only 1.5 per cent among the Bhaktapur *Jyapus* were found in business (Acharya et al, 1980: 111). The primary occupation of the upper caste Newars is trade and business. Another major source of their income is service. So social and economic changes taking place in Bhaktapur are not for the interest of the upper caste Newars, which led them to seek alternative place for their betterment. Migration by the upper caste Newars to Kathmandu for better economic opportunities and career development is high. The *Jypau* is less mobile community in terms of migration from hometown to other areas. Such a picture of migration also favours the *Jyapus* for continuing in powerful positions in local politics.

The sociology of leadership transformation in Bhaktapur city suggests that social and economic changes taking place since the early 1950s made a background for the emergence of new political situation. The most remarkable one was land reform programme in introducing caste/class conflicts against the traditional system of hierarchical interdependence in relations among the Newars of Bhaktapur city. Its contribution did not only limit to improving economic conditions of *Jyapus* but also in injecting a new culture that they have largely overcome the tradition of their submissive culture vis-à-vis the upper caste Newars. The availability of other sources of cash income led to reduce their dependency on the upper caste Newars. Over time, the caste-based economic disparities between these two groups no longer exist. The economic prosperity of the *Jyapu* community rendered help to lessen the rigidity of caste hierarchy in social life of Bhaktapur city.

The exposure of the *Jyapu* community in the educational sector has also brought about changes in the social and economic spheres of Bhaktapur city. In the past, education was limited to the members of high caste Newars. The entry of new generation of the *Jyapu* community in educational field has led to bring distinct changes in decision-making power in family and in relations with other caste groups. The aged people are respected in family affairs and in cultural activities, but on the issues of public affairs i.e. politics, the younger men in the family, who have been to school and campus, feel more qualified to deal. The older generation of *Jyapu* community still believes in fatalism, but the younger generation has discontent against their hereditary subordinate positions vis-à-vis the upper caste Newars. Their aspiration and exposure to secular values i.e. democracy and equality have been largely respected by the NWPP. The NWPP, rather than any other party, addressed the *Jyapu* community's aspiration for changes in social, economic and political aspects of Bhaktapur city.

Another important reason behind leadership transformation in Bhaktapur city could be found in observing social psychology of the city dwellers. "Newars of Bhaktapur identify first with their family, then with their caste, next with their *guthi*, and finally, with their *tole*" (Haaland, 1982: 19). Each caste group of Newars see themselves as "We" and treat other caste groups as "They" and all Newars consider the non-Newars as "Outsiders" and lump them as "*Khaen*" for hill caste Brahmin/Cheetri and "*Saen*" for hill ethnic groups and "*Marsya*" for plain caste/ethnic groups. This explains the absence of non-Newar community in leadership of BM, except for one lone case of the victory of Surya Pratap Rana (Thakuri Chhetri) as Ward Chairman in 1957. Tilak-Kayastha viewed that the part of reason why his party (NC) failed to penetrate into the *Jyapu* community of Bhaktapur in the 1950s was that the party front organization, Kisan Snagh, was constituted by *Khain* to whom the city dwellers saw as "Outsiders". The district level leadership of the NC has been dominated by *Khains* since its inception. Its City Committee is mostly constituted by the upper caste Newars. The RPP and the UML are dominated by *Khains*, nevertheless the local Newars constitute the leadership of their own party City Committee. The NWPP' leadership, both at district and city levels, is mostly constituted by Newar *Jyapus*. The social psychology of 'We, They and Outsiders' has its own impact on the politics of Bhaktapur city.

Among the Newars of Bhaktapur city, *Jyapu* is more homogeneous group bound by intra-caste marriage and by *guthi, bhajan* and *dafa* systems that provide platforms for their collective activities in cultural affairs. The upper caste Newars are divided into three hierarchical groups – Brahmin, *chha-thari* and *panch-thari*. The untouchables have also three ranking, *Jugi, Nae* and *Pore*. Those under the category of the low caste Newars are most heterogeneous. The *Jyapu* being a coherent community, a majority group in total population of city, their caste consciousness, and their assertion for political power work as forces behind their domination in urban politics of Bhaktapur city. The first-past-the-post (FPTP) electoral system provides a ground for transforming social strength into political power. It is indeed need to recall a general trend of Nepali politics that political parties usually recruit their own local leaders from the locally dominated population.

Political Parties and Candidate Selection

Bhaktapur is the stronghold of the NWPP and other parties like the NC, the UML and the RPP are too weak to challenge its dominant position. Despite the NC's long record of working in Bhaktapur since the late 1940s, it had always been poor showing in elections of Bhaktapur municipality.

The 1960 royal coup, which forced its local leaders to be in jail for long time or in exile in India, was a big setback. Nevertheless, the NC had never been rooted out from Bhaktapur in adverse situations. The party tried to reactivate itself after the 1980 referendum but only through the student politics. Before it entered into competitive mass politics after the restoration of democracy in 1990, Bhaktapur city had already turned into the NWPP's pocket area. In the post-*Jana Andolan* period, the NC appeared as the most "inactive opposition vis-à-vis NWPP" in the context of Bhaktapur city. The president of NC' Bhaktapur City Committee confessed that the party local leaders did not have vision, programme and strategy to penetrate into the *Jyapu* community, the majority population of Bhaktapur city (Interview with Babu Raja Joshi, 26 December 2001).

The condition of other parties is not much different from that of the NC. In the context of Bhaktapur city, the panchayat system produced only few individuals as leaders without mass followers so the RPP could not sustain its old strength in the changed political context after the restoration of democracy in 1990. One of its local leaders said that the RPP existed in Bhaktapur city only in paper not in action and programme (Interview with Uttam Bati, 27 December 2001). The UML or the former ML entered late in Bhaktapur politics. Before this party started its activities in the late 1970s, another communist party, the NWPP, had already expanded its organizational base. A local leader of the UML opines that Bhaktapur city politics can be understood with its two distinct characteristics. First, the NWPP has strong support base among the *Jyapus* and other parties could not penetrate into this majority community. Second, in the given condition, other parties were competing for their own influence among the non-*Jyapu* communities (Interview with Raja Ram Ranjit, 27 December 2001). Parties' influence in caste-based society of Bhaktapur city can be roughly divided into following: *jyapu* with the NWPP, upper caste Newars with the NC, low caste, untouchable and Buddhist Newars with the UML. The RPP has some influence in all above mentioned caste groups. Irrespective of a rough estimate of caste-based political equation, all parties have given preference to the majority community of the city while selecting their candidates for the elections of Bhaktapur city.

The table reveals that more than two-thirds candidates of different parties contesting the 1992 and the 1997 elections to BM were from the *Jyapu* community. In both elections, the NC candidates from this community figured around 60 percent. Elections contesting by *Jyapus* from the RPP went down considerably from 84 percent in 1992 to 43 percent in 1997 elections. Similarly the UML's *Jyapu* candidates were reduced from 58 percent to 40 percent in corresponding period. But the NWPP gave its more candidates from the *Jyapu* community, i.e. 79 percent in 1992 and 84 percent in 1997 elections. The overall pictures of parties' candidates to elections of BM corresponded to a general trend that political parties usually recruit their own local leaders from the locally dominated population.

To see it in retrospect from the result of elections, candidates contesting from the same caste status group did not carry the same meaning for all parties. The victory of *Jyapu* candidates from only the NWPP and not from other parties suggested the significance of party affiliation. The caste and party identity were two vital factors in determining the result of the local elections of Bhaktapur city. The NWPP has already gained an image as pro-*Jyapu* party by its long political standing. It has outstanding record of making substantial contribution for the cause of *Jyapus* at the most important time of tenant-landowners conflicts in the 1960s. Besides, the party has always been with the mass of Bhaktapur city even during the ban on political parties under the partyless panchyat regime (1960-1990).

Before the NWPP came up as a splinter communist group, communists of Bhaktapur penetrated into panchayat since its inception, and Rohit, the then in-charge of CPN-Bhaktapur, himself held the post of chairman of Ward 8 in the early 1960s. Before 1980, persons with a communist background had considerable representations in Bhaktapur *Nagar*

TABLE 9:3
Caste Background of Parties' Candidates for BM, 1992 and 1997 Local Elections

	1992					*1997**				
Caste/parties	*NWPP*	*NC*	*RPP*	*UML*	*Total*	*NWPP*	*NC*	*RPP*	*UML*	*Total*
Upper Castes	2	7	3	-	12	2	1	4	1	8
Jyapu	15	11	16	7	49	16	3	3	2	24
Low Castes	1	-	-	1	2	-	-	-	1	1
Untouchables	-	-	-	-	-	-	-	-	1	1
Buddhist Newar	1	-	-	4	5	1	-	-	-	1
Non-Newar	-	-	-	-	-	-	1	-	-	1
Total No.	19	18	19	12	68	19	5	7	5	36

* NC, UML and RPP made an alliance in contesting elections.
Source: ECN (1992, 1997). Breakdown into different social groups is done by the author.

Panchayat and three of them (Bishnu Prasad Nepali, Babu Kaji Basukala and Lakhan Das Banepali) even succeeded in holding the post of *Pradhan Pancha*. Such a penetration strategy later turned into participation in panchayat elections after the 1980 referendum. The NWPP captured almost all seats of Bhaktapur *Nagar Panchayat* in the 1982 and the 1987 local elections. The party's candidates, Karna Prasad Hyaju and Govinda Duwal, got victory in the elections of National Panchyat held in 1981 and 1986 respectively. The party justified its involvement in panchayat with an explanation that "Election also provides a political platform to wage class struggle." This strategy was formally expressed in words, "NWPP decided to adopt and apply the Leninist doctrine of using bourgeois elections in order to arouse the class consciousness among the masses on the one hand and to expose the bourgeois exploitation on the other" (NWPP, 1994). This line of thinking remained unchanged despite the NWPP appeared as one of the parliamentarian parties and the numbers of its representations in the House of Representatives (HOR) were: 1, 4 and 1 in the first, second and third tenure of parliament respectively.

Being a non-conformist party vis-à-vis parliamentary democracy, it professes Marxism and Leninism as its ideology and Mao's thought as its guiding principle (NWPP, 1991:5). The NWPP asserted its ideological position, "Participation in bourgeois elections does not mean that we expect to emancipate the working class from the suckles of bourgeois slavery through parliamentary means. Parliament is merely a legal mean to wage life and death struggle against the parasitic bourgeois system" (NWPP [b], 1991:3). Though the NWPP has projected itself as a non-conformist force to the panchayat and the parliamentary system, the party, through making a tactical alliance with the establishment, has always taken advantage in activating itself through underground and open politics. This rendered help it to be in touch with the mass either way.

The NWPP had some influence in the mid-west hill districts in addition to Bhaktapur, as shown by victory of its two candidates, one from Jumla and other from Kalikot district in the 1994 mid-term elections. But defection from the party by these two members of the HOR led to localize the NWPP in Bhaktapur district only. Though the party contested for 43 constituencies from 19 districts but it could gain only one seat from constituency-1 of Bhaktapur district in the 1999 elections. One of the reasons for making the NWPP popular among the *Jyapus* of Bhaktapu is that the party Chairman Rohit took shelter in their houses during his underground period. Despite being an upper caste Newar, he crossed the caste barrier in accepting meals from *Jypau* families. By this way, Rohit capitalized *Jyapus*'s psychology that they become happy if an upper caste Newar takes meal in their house.

Coming back to the question of candidate selection, parties would consider a number of factors before they took a final decision. As Bhaktapur is the stronghold of the NWPP, other parties have no more choice though they selected their own candidates for the post of Mayor among the local leaders having long service to the party. For other posts like ward chairman and members, they always faced problems to give candidates from all wards of Bhaktapur municipality. So this section primarily deals with candidate selections by the NWPP.

The NWPP is personality-based centralized party dominated by Rohit who has held the post of party chairman continuously since its establishment in January 1975. This factor counts though the party City Committee has formal authority in selection of candidates for the elections of BM. But taking into consideration three things— one party Chairman Rohit being inhabitant of Bhaktapur city; two the party City Committee is headed by one of the members of the Central Committee; and three status of party's candidate for Mayor post being a member of the party Central Committee — one can easily assume the centralized tendency in the NWPP in producing its local leaders. It, however, does not mean that the party completely overlooked the opinion of party activists. For both the 1992 and 1997 elections, the party called meeting in each of 17 wards of Bhaktapur city in which the party organization leaders of the ward level, party sympathizers, and voters participated and gave their own opinions regarding the appropriate candidates for their own ward. At institutional level, the party Ward Committee, City Committee and some central leaders involved in candidate selections for the elections of BM except for the post of Mayor and Deputy Mayor for which the party Central Committee decided directly. A mixed of centralized and decentralized way of decision-making in candidate selection could be found in expression of Prem Suwal, "I contested to the post of Mayor as per requested by the party City Committee and instruction of the Central Committee" (Interview, 19 December 2001).

Among several factors to be considered for candidate selection by the NWPP, the primacy of caste factor is too obvious since most candidates to the elections of BM were from the *Jyapu* community. The party had also maintained caste balance in all local elections that its candidate to the second top post, Deputy Mayor, had always been from non-*Jyapu* community, mostly Buddhist Newar. For Ward 4 and 8 of Bhaktapur city the party had picked up persons from the upper caste Newars while giving its candidates to the post of ward chairman in all the last four local elections considering the fact that non-*Jyapu* communities are in majority in these wards and also in ward 16. Furthermore, the party had also maintained area balance in giving 5 candidates, one chairman and four members, for the election of Ward Committee. Each ward constitutes with four or five *toles* and the party had usually given candidates from each *tole* that there would be representations from each *tole* in the elected body of Ward Committee. Moreover, the NWPP tried its best to avoid the rich person to be involved in popular politics. Gyan Bahadur Nyanchain told his case that the NWPP offered him to contest the post of *Pradhan Pancha* in the 1982 local election but at the cost of leaving his involvement as owner of brick factory (Interview, 27 December 2001). Besides, personalities, party loyalty, educational background, willingness to serve the people are some of the factors the party considered in selecting its candidates for the elected bodies.

Personal Profile of Municipality Members

Some aspects related to social and economic characteristics of BM members (including Mayor and Deputy Mayor) distinctly showed the transformation of urban leadership of Bhaktapur city from the traditional elite of the upper caste Newars to the *Jyapas*. The upper caste Newars constituted only 3 in addition to 1 Buddhist Newar. They had distinct characteristics from other fellow members belonging to *Jyapu* in their occupation and family background. They were from elite family background and their major occupation was business. But none of the BM members from the *Jyapu* community, which constituted majority among the elected members of BM, was from the elite family background. They were from a peasant family and their major occupation was agriculture. But irrespective of different caste status among the BM members, all of them had common class background since they were all from the middle class.

Among 19 BM members including the Mayor and the Deputy Mayor, 11 were from the middle-aged group followed by 5 youngsters and 3 old-aged groups. All were Hindus except one Buddhist holding the post of Deputy Mayor. This figure corresponded to religion-wise population distribution of Bhaktapur city. Only three of 19 BM members were less educated whereas majority of them had attended higher education, suggesting the education as one of the important factors for leadership building in the urban area.

The NWPP had an absolute control in the local government of Bhaktapur city except for one representation from each of the NC and the RPP in total 19 elected members of BM. Most of their political career started in the post-referendum period through their involvement in party activities. Some of them had long political career and record of being political sufferers. Most elected leaders came from those persons who served in the party's local committees – ranging from Ward to District Committee. Twelve out of 19 BM members held post in different levels of the party local committees. Three, including Mayor and Deputy Mayor, were members of the NWPP' Central Committee. Nevertheless, majority of BM members lacked non-political support base, except the caste factor, for their emergence as local leaders. Few could have influence the business and teaching communities by their affiliation and previous job. Most of them had simply identified themselves as 'social workers' for their convenience without record of substantial contribution to social service sectors. The caste and party identity were the two major sources of their political power.

TABLE 9:4
Social, Economic and Political Profiles of Municipality Members

		Subjects	*Mayor*	*Deputy Mayor*	*Members*
Sex	1.	Male	1	1	16
	2.	Female	-	-	1
Age	1.	Young (18-35)	-	-	5
	2.	Middle (36-50)	1	1	9
	3.	Old (51-)	-	-	3
Education	1.	Literate/School Level	-	-	3
	2.	Higher Education	1	1	14
Religion	1.	Hindu	1	-	17
	2.	Buddhist	-	1	-
Economic Status	1.	Rich	-	-	-
	2.	Middle	1	1	17
	3.	Poor	-	-	-
Occupation	1.	Business	-	1	4
	2.	Agriculture	1	-	12
	3.	Service	-	-	1

Caste	1.	Upper Caste	-	-	3
	2.	Jyapu	1	-	14
	3.	Buddhist Newar	-	1	-
Family Background	1.	Elite	-	1	3
	2.	Farmer	1	-	13
	3.	Service	-	-	1
Political Background	1.	Party Activism	1	1	14
	2.	Panchayat	-	-	2
	3.	Nothing	-	-	1
Party Affiliation	1.	NWPP	1	1	15
	2.	NC	-	-	1
	3.	RPP	-	-	1
Status in Party	1.	Suppporter	-	-	1
	2.	Members	-	-	3
	3.	Party local committee member			
	4.	Central committee	-	-	12
		member	1	1	1
Affiliated area	1.	Business	-	-	2
	2.	Teaching	-	-	4
	3.	Social worker	1	1	10
	4.	Other	-	-	1

Source: Information collected through interview included questions related to above mentioned profiles of the respondents and their fellow BM members.

In retrospect, the caste, class and sex composition of BM members raised doubts to the NWPP's ideological credential as a communist party committed for the cause of 'have not' class and deprived sections of society. All members of the BM constituted middle class, showing a complete absence of representation from rich as well as poor classes. One could find a broad combination of caste and class in Bhaktapur city that the low caste Hindu Newars and untouchables are relatively poor and deprived sections of society. With a realization of non-representation of downtrodden strata of society in power structure of the country, the state provided a legal provision to co-opt them in the local leadership structure.[1] But this legal provision was not properly followed by the BM and the NWPP since only two from the low caste Hindu Newars were selected from among 18 nominated members of Bhaktapur Municipal Council. Sixteen nominees were from the *Jyapu* communities and the two nominated members of BM were also from the same group, showing the NWPP's bias against untouchables and non-*Jyapu* communities. The logic of Rohit can be referred here, "The NWPP has tried to win the heart of both socially low caste *Jyapus* and also those upper caste Newars who suddenly turned into poor class after the implementation of land reform programme. But the party is not yet successful in gaining the confidence of the later groups mainly because of the party's past role during the land reform programme, which really hurt the interest of the upper caste Newars. The party could not yet build its support base in the upper caste and untouchable communities (Interview, 26 December 2001). So, one can draw a conclusion that the NWPP was overwhelmingly preoccupied with caste politics rather than class ideology in producing local leaders for Bhaktapur city.

Governance

This section focuses on leadership's capacity to provide good governance. While dealing with leadership-governance interface in the context of Bhaktapur city, two things need to be highlighted. One, as the NWPP being a personality-based party, the party leaders working in organization or in elected bodies were overwhelmingly subdued by dominant personality of Rohit. This could be seen in BM leaders' self-perception about their position. Mayor Prem Suwal considered himself as merely an agent carrying out his party's vision embodied in the election manifesto (Interview, 19 December 2001). Similarly, Ash Kumar Koju used a metaphor of *Hulaki* (postman) in defining his role and function as an elected representative. He said, "As ward chairman, my primary duty is to link the needs of *wadabasi* with municipality's development projects" (Interview with Ash Kumar Koju, 24 December 2001). So it would be more appropriate to treat BM members from the perspective of institutional leadership in analysing BM's vision, policy and programmes.

Another significant part related to leadership-government interface is empowerment of the local elected bodies in both content and volume of their power, authority, and responsibility after the enactment of Local Self-Governance Act (LSGA) 1999. "The LSGA has empowered the municipalities of Nepal, with challenging roles, responsibilities and functions, so that they could eventually perform as full-fledged decentralized, autonomous, and self-governing local bodies, to cater to the needs of their townsfolk" (Jayarajaan, 2001:1). How far the BM succeeded to cope with its new challenges and opportunities in its objective to provide good governance. Resource generation and mobilization are important to enhance its capacity to serve the city and city dwellers. Another vital part is the people's participation in local governance. Of many mobilizing agents, political parties and civil society have crucial role in bringing the masses in development projects and other activities related to local governance. This section will try to analyse the performance of BM leaders under three sub-headings: vision, resource generation and mobilization, and people's participation.

Vision: Making Bhaktapur a Cultural City

With a slogan "Creation of our predecessors – our art and culture", BM has been heading towards making Bhaktapur a cultural city. Its other objectives such as city cleaning, promotion of tourism, educational development, sewerage facilities, conservation of historical monuments and heritage were integrated into its main thrust of developing itself as a cultural city. The table below showed a combination of BM's vision, its policy/programme and its development projects.

The idea of making Bhaktapur a cultural city is motivated by many factors i.e. preservation of beauty of an old city, generation of financial resources, and retention of political support. In efforts to draw the attention of government and people to the proposal of making Bhaktapur a cultural city, the NWPP and BM highlighted a number of unique characteristics of Bhaktapur city. Bhaktapur has rich architectural and urban heritage; it has remained ethnically, religiously and culturally homogeneous in comparison to other cities of Nepal; built urban and architectural heritage dating back to 14-15 centuries has remained relatively well preserved; the city has largely maintained the traditional culture, custom, art and craft; and it is enlisted in the World Heritage list. It would be relevant here to recall the observation of E.A. Powells, "Were there nothing else in Nepal save the Durbar Square of *Bhatgaon* (Bhaktapur), it would still be amply worth making a journey halfway round the globe to see" (Quoted in BM 1, 2001: 2) Since the preservation of heritage is the main ground for the justification of making Bhaktapur a cultural city, credit should be given to BDP (1974-1985) for its catalyst role in launching programme of city cleaning and renovation of historical monuments of Bhaktapur city. After the termination of the BDP project, BM has expedited these programmes and eventually proposed for the formal recognition of Bhaktapur as a cultural city after the 1997 elections.

The proposal of developing Bhaktapur as a cultural city is closely linked with BM's objective to convert Bhaktapur as a tourist destination and thereby generate a new source of income. From July 1993 (when BM introduced the tourist entry fee) to June 2000, BM collected US $ 332,320,9

TABLE 9:5
BM's Vision, Policy and Project

Vision	*Policy/Programme*	*No. of Projects Undertaken (1954-1998)*	
1. Declare Bhaktapur as a cultural city 2. Preserve heritage and traditional culture 3. Make it pollution-free and cleanest city of Nepal 4. Develop it as a tourist centre 5. Restore traditional art and craft 6. Make it corruption-free and transparent 7. To have 100 % literacy rate and produce at least one graduate from each household	1. Assist to conserve individu-ally owned private houses with archaeological values 2. Fund to encourage and protect traditional folk dance, prayers, *dafa and guthi* 3. Build treatment pound for sewerage 4. Making Hanumante river pollution-free 5. Expand skill and employ-ment oriented education 6. Take preventive measures for public health 7. Financial aid to promote education and sport 8. Integrated Town Planning 9. Establish children's park, model school and kinder-garten 10. Mobilization of civil society and other social groups to promote people's participa-tion in local governance	1. Sewerage 2. Renovation of Temples 3. Renovation of satal and pati 4. Renovation of stone taps 5. Renovation and recons-truction of ponds 6. Stone/brick roads 7. Renovation of wells 8. Building construction 9. Others	55 57 70 11 31 291 49 54 161

Source: NWPP's election manifestos, 1992 and 1997; Interviews; BM (2000).

from tourists who visited city core area (BM, 2001: 3). The tourist entry fee has become good source in generating internal resources which has contributed more than 50 percent of BM's annual income since the last few years. The NWPP's interest to sustain its political influence in Bhaktapur also counts as a factor behind BM's proposal of making Bhaktapur a cultural city. The land reform is now an outdated issue for Bhaktapur. The city is equipped with the minimal level of infrastructure development, i.e. electricity, roads, drinking water, transportation and communication, etc. The prospect of industrialization is not feasible nor can it be developed as an agricultural city. So the best alternative way is to convert it into a tourist destination centre. In a cultural city, city-dwellers would have less burden to pay (tax) the cost of development and it also discourages migration from outside. The projection of Bhaktapur as a cultural city has become a political strategy and programme to maintain demographic balance, which is also a political interest of the NWPP.

For heritage conservation, tourism promotion and city cleaning— three major ingredients of making Bhaktapur a cultural city— the BM has taken some notable steps, such as restoration and maintenance of historical monuments; conservation of traditional art, culture and heritage; regulation for construction and reconstruction of private houses in old architectural style in the areas of Protected Monument Zone; subsidy (up to 100 percent) in materials required for the reconstruction (in the old architectural style) of private houses with archaeological value; financial and other incentives to *bhajan*, *dafa* and *guthi* for the protection and promotion of traditional music and folk dance; restriction for pollution-prone industries and relocation of previously established industries from the core city area; and ban for heavy vehicles to enter into the city and prohibition of all kinds of vehicles in Durbar Square area. In addition to BM' own initiations in creating a conducive environment for developing Bhaktapur as a cultural city, the NWPP has constantly pursued to get formal recognition of the government. The party chairman and member of HOR, Narayan Man Bijukchhe, has pushed and pressed for it in one way or the other. He presented a private bill (Conservation of Art and Culture) and drew the attention of parliament several times for the constitution of a National Committee for the Preservation of Art and Culture, a separate court to look after the subjects of Protected Monument Zone, and the establishment of University of Traditional Art, Culture and Architecture. He even put the case before the king during his audience. His efforts brought out results but in different shape that the government documents, i.e. Ninth Plan and LSGA (NPC, 1998: 559; LSGA, 2000:70) had made provision for the declaration of cultural city, though the government has not yet formally recognized Bhaktapur as a cultural city.

The scope of the proposed idea of making Bhaktapur as a cultural city goes beyond the conservation of urban heritage. The overall activities carried out by BM are put under its broad objective of developing the town as a cultural capital of Nepal. BM has broader responsibilities. The running of two colleges for three subjects (science, management, and engineering) by the BM with a modest and reasonable tuition fee is widely appreciated. But its emphasis on conservation of urban heritage, tourism, and city cleaning has led to its lesser involvement in other areas. Lack of pure drinking water and the poor state of health services are two major problems facing the city dwellers to which BM shows least concern. A study shows a trend of BM's decreasing investment in the health and education sectors (MLD and UDLF, 2000: 33). Its commitment for the establishment of employment-generated industries was limited to direct benefit for only 36 persons in the last five years from 1997-2002 (Bhaktapur, 2001: 1). The NWPP's promises, made during the 1997 local election, to build a city hall and treatment ponds, were listed in the failed areas in the party's evaluation to the performance of BM (Bhaktapur, 2001: 4). In fact, BM has given overdose to the conservation of urban heritage, city cleaning and tourism promotion at the cost of development in other areas. Yet it continues to push its objective to make Bhaktapur a cultural city.

Of course, Bhaktapur deserves to be a cultural city because of its unique characteristics. But the leadership of the NWPP and BM had not given specific contents and characteristics for the proposed cultural city. Neither was this agenda put for public debate and discussion nor could consult with members of civil society and political parties. Rabindra Kharbuja, a local leader of NWPP and chairman of Ward-15, confessed that BM's proposal of cultural city was discussed only in the Municipal Council meetings and in a seminar organized by BM and participated in by experts and the officials of concerned ministries. The proposal of a cultural city could not get much publicity except in a weekly newspaper *Sramik* and a monthly magazine *Bhaktapur*, run by the NWPP and BM respectively. It had yet to put forth before civil society members and parties' local leaders and the idea as such had yet to reach the masses of Bhaktapur city (Interview with Rabindra Kharbuja, 27 December 2001). So the citizens and leaders of Bhaktapur were not sensitised for developing Bhaktapur as a cultural city.

In response to a question about type of visitors to the leaders' house and office, BM members identified ordinary people first in ranking order, followed by the NWPP workers and other parties' activists respectively. The purpose of visits, in ranking order, was to seek help and assistance from their respective ward chairman for their work related to government offices. A tendency of seeking leader's help for personal interest, i.e. jobs, business, family dispute, etc. was also strong. The BM members expressed that the issue related to collective interest and development also figured in the list of people's demands. On leaders' response to citizens' demands, eight BM members said that they entertained only those issues that come

TABLE 9:6
Leader-People Interface

Nature and Ranking of Visitors	*Ranking*		
	1	*2*	*3*
Party Workers	-	9	6
Other Party Activists	-	6	8
Ordinary People	16	-	-
Opportunists	-	1	-
People's Demands in Priority Order	*Ranking*		
	1	**2**	**3**
Individual Interest	1	6	10
Recommendations for Official Work	15	3	-
Collective Interest and Development	2	9	7
Response			
Use of Position to Influence in Decision-Making	4		
Recommend to Concerned Authority	6		
Do Only Under Own Jurisdiction and Discretion	8		
Tactfully Avoid	-		
Others	-		

Source: Interview.

under their own jurisdiction. Those who said that they used (abused) their position in favour of their clients were smaller in number (only 4). On the whole, the proposal of making Bhaktapur a cultural city did not figure in people-leader dialogue, suggesting that this agenda was top heavy. Even the Municipal Council members appeared least concerned with the agenda of cultural city. This was reflected in the list of 48 point suggestions made by Municipality Council members during its 8th session in March 2001; out of which 10 points were related to improvement in municipality administration, 8 on city cleaning, 7 on education, health and road, 5 on conservation of urban heritage, 5 on welfare to women and children, and 3 on income generation (Bhaktapur, 2001: 28 29).

In principle, local leaders of other parties affirmed the idea of developing Bhaktapur as a cultural city, but they had complained against the NWPP and BM for not pursuing an all-party consensus to such a big agenda and long-term goal. To what extent the leadership of BM bypassed other parties could be found in reaction of the president of the NC's City Committee. He said, "I have come to know BM's decision to convert Bhaktapur as a cultural city through media. My party was never consulted before and after this decision" (Interview with Babu Raja Joshi, 26 December 2001). The failure of BM to take confidence of the local leaders of other parties had negative impact in its pursuance for formal recognition to its proposal of cultural city by the central government. BM leaders largely perceived the central government and bureaucracy in a negative light while identifying major problems they were facing to work as people's representative at the local level.

TABLE 9:7
Responsibilities and Obstacles

Three Major Responsibilities		*Three Major Obstacles*	
Empowerment of people and local elected bodies	18	Party's intervention and pressure	-
Social mobilization and change	18	Lack of coordination between government and party	-
Institutionalization of own party	10	Lack of opportunity to increase leadership capability	3
Uplift of disadvantaged and handicapped	4	Lack of resources	12
Infrastructure development	3	Non-cooperation from or lack of coordination with local line agencies	11
Others	-	Lack of adequate rights and power	11
		Centre's control and intervention	9
		Corruption	-
		Others	4

Source: Interview.

While responding to the question about three major responsibilities of people's elected representatives, all BM members stood for 'empowerment of people and local elected bodies' and 'social mobilization and change'. Ten of them identified 'institutionalization of own party' as one of their major responsibilities. The agendas like 'uplift of disadvantaged and handicapped' and 'infrastructure development' received least priority. They had faced a lot of problems in holding their responsibilities. The major obstacles as they pointed out were: 'lack of resources', 'lack of proper coordination with bureaucracy', 'lack of adequate power' to the local government, and 'the central government's control and intervention.' All indicated their perception and experiences that the NC government at centre did not provide proper support and cooperation to local government of Bhaktapur city dominated by the NWPP. Such a general pattern of relationship between the central and the local government, in a situation that two different parties hold power at the central and local levels, suggested the difficulty of BM in pursuing for the government recognition of Bhaktapur as a cultural city. Both the central government and local leaders of other political parties were non-cooperative to the NWPP and BM's proposal of making a cultural city. Parties' position reflected citizen behaviours vis-a-vis BM. For instance, many houses in the main road of Bhaktapur city belong to the upper caste Newars and most of them are hostile to the NWPP. So the BM was facing problems to implement its project of reconstructing the private houses in the old architectural style.

Resource Generation and Mobilization

During the operation of BDP (1974-1985), which looked after the town development of Bhaktapur city, BM or the then Bhaktapur *Nagar Panchayat* existed mainly as political and administrative unit. After the termination of this project, BM has come up as a development unit as well. Moreover, the LSGA enlarges municipality's responsibilities into 82 specific functions, which are categorised, by a scholar, into six broad areas: financial management, physical and infrastructure development, environment, health and education, social, cultural and community welfare, municipal administration and management, and legal affairs (Jayarajan, 2001: 4). To quote Nepal: Human Development Report 2001 for increased role of local elected bodies, "Local governments are now responsible for health, education, quality and standards; drinking water and sanitation; women's development, service to the elderly, deprived, and children; protection of culture, heritage, and ethnic traditions; education in mother tongue; etc. They must also provide services in agriculture, livestock, and marketing; promote tourism; create income and employment opportunities at the local level; promote cottage industry; handicraft, and small industry, develop commerce; build and maintain trails, roads, bridges, irrigation, embankments, community building, dumping sites, and solid disposal sites; and undertake land use planning and zoning" (UNDP/Nepal, 2002: 77). To fulfil such increased roles and responsibilities, a municipality obviously needs more financial and other resources.

Bhaktapur is neither an industrialized city nor is it a big business centre. This indicates BM's limitation to collect revenue from the city dwellers. It could collect less than Rs.10 million from 110 tax items in the Fiscal Year (FY) of 2000/2001, which contributed only 6.41 percent in total annual budget of Rs.143,92,3,528. The grant from the central government was also negligible, Rs. 300,000 (BM, 2001: 1). BM received a share of estimated Rs. 216, 000,00 from Local Development Tax, accounting for just 15 percent of total budget. But, Bhaktapur being a tourist destination, it has potentiality of generating internal source from tourism sector. Most remarkable is introduction of tourist entry fee since July 1993 and the rate increased from US $ 1 to 5 in July 1996 to US $ 10 from January 2001.

Tourist entry fee has become a substantial source of income of BM. A year before the introduction of this system, its annual budget was only Rs. 21.9 million which was increased rapidly to Rs. 169. 6 million in FY 2001/2002. In the initial period, the contribution of tourist entry fee was 10-12 percent in total budgets and 19-24 percent in BM's internal revenue. This figure suddenly increased to 41-52 percent of total annual budget and it alone covered 56-70 percent of total internal revenue of BM after the rate of tourist entry fee increased in 1996 and 2001.

TABLE 9:8
Budgets of BM from FY 1992/1993 to 2001/2002

'000

FY	*Total Budget*	*Internal Source*			
		Total	*Tourist Entrée Fee*		
				% in total budget	*% in total internal income*
1992/93	219,23	103,51	-	-	-
1993/94	357,99	226,66	436,7	12.19	19.26
1994/95	510,45	200,59	488,8	9.57	24.36
1995/96	469,27	246,15	570,9	12.16	23.19
1996/97	752,69	577,99	322,06	42.78	55.72
1997/98	919,72	621,82	379,07	41.21	60.96
1998/99	100,869	625,74	439,84	43.63	70.29
1999/2000		756,08	461,30		61.01
2000/01	143,924*	111,974	745,02	51.76	66.53
2001/02*	169,613	128,399	800,00	47.16	62.30

* Estimated
Source: Budgets of Bhaktapur Municipality

BM had a fairly good record of mobilizing its resources for development budget. Nearly 50 percent of its total budget of the FY 2001/02 was allocated for development budget. Out of Rs 80 million development budget Rs. 8 million was allocated under the heading of ward budget and distributed approximately Rs. 500,000 to each of total 17 wards. The rest, 90 percent of development budget was handled by municipality suggesting centralization in fiscal administration. Small projects, which cost less than 300,000 were generally conducted through ward level projects and other projects of higher cost were handled under the municipality level project. Planning of both the ward level and municipality level projects was a long process in which a number of people and institutions i.e. party, elected representatives, citizens, etc. got involved. Rabindra Kharbuja, Convenor of Construction and Physical Development Committee of BM, informed that the development planning had to pass seven stages: opinion collection in different *toles* of a ward, consideration of the party (NWPP) Ward Committee's agendas, aggregation of demands by the elected Ward Committee consisting of ward chairman and four members, submission of list of projects to Municipality Board, site visit by members of Construction and Physical Development Committee, decision by Construction and Physical Development Committee in presence of chairman of concerned ward committee, submission to Municipality Board for approval, and passed by the Municipal Council meeting (Interview, 27 December 2001).

BM, dominated by the NWPP's representatives, had largely maintained economic discipline in management of development projects. Perhaps this is an exceptional case that an applicant for party membership to the NWPP must inform his/her property (NWPP [a], 1991: 21) and this is the first party, which publicly disclosed the party expenditure in the 1999 general elections. BM is the first among the local elected bodies, which made an agreement with Transparency International, Nepal on 26 February 1999 for an integrity system. According to this agreement, "an integrity system will be implemented in all activities of public offices in Bhaktapur. Transparency will be maintained in providing services, supply of goods, services or materials, decision making process and other activities of public concerns" (TIN, 1999. 2). Berlin based Transparency International also gave a title of "Island of Integrity" to BM.

BM has never entered into *theka* (contract) system for its development projects and the logic behind it is to keep people's representatives far away from corruption and commission. For the mega project i.e. Libalibi town planning of Rs. 60 million, BM handled itself under the *amanat* system. All projects in Bhaktapur were being implemented through user group, not through contractors. The local leaders of other parties suspected of BM's public posture as least corrupt institution but they failed to give evidence except making point of financial irregularities mentioned in Audit Reports. They also blamed for not including non-NWPP persons in constituting user group. NWPP's representatives to BM acknowledged the domination of pro-NWPP among the members of user group but dismissed the charge of complete exclusion of other parties' sympathizers from development projects. BM members also did not completely deny the case of small leakage of money and material of development projects handled by user groups. However, Dhruba Livi (a local leader of RPP, chairman of ward 11, and member of Planning Supervision and Monitoring Committee of BM) felt the existence of a separate monitoring system of the NWPP, which operated clandestinely and checkd the user groups (Interview, 24 December 2001).

Handling of development projects through user group is a slow process for two reasons. One, it is non-paid job and the second is bureaucratic hurdle to get second and third instalment of money allocated to development projects. Moreover the leaders of BM felt the decline of people's volunteer participation/contribution, which would have natural effects in implementation of development projects. A mid-term review of development projects of FY 2000/01 showed that out of total 114 ward level and municipality level projects approved, only 26 were completed, 24 were being undertaken, and 64 were untouched (*Bhaktapur*, 2001: 33). This indicated a fact that the NWPP had of course received votes from city people but it largely failed to mobilize them for development activities.

People's Participation

Political parties and civil society are two major mobilizing agents. The ability of BM leadership to cultivate political and civil society would largely determine the degree of people's participation in local governance of Bhaktapur city. Its relations with the NWPP, ruling party in Bhaktapur context, were regulated by a premise of party's supremacy over elected bodies. Since the headquarters of the party is in Bhaktapur and the party chairman is inhabitant of Bhaktapur, BM received order and instruction from the central level very frequently. At institutional level the NWPP's Bhaktapur City Committee controlled over its representatives in the BM. In addition, there was a separate unit in party— Elected Committee—

constituted by some core leaders among the party organizers and elected representatives, which took major decisions on policy matters and BM was bound to follow it, according to Mayor Prem Suwal (Interview, 19 December 2001). The meeting of Elected Committee preceded meeting of Municipality Board. BM members belonging to other parties felt that their counterparts of NWPP enjoyed individual freedom at the level of debate and discussion but they followed their party's instruction while taking decisions by Board meeting on all issues and questions. Since BM leaders perceived themselves as an instrument to carry out the party's policy and largely operate under the control of party organization leaders, they obviously received cooperation from the party. In fact, the NWPP has supplied its cadres and sympathizers to development projects and other activities launched by BM.

BM's relations with other parties appeared unfriendly. Rabindra Kharbuja saw it at two levels. At ward level, the ward chairman generally consulted local leaders of other parties, but at municipality level mutual consultation and cooperation between BM and leaders of other parties was very low. Part of its reason was that BM did not need to take confidence of other parties as their representation in this elected body was very nominal. Parties were too weak to check and control the activities of BM. To what extent BM disregarded other parties could be observed by a case. The president of NC City Committee said there was a lone case of receiving a letter of invitation to his party from BM to consult on the pity issue, holding *amanat* system. (Interview with Babu Raja Joshi, 26 December 2001). Leaders of other parties also felt that they had not been treated more than as the members of civil society by BM. Moreover, opposition accused BM of its discriminatory behaviour against non-NWPP voters. Such political parochialism was observed in BM's administrative and judiciary works. Besides, BM administration was widely criticised for its delay and slow service to citizens, particularly in getting permission for construction and renovation of private houses. Politicization of municipality administration was too obvious. Opposition parties largely appeared indifference and uncooperative to BM. The state of poor relations between BM/NWPP and other parties had negative impact on the involvement of civil society in local governance.

The LSGA states that participation of civil society in local governance is mandatory. But BM followed it partly. The civil society existing in Bhaktapur could be broadly categorized into four groups: NGO, interest group/professional organizations, club/team and traditional social groups, i.e. *guthi, bhajan, dafa* etc. The first two kinds of civil society groups are largely dominated by non-NWPP persons and have been largely excluded in BM's programmes and activities. To make NWPP's own space to the upcoming trend of civil society, BM had adopted a separate rule of NGOs registration in its office against the law of NGO registration only in the district administration office or in the Social Welfare Council. There were altogether 43 NGOs registered in BM and most of them were sport related and run by the NWPP's activists. These clubs and teams received financial assistance from BM and they reciprocated with their involvement in different programmes and activities called by BM and the NWPP. The most important and active social institutions in Bhaktapur are *dafa, bhajan* and *guthi,* which have been patronized by BM. They participated actively in cultural programmes organized by BM. The NWPP's political bias and BM's partition behaviour to certain types of social organizations led to a state of non-cooperation between the modern form of civil society and the elected leadership of Bhaktapur city.

In conclusion, to understand the question that why the NWPP had constantly received support from the majority voters of Bhaktapur city, some points that described above need to be recapitulated. The most important contribution made by the NWPP is building of confidence among the *Jyapus,* hitherto suppressed community, through providing them opportunities to play a lead role in political, social and cultural affairs of the country. Though BM lacked charismatic leader, its members had individually and collectively maintained personal integrity and economic discipline, which helped them to foster their public image. BM had also maintained transparency particularly in financial matters and development projects. It has constantly pursued the agenda of cultural city and has invested extensive financial and human resources. Some other works of BM, which were appreciated by leaders of other parties too, were noteworthy, i.e. generation of financial resources through tourist entry fee, city cleaning, renovation of historical monuments (temples, *pati, pauwa,* and *math*), conservation of urban heritage, revival of traditional art, culture, custom, music and folk dance. Despite such works carried out by the BM, there was a feeling that this local institution continued to be biased against its adversaries. It, therefore, needs to overcome its prejudices in order to ensure wider people's participation in its endeavours.

Chapter 10

CIVIL SOCIETY

Do we have civil societies in Nepal? If yes, in which form they exist? How are they different from other associations of citizens, i.e. non-governmental organizations (NGOs) and community-based organizations (CBOs). To what extent Nepali civil societies are independent from the state and foreign donors? How are they contributing to promote people's participation in governance? This chapter attempts to address these questions in theoretical and contextual perspectives.

Concept

The first question about the existence of civil society in Nepal demands an understanding of its concept in both theoretical framework and discourse in the country. Civil society is a public space between state and citizens. Does it mean all types of intermediary institutions between state and citizens are civil societies? The pioneer writings on the origin and evolution of civil society in the West, i.e. John Locke's 'civil state', Hegel's 'ethical life' and De Tocqueville's 'associational life' loosely incorporated all types of citizens' groups in the basket of civil society. Theorists of social capital, i.e. James Coleman and Robert Putnam broadened the boundary of civil society. Its meaning gets complicated since it is a new phenomenon to rename as civil society to those associations which were conceptually dealt with distinct meaning as interest groups, pressure groups, professional/occupational groups, ethnic groups, etc. in the text of political theory of the 1960s and 1970s. The core notion of civil society varies from one world to another. In the West, civil society is a means of rejuvenating public life; in the East, it means – besides political and civil liberties – private property rights and markets; and in the South, it refers to those forces and agents which oppose the state and its efforts at regulation (Khilnani, 2002). Putting such varieties into one basket, it obviously enlarges the concept and scope of civil society. For an elastic definition of this concept, two statements are cited below.

> The elements of civil society range from groups based on religion and ethnicity to more fluid voluntary associations organized around ideology, professionalism, social activities or the pursuit of money, status, interest, or power. They range from circles of friends ... to single purpose political advocacy groups. Civil society also includes communities, like formally organized religious settlements, with their implication of primary socialization, strong attachment, and common history and expectations (Rosenblum and Post, 2002: 3).

> Nor is there any disagreement about including in civil society the great variety of social movements, village and neighbourhood associations, women's groups, religious groupings, intellectuals, and where they are reasonably free, the press and other media, civic organizations, associations of professionals, entrepreneurs, and employees, whose purposes and direction are not controlled by the institutions of state (Hawthorn, 2002: 276).

Definitional problem is somehow sorted out in two ways, listing organizations that are not civil society and qualifying virtues of civil society. Those excluded from civil society are: organizations from within the state structure and market (Young, 1999) and primordial kinship groups or institutions (Mouzelis, 1996: 52). Civil association is not enterprise association (Oakeshott, 2000:139). Civil society is not the sum total of the NGO community (James, 1995: 69). A strong civil society entails:(a) the existence of rule of law conditions that effectively protect citizens from state arbitrariness,(b) the existence of strongly organized non-state groups, capable of checking eventual abuse of power by those who control the means of administration and coercion and (c) the existence of balanced pluralism among civil society interests so that none can establish absolute dominance (Mouzelis, 1996: 52). Phillippe C. Schmitter viewed that to be qualified an intermediary organization as a civil society requires four characteristics: its dual autonomy from both the state and primary social units of production and reproduction; its capacity for collective action in defence of the interests and passions of its members; its self-limitation with regard to governing the polity as a whole; and its willingness to act in a civil fashion (1995: 59). Distinction of a civil society from other intermediary organizations, i.e. interest groups, pressure groups, NGOs,

CBOs, religious organizations, ethnic organizations, professional associations, etc. calls for a tight definition. Civil society is a secular forum that crosses religious, ethnic and political boundaries, and its backbone comprises independent, conscious and educated people.

Relations between civil society and state are conceptually contested. Marxism and Liberalism stand on two opposite poles. For Marxists, civil society is an outcome of transformation of state and society from feudal to capitalist world. Civil society did not exist in feudalism as economy, state and politics all fused. This argument is close to liberal interpretation, for instance, Hegel stated, "the creation of civil society is the achievement of the modern world" (quoted in Rostenblum and Post, 2002: 10). Marxists and Liberals clash in views of civil society's relations with the state. For Marxists, civil society is a bourgeois state and anti-proletarian articulation. In the context of the communist upsurge in Central Europe in the post-First World War period, Gramsci concluded, "the revolutionary wave was defeated by a combination of bourgeois state and bourgeois civil society" (quoted in Gibbon, 1996: 28). The communists, therefore, believe that civil societies play an organically conservative role by serving as a barrier protecting the state from spontaneous popular impulses. In liberal philosophy, civil society is primarily seen as a guard of citizens' rights and interests against the state as the idea of civil society was "developed along the tradition of European anti-absolutist thinking" (Chatterjee, 2002: 171). In the context of transforming the West into the modern world and in consideration of the Western political system as the most advanced democracy, has civil society retained an anti-state posture as it was at the time of its birth? The reality lies on what some said in suggestive form, "civil society must not develop simply in antagonism to the state; some elements of positive engagement with the state are essential. "Society against the state" should be matched by "society for the state" (INPR, 1995: 6; Young, 1999:161; Rostenblum and Post, 2002: 23). Civil society-state relations are a mixture of both conflict and cooperation.

In the new discourse of civil society, anti-state authority approach is more pronounced. In fact, rediscovery of civil society is associated with the 'third wave" of democracy in Asia, Africa and Latin America, particularly the resistance movements of the ordinary citizens in voluntary associations against communist regime in East European countries. "The return of civil society to political vocabularies has in part been the result of neo-liberal projects such as privatization, de-nationalization, deregulation and de-stabilization which seek to roll back the state"

(Chandhoke 1995: 10). Much weight is given to civil societies of newly established democratic countries as an important instrument for the consolidation of democracy, linking them with global project of good governance and democratization.

After the collapse of different forms of dictatorship, logically civil societies of the respective countries should go back or move forward in different direction semblance to the Western world. But it does not happen mainly because of the threat of reversal to democracy and baggage of authoritarian legacy carried out by new rulers under democratic tag. In many third wave democracies, it is generally observed, civil society organizations have had difficulty in overcoming the old uncivil structures and habits of the past, and in moving beyond simple opposition politics (INPR, 1995: 6). Civil societies of new democracies are functioning mainly as opposition to the state authority rather than developing themselves as apolitical organizations. For several reasons, it is unlikely that civil societies of new democracies will develop in the Western model. Civil societies in the West are largely apolitical but those in new democracies are greatly influenced by uneven political developments in their respective countries. High voting turn out in Third World countries is an indication about the location of civil societies in new democracies different from the Western world. Decline of volunteerism and increasing dependency on foreign donors also make differences between civil society of new democracies and established democracies. Civil society in new democracies is broadening its scope to arrest new social movements against injustice and for promotion of particular interest of a group bound together by common history, culture and language.

Nepali Discourse

The concept of civil society in Nepali discourse is contested and to some extent self-contradictory and confusing. Part of reasons is a phenomenon that civil society is legally and analytically equated with NGO which is a 'de facto definitional amendment' of civil society, but also manifestation of 'inability of academics and analysts' to differentiate between these two terms (Tamang, 2003: 15-17). An edited book – *NGO, Civil Society and Government in Nepal* – of 15 titles (articles, comments and lectures) entertains the term of civil society only in its jacket not in text (2001), suggesting how civil society is blended with NGOs. Those who loosely undertake civil society slotted other types of social groups, i.e. traditional community organizations like *guthi, bihar, dhikur, parma* (Dahal,

2001; Bhattachan, 2001; Chand, 2001;Pokhrel, 1996), and modern CBOs such as User Group, Mother Group, Self-help Group, Small Farmer Cooperative Limited and Saving and Credit Organizations (Shrestha, 2001) under its purview. A book entitled *The Role of Civil Society and Democratization in Nepal* inserts trade union, gender, NGO, media, human rights, and ethnicity as core constituents of civil society (1998). Some depicted minorities' initiatives, i.e. women, Dalits, ethnic, and religious groups, etc., to promote their respective particular interest are part of civil society movements (Gurung, 1998; Bhattachan, 2003). The impact of Tocqueville's 'associational life' in understanding of civil society in Nepal in a larger canvas is well reflected in the following statement:

> Since 1990, the civil society is beginning to emerge into the mainstream of national activities. The growth of civic associations and NGOs during this period has been phenomenal. Occupational and professional associations have sprung up as never before. Trade unions have grown in size and diversity. Human rights groups taking special interest in the rights of women, children, the disabled and consumers have grown. Corruption, though growing rampantly, is being challenged. The interest of environment conservation is being expressed similarly – as in the case of Arun III project, Bagmati pollution, Godavari marbles and Bara forests. Individual citizens are inducing 'judicial activism' by increasingly filing petitions at the Supreme Court (NSAC, 1998: 139).

In defence of their argument of broader civil society boundary including those of traditional community association, the maximalists asserted that tradition of civility is not an alien concept in Nepal (Dahal, 2001); and the history of indigenous volunteer organizations predates induced NGOs (Bhattachan, 2001). In contrast, some tried to measure civil society of Nepal from the window of Western concept and made sceptic conclusions such as "absence of civil society' in Nepal (Shrestha, 1998); and "genuine civil society is yet to evolve in Nepal" (Dahal, 2001: 42). Minimalists viewed that traditional community associations are different from what we understand as civil society and NGOs today (Gyawali, 2001; Shah 2002). NGOs are new innovation and outcome of the expansion of the global multilateral assistance programme and the expansion of the Northern INGOs into the South (Mishra, 2001; Dahal, 2001). Following the restoration of democracy in 1990, NGOs booming in Nepal is witnessed by a record of registration of 15,520 NGOs in the Social Welfare Council till November 2003 (*Rajdhani Daily*,14 November 2003), in addition to 20,000 NGOs registered in Chief District Offices in 75 districts till 1999 (Mathema, 2001: 174).

Two contrast opinions are found in assessment of Nepali NGOs and civil societies. For appreciators, the impacts of NGOs and civil societies are visible: increasing awareness of masses and empowerment of marginalized groups (Chhetri, 2001: 37), people's mobilization for local development (Shrestha, 2001), people's participation in governance (Pokhrel, 2001), employment of educated youth (Shah, 2002), and in preventing from the Maoist insurgency (Chand, 2001). Ramesh Parajuli had a long list of NGOs and civil societies' successful interventions against the Arun III project, Anti-Terrorist Act of 1997, parliamentarians' privilege of duty free import of vehicle, and in favour of women's inherent property rights, empowerment of Dalit and marginalized groups, minority rights, abolition of bonded labour system, etc. (2003). These achievements are, however, of secondary importance for critics of NGOs and civil society. Most NGOs and civil society platforms are run by the same privileged caste and groups who have long dominated political and administrative spheres of the country. Lack of internal democracy, transparency and accountability are common to most NGOs of Nepal. Most of them are attached to private rather than public interest. As they are highly dependent on foreign donors only a few English-speaking elites are benefited by NGOs business (Tamang, 2003; Bhattachan, 2003; Kumar, 1999; Mishra, 2001). Dilli Ram Dahal stated, "Almost all NGOs in Nepal survive on donor funding. Once the donors withhold the money for some reason, most of those NGOs will collapse immediately (2001:113).

Since public debate on social space is over-dominated by NGOs issues, relations between state and civil society of Nepal is less talked. Obviously the legal and plan documents acknowledge all non-state organizations, i.e. civil society, NGOs and CBOs as partners of national development. Functionally and psychologically, relations between state and NGOs are uneasy, contentious and full of rivalry (Shah, 2002; Dahal, 2001). A study found that civil society's relation with the state is both conflictual and cooperative: cooperation by opposition parties in parliament and conflict with the government (Parajuli, 2003).

This chapter now concentrates on Nepali civil society and its functions of popular mobilization and participation. I am not going to copy the Western notion of virtues of civil society, i.e. autonomy, independent, self-determination, intervention in public spheres etc. while contextualizing the meaning of civil society in Nepali milieu. It is obviously because Nepali civic organizations possess some or parts of all characteristics of the Western civil society. For instance, a number of civil society organizations of Nepal, like most NGOs, are financially dependent upon foreign donors. Dependency of individual members of civil society upon state authority and partisan and inclination of non-state organizations with political parties are other factors limiting Nepali civil society so far independence and autonomy are concerned.

This chapter excludes NGOs since NGOs are primarily an agent of development though some of them occasionally undertake civil society's role particularly in awareness and advocacy campaigns. Distinction between civil society and NGOs is made by some previous studies. One stated, "...unlike NGOs and INGOs whose *de facto* and *de jure* operation in Nepal requires their registration with Social Welfare Council, civil societies operate under a diffused mandate and many of them work as informal organizations without any need for registration at all" (Dahal, 2001: 33). In respect of turning SAP/Nepal from INGOs to an NGO to a debate forum most recently, its Executive Director Rohit Kumar Nepali requested to designate his organization as a civil society than an NGO. Similarly Gopal Sivakoti Chintan, founder of Rashtriya Sarokar Samaj – an organization involving in advocacy and people's right – requested for not consideration of this organization as NGOs (2001). The plea of Nepali and Chintan give a sense that civil society, unlike NGOs, refers more to public debate, interest articulation, lobby, advocacy, people's rights and civil campaigns. Human rights organizations and Transparency International/Nepal have greater virtues of civil society. However, other organizations – irrespective of their own good reputation and credibility and irrespective of occasionally involving in advocacy and campaigning activities – working for the promotion of particular interest of a group (i.e. Women Pressure Group and other women's organizations for gender empowerment, Maiti Nepal and similar organizations against girl trafficking, Federation of Nepali Nationalities and indigenous Janajati organizations for inclusion, Federation of Dalit NGOs and Dalit organizations against untouchability and social injustice, etc.) are beyond the scope of this chapter. This chapter also excludes both traditional and modern CBOs nevertheless the former type of CBOs are apolitical and some modern CBOs i.e. Mother Groups have a successful story of greater people mobilization against anti-alcohol and anti-gambling campaigns. Several scattered micro civil associations functioning at local level, such as BASE, are also left out by this chapter.

This chapter narrows down civil society at macro level in its scope. The limitation of boundary calls further specification about definition of civil society in the Nepali context. In Nepal, civil society exists as a forum, both formal and informal, of enlightened people with different tags: academics, lawyers, professionals, journalists, human right activists, NGO holders, ethnic activists, women activists, Dalit activists, and to some extent retired bureaucrats and politicians holding double constituencies, politics and civic organizations. The Professional Solidarity Group, formed on the eve of the 1990 mass movement, is the immediate predecessor of the present civil society of Nepal. Since it is a conglomeration of people involving in different fields, Nepali civil society generally shows its concern to broader issues, i.e. human rights, governance, democracy, peace and conflict resolution. It sometimes picks up and involves in promoting particular interest of different groups, i.e. women's empowerment, Dalit upliftment, minority rights, etc. It has been largely appearing in public debate (meeting, seminar, workshop and conference); reacting against state policies and decisions; producing ideas and knowledge; and occasionally taking to the streets for public campaigns.

The strength and limitation of Nepali civil society for people's mobilization and participation is dealt with three propositions. One, origin and evolution of civil society are closely tightened with struggles for democracy in Nepal. Two, Nepali civil society, though it is non-state organizations, is not apolitical. Three, its main agendas and concerns have changed constantly in responding to changed political context.

Origin, Revival and Reconstruction

The genesis of modern civil society in Nepal goes back to the pre-1950 period and associated with a struggle against the century long Rana oligarchy (1846-1951). Literates are pioneers in creating civil society in the form of idea than organization who used non-political spaces in producing new ideas of social reformation and political change. As one historian observed, "Many writers in the Rana period emerged out of their traditional role of composing prose and poetry just for the sake of aesthetics. They rather wrote for the need for reforms in the society; but in a very subtle way. As emerging communicators, they began to disseminate a new vision of reality and awareness of potentialities of politics. They distinctly occupied the vanguard role in urging their fellow countrymen to widen their narrow horizon and absorb the spirit of the modern world. Their slow, yet, a gradual diffusion of new ideas and the stir of new emotions and feeling all had the ultimate consequences for politics" (Uprety, 1992: 19). Some other prominent figures that made organized efforts from social spaces for the same causes were Madhav Raj Joshi (Arya Samaj), Tulsi Mehar (Charkha), Shukra Raj Shastri (Nepal Nagarik Adhikar Samiti) and Daya Bir Singh Kansakar (Paropakar Santsthan).

The advent of democracy, following the fall of the Rana regime in February 1951, opened up new spaces and opportunities for expansion of civil societies. Some organizations championing particular interest of their respective groups related to women, Dalits and ethnic groups appeared, but they were not active and effective as it should be under democratic disposition. The absence of a broader civil society working for general interest of the masses across the social segments also indicated something lacking and inadequacy. Perhaps Marxist philosophy can explain better the question why political openness and fundamental rights, including freedom of association, are not sufficient for the emergence of a vibrant civil society. Despite democracy in the 1950s, Nepali society at large was feudal and in feudal set up economy, state and politics all fused. To see the problem from theoretical frame of liberalism, the nonexistence of strong civil society in the 1950s was not amazing since the country was just steeped in towards modernization. The limited numbers of educated Nepalis, backbone of civil society, were absorbed into state apparatus and party structures. The break of democratic exercises by a royal coup in December 1960 and revival of royal absolutism in the name of partyless panchayat system ended the possibility of gradual evolution of civil society in Nepal.

As of its nature, the authoritarian panchayat system provided only limited fundamental rights. Freedom of association against the state authority was not granted at all. Civil society cannot exist without liberal democracy, except for the case of East Asia (quoted in Khilani, 2002: 25). The monopoly of state in social spheres was reflected by the Panchayat's conscious and deliberate formation of six class/occupation organizations, like youth, women, peasant, ex-army etc. as core partners of partyless regime. To coup up global wave of NGOs, Social Service National Coordinate Council was set up with the then Queen as the Chairperson. The Council did not only register NGOs it also controlled them. The state's hegemony over society is also reflected in words of the legal provision. According to Society Registration Act 1977, the chief district officer (CDO) would register, guide, direct, control and supervise social organizations, i.e. clubs, public libraries, literary societies, self-help groups, NGOs and cultural groups. However in the 1980s, in the pretext of political relaxation in the post-1980 referendum time, a new form of civil societies appeared, different from those constituted during the Rana period on character if not in goal.

Revival of civil society in Nepal in the 1980s was synchronized with the emergence of new trends in national and international politics. Two most remarkable developments, within the country and world politics, are: entry of Nepali communist parties in broader democratic movements through forming and activating front/occupational organizations; and resurgence of civil societies' resistance movement against authoritarian regime at the global level, known as third wave of democracy. Formation of five open forums – Democratic National Unity Forum, National People's Forum, Civic Rights Forum, People's Right Protection Forum, and Human Rights Protection Forum – in 1985 by the Communist Party of Nepal (ML, later renamed as UML) was an example of overlapping between civil society and political society. Besides, each occupational and professional group, i.e. students, teachers, professors, lawyers, doctors, engineers, journalists, etc. had their own separate organizations with ideological/party brand: democrat/Nepali Congress party (NC) and progressive/communist parties. This makes a distinct of the civil societies of the1980s from those formed purely in social space in the 1930s-1940s, nevertheless both originated and activated for change of the then non-democratic regime.

The forums and professional organizations of the 1980s were civil in name but political in objective. So distinction between banned political party and civil society was thin as both were outside the state structure and had a common goal. The civil society in the 1980s meant a joint front or forum where professional/occupation groups belonging to democrat and progressive camps worked together for a common goal. The ideological profile of all 89 founder members of Nepal Human Right Organizations, founded in December 1988, clearly revealed that it was/is a forum of critical mass belonging to different ideological camps. The formation of the Professional Solidarity Group on the eve of the 1990 mass movement against three decade-long partyless panchayat system epitomized the basic nature of revived civil society. The way civil society constituted in the 1980s has greater impact in the reconstruction of civil society in the changed context after the restoration of democracy in Nepal.

Restoration of democracy in 1990 has brought a paradoxical situation, broadening the space of civil societies at the one hand and declining the spirit of civil-ness on the other. Deviation of civil society in the post-dictatorial time is a common phenomenon of new democracies. In the context of the East Europe where civil societies stood on frontline during movements against communist regime, Aleksander Smolar observed, "The myth of civil society – united, anti-political, supporting the programme of radical reforms – was quickly undermined, discredited and forgotten" (1995: 62). About African case, it is stated, "the unity of civil society appears to last only enough to initiate the movement from authoritarian to democratic rule. In one African country to another, the movement for democracy has been fractured along ethno-regional and sectarian lines either in the course of the transition to democracy or immediately thereafter" (Gyimah-Boadi, 1995: 64). Fragmentation of civil society in Nepal has undertaken in political party line. In the early period of democracy, it was almost difficult to find civil society even in the form of its existence in the 1980s, a joint forum of enlightened people with different ideologies.

In the early period of democracy, Nepali society was highly politicized in party line and many persons who claimed themselves as civil society members did not hesitate to carry out party flag of their inclination. Domination of politics over society happened due to parties' excessive encroachment to social spheres. Taking advantage of excessive politicization of social groups in the early phase of democracy, political parties set a trend of 'partyness' creating several ancillary and affiliated organizations from caste, community, class, occupation and professional groups to satisfy their quest for new avenues and platforms (Hachhethu, 2002). This led to the mushroom growth of party-inclined formal groups at all segments of society, even among civil servants, human rights activists and ethnic activists. Almost all parties have their own separate platform for ethnic groups and Dalit community. Aside from constituting affiliated organizations in several numbers, the NC had, at once, 8 ancillary organizations. The number of such organizations in the Communist Party of Nepal (UML), Rashtriya Prajtantra Party, Nepal Sadbhawana Party (NSP), Jan Morcha and Nepal Workers and Peasants Party (NWPP) was: 11, 8, 6, 6 and 8 respectively. Parties' deliberate attempts of creating partyness society were facilitated by civil society members. Following the restoration of democracy in 1990, there was a wave of forming organizations that were civil in name but political in purpose. Among more than a dozen human right specific organizations formed in the post-1990 period all, except three, are inclined to the communist parties. The nature of party politics till the first half of 1990s – dominated by stiff conflicts and confrontations between the NC and communist parties – highly impacted for fragmentation of civil societies. For instance, those political scientists who don't have democratic identity in conventional sense separated themselves from the original Political Science Association of Nepal (POLSAN) and formed a separate forum of the same name.

A new pattern of party politics has emerged since the mid-1990s and in the changed political context Nepali civil society has been reconstructed largely in the format of the 1980s but with new contents and wider space. At the outset, the UML's ideological modification in line with liberal democracy in the name of *bahudaliya janabad* (People's Multiparty Democracy) contributed to reducing ideological gap among ideology-oriented civil activists, intellectuals and professionals. Inter-party relations had changed from that of stiff conflicts in the first tenure of parliament (1991-1994) to coalition building in second parliament (1994-1999) to consensus building in the third parliament (1999-2002) and thereafter. This had spilled over effect in bringing a favourable environment for cohesive actions among fragmented civil society organizations and members. The degeneration of Nepali politics – marked by power centric party politics, abuse of state resources, corruption, mis-governance, political instability and crisis, violence and armed conflict, regression – has widened the space of civil society in both aspects, increase the number of civil society members and enlarge the contents for activism. Increasing apathy to politics and disillusion with parties and their leaders provide a hope of reconstruction of Nepali civil society in a way that it will keep itself at a certain distance, if not break completely, from party politics. Civil society's stands taking against the king (for his actions of taking back executive power since October 2002) and against the Maoists (for continuation of armed insurgency) seemed relatively free from the parties' position vis-à-vis monarchy and the Maoists.

Motivation, Mobilization and Participation

It is generally considered that civil society promotes democracy and its resistances against the state help in making political society accountable to citizens and societies. How does it contribute for the consolidation of democracy? Schmitter listed: it stabilizes expectations within social groups; inculcates conceptions of interest and norms of behaviour that are civic; it provides channels for self-expression; serves to govern the behaviour of its members with regard to collective commitments; and provides important reservoirs of resistance to arbitrary action by rulers (1995: 60). Whether civil societies of newly established democracies are functioning in conformity to such checklists is questionable. But the way it revived in the

East and the Third World as resistance movements against authoritarian regimes undoubtly suggests that civil society is an ally of democracy. Nepali civil society, unlike its counterparts of the Eastern Europe, is not the foremost instrument of bringing democracy back, but its origin and revival is closely tied with struggles for democracy.

Recall the 1990 mass movement – that was called jointly by the NC and United Left Front of seven splinter communist parties – revealed the contribution of Nepali civil society. A study found that "after the first week of the movement, actors other than the political activists became the most visible and mobilized" (Sharma, 2001). Its noteworthy contribution was: giving continuity to the movement, paralyzing the machinery of the regime and motivating the rest of the population" (see Chapter 1). Though it was parties led movement with specific limited demands – freedom of party and interim government – civil society's pressures forced the leaders to upgrade achievements. During 8 April 1990 (release of ban on party) to 9 November 1990 (promulgation of new constitution), civil society backed for four successive upward revisions on the goal of the movement. First, legalization of political parties, second, abolition of all Panchayat institutions, third, formation of a constitution drafting committee on the recommendation of PM against the traditional prerogative of the king, and last constitutional monarchy (see Chapter 2). It became possible because, what Ganesh Man Singh (commander of the 1990 movement) said, "People moved ahead faster" than leaders and parties. This was a clear acknowledgment of civil society's role in advancing and upgrading the achievement of the 1990 mass movement. Civil society appears most advanced than political parties in setting agendas of state restructuring, a dominant issue of current discourse. This part will deal with after reviewing briefly how civil society functions after the restoration of democracy in 1990.

Though biased and fragmented, Nepali civil societies have kept themselves active resisting against the state on a number of issues and problems. The dominant issues in the early phase of democracy, what civil societies showed their concern, were: government's repressive measures against communists' state protests, transparency of Tanakpur treaty with India, and grievances of groups, i.e. civil servants, landless people etc. Over the time, focus of civil societies shifted to the emerging questions: abuse of power and resources, i.e. corruption, instability, mis-governance, erosion of democratic norms and values, accountability and transparency, internal democracy in parties. Withdrawal of members of parliament (MP)'s privilege of duty free import of vehicle, disqualification for candidacy in the 1999 general election by political parties to those involved in scandal of abuse of red (diplomatic) passport, making of party regulation act, and abolition of bonded labour system were few to mention as outcome of civil society's successful assertions for the betterment of society. Nepali civil society has gradually widened its spaces picking up outstanding social problems and involving in social movements against exclusion and injustice, i.e. Dalit campaigns against untouchability and ethnic movements for inclusion.

Currently civil society is engaging on the most ambitious state restructuring project addressing several complicated and interrelated issues, i.e. human rights, peace and conflict resolution (directed against the Maoist violent insurgency and militarization by the state); and constitution amendment or framing of a new constitution through election of Constituent Assembly (targeted against the political regression under the leadership of the King Gyanendra). Civil society's agenda of state restructuring was progressive and radical than parties' demand for revival of political and constitutional course through constituting of all-party interim government and reinstating of the dissolved House of Representatives (HOR). It seemed that civil society stood against all forces – monarchy, Maoist and parliamentary parties – representing political society in different capacities. In a given context, is it possible that civil society mobilizes masses for its radical agendas?

The ways it originated, revived and reconstructed in different time frames suggest that Nepali civil society, unlike its counterpart of the Eastern Europe, has rarely opted for the mass mobilization. Its capacity and potentiality of mass mobilization is constrained and limited by several factors i.e. financial dependency on foreign donors, dependence of civil society members upon political leaders for their own personal ambition, absence of non-state institutions to support civic activities, and the financial cost of constant involvement and participation. Its strength is to motivate and mobilize gradually the critical section of society than general mass. For instance, till the end of 1990s and the beginning of the 2000s, there are only few intellectuals who suggested for Constitution Assembly to resolve the Maoist problems, but now this approach has been bought by several hundred enlightened people. Even several contents of the18-point forward-looking agenda of the five parliamentary parties were first brought out into public debate by civil society members. So the greatest achievement that Nepali civil society has gained throughout its history is to leading the country in terms of idea and thought. So civil society as idea/thought giver rather than organization for mass mobilization has been very much alive and active in Nepal.

Conclusion

Nepali civil society originated and revived as a part of democratic movements. And it has been engaging mainly on high political issues even after the dawn of multiparty system in 1990. The simple answer to a big question– why politics has remained the main concern of civil society?–is that the project of democracy in Nepal has not yet been completed. In a situation of a prolonged political crisis that aggravated one after another around the events – escalation of the Maoists armed insurgency, absence of any elected bodies both at local and central levels since October 2002, and assertion of power by the most ambitious King Gyanandra since October 2002 – it was quite natural that the question of settlement of political problem override other issues of social and economic developments. It, however, did not mean that civil society kept its eye closed to emerging social movements. Participation of civil society members in personal capacity or representing organization they belonged to in Dalits' campaign against untouchability, Janajatis' movement against exclusion, and other activities related to empowerment of women and marginalized groups is quite visible. Again, politics remained the key issue in public debate and discourse. Part of reason behind over politicization of Nepali civil societies is their inclination with different political parties. The strict definition of the difference between civil society and political society does not work very well in Nepal. It is, however, a thing to be celebrated that a distance is widening between civil society and parties. A trend of de-politicization and de-partyzation of civil society has gradually been emerging since the last half of the 1990s. Reconstruction of civil society against partisan line is an outcome of the people's apathy, dismay and disillusionment with politics, party and leaders. In the future, one can hope that such a reconstructed civil society of Nepal will intervene on wider issues of public concern with its greater strength of autonomy and independence.

BIBLIOGRAPHY

Documents

CPN (Maoist) [a]. 1995. *Text of the Strategy and Tactics of Armed Struggle in Nepal* (March 1995).

—— [b]. 1995. *Text of the Plan for the Historic Initiation of the People's War* (September 1995).

—— 2001. *Text of the Resolution Passed by the Party's Second National Conference* (February 2001).

—— 2003. *Text of the Forward Looking New State System and a New Constitution* (April 2003).

CPN (Marxist). 1990. *Text of the Recommendations Submitted to the CRC* (June 1990).

CRC (a). 1990. *Text of the Draft Constitution.*

—— (b) 1990.*Text of the Analytical Note of the Draft Constitution.*

FC. 1990. *Text of the Press Note of the Fourth Convention* (9 June 1990).

JSP. 2005. *Text of the Political Resolution Passed by the Central Committee of the Jana Shakti Party* (11 September 2005).

ML (a). 1990. *Text of the Statement of Madan Bhandari, Spokesman of the Party* (1 June 1990).

—— (b). 1990. *Text of the Recommendations of the Party Submitted to the CRC* (June 1990).

—— (c). 1990. *Text of the Present Situation and the Party's Responsibility* (November 1990).

—— 1991. *Text of the Present Situation and the Party's Responsibility* (January 1991).

NC (a). 1990. *Text of the Situational Paper* Presented *by G.P. Koirala at the Party's Conference* (18 January 1990).

—— (b). 1990. *Text of Surya Bahadur Shakya's Speech at the Party's Conference* (18 January 1990).

——(c).1990. *Text of M.J. Akabar's Speech at the Party's Conference* (18 January 1990).

—— (d).1990. *Text of the Press Note of the Party* (17 April 1990).

—— (e). 1990. *Text of the Political Resolution Passed by the Party's Central Committee* (25-27 April 1990).

—— (a). 1991. *Text of the Political Resolution of the Party* (1991).
——(b).1991. *The Election Manifesto of the Nepali Congress.*
—— (a). 1992. *Text of the Economic Resolution, Passed by the Party's Eight National Convention* (February 1992).
—— (b). 1992. *Text of the Political Resolution Passed by the Party's Central Committee* (December 1992).
—— (a). 1994. *The Election Manifesto of the Nepali Congress.*
—— (b). 1994. *The Constitution of Parliamentary Party of the Nepali Congress.*
—— (c). 1994. *A Short Description of Elected Government's Notable Performance in Three Years.*
——(a).1995. *The Constitution of Nepali Congress 1960* (Amended in 1995).
—— (b).1995. *The Nepali Congress in the Eighth Session of Parliament.*
—— 1999. *The Election Manifesto of the Nepali Congress.*
—— 2000. *Text of the Recommendations to Resolve the Maoist Problems Submitted to the Deuba Commission.*
NPF. 1999. *The Election Manifesto of the National People' Front.*
NSP. 1991. *The Election Manifesto of the Nepal Sadbhabana Party.*
—— (a). 1994. *The Election Manifesto of the Nepal Sadbhabana Party.*
——(b).1994. *The Constitution of the Parliamentary Party of the Nepal Sadbhabana Party.*
——1999. *The Election Manifesto of the Nepal Sadbhabana Party.*
NWPP (a). 1991. *The Constitution of the Nepal Workers and Peasants* Party (Amended in 1991).
—— (b). 1991. *The Election Manifesto of the Nepal Workers and Peasants Party.*
—— 1992. *The Election Manifesto of the Nepal Workers and Peasants Party*
—— 1994. *The Election Manifesto of the Nepal Workers and Peasants Party.*
—— 1992. *TheElection Manifesto of the Nepal Workers and Peasants Party.*
—— 1999. *The Election Manifesto of the Nepal Workers and Peasants Party.*
RPP. 1990. *The Constitution of the Rashtriya Prajatantra Party 1990.*
—— 1991. *The Election Manifesto of the Rashtriya Prajatantra Party*
—— (a). 1994. *The Election Manifesto of the Rashtriya Prajatantra Party*
—— (b) 1994. *The Constitution of the Parliamentary Party of the Rashtriya Prajatantra Party.*
—— 1999. *The Election Manifesto of the Rashtriya Prajatantra Party.*
Text of His Majesty King Gyanendra's Royal Proclamation (1 February 2005).
Text of the Advice Submitted by the Majority of 6 Against 3 Supreme Court Judges to the King on the Subject of Constitutional Provisions of Article 53 (3)(February 1998).
Text of the Constitution, Revised and Approved by the Cabinet (October 1990).
Text of the Letter Jointly Sent by Six Members of the US Congress to King Birendra (18 January 1990).
Text of the Memorandum Presented to PM G.P. Koirala by a Group of Donors Representing an Overwhelming Majority of Donor Agencies Working in Nepal, Nepal's Development Partners (15 May 1998).
Text of the Palace Draft Constitution (October 1990).
Text of the Speech by PM Krishna P. Bhattarai to the House of Representatives (16 March 2000).
Text of the Statement of John Kelly in Regard to the US Stand on the MRD in Nepal (16 March 1990).

Text of Statement of the Secretary of the BJP (n.d).

UML (a). 1991. *Text of the Political Declaration, Approved by the Meeting of National Council* (January 1991).

—— (b).1991.*The Election Manifesto of the Communist Party of Nepal (UML).*

—— (a). 1993. *Text of the Programme for Revolution in Nepal: Multiparty People's Democracy* (February 1993).

—— (b). 1993. *Text of the Organizational Report Passed by Eight National Congress of the UML.*

—— (c). 1993. *The Constitution of the Communist Party of Nepal, Unified Marxist-Leninist Party.*

—— (a). 1994. *The Election Manifesto of the Communist Party of Nepal (UML)*

—— (b). 1994. *The Constitution of the Parliamentary Party of the Communist Party of Nepal, UML.*

—— 1996. *Text of the Political Report Presented by the General Secretary of the UML to the Party's National Council Meeting in Janakpur* (February 1996).

—— 1999. *The Election Manifesto of the Communist Party of Nepal (UML).*

—— 2001. *Text of the Summary Report of the UML on Violence and Terror Created by the State and the Maoist* (July 2001).

UPF. 1991. *The Election Manifesto of the United People's Front.*

—— 1994. *The Election Manifesto of the United People's Front.*

—— 1999. *The Election Manifesto of the United People's Front.*

Books

Acharya, Nara Hari. 2000. *Nayan Nepal ko Prastabana* (Proposal for Making New Nepal). Kathmandu: Sambatsar Publication.

Acharya, Rajeshwar and Hamid Ansari. 1980. *Basic Needs and Government Services: An Area Study of Bhaktapur Town Panchayat, Nepal.* Kathmandu: Centre for Development and Administration.

Anderson, Mary M. 1970. *The Festivals of Nepal.* Delhi: Rupa and Co.

Anderson, Charles W. 1977. *Statecraft: An Introduction to Political Choice and Judgment.* New York: John Wiley & Sons, 1977.

Baral, Lok Raj Baral. 1977. *Oppositional Politics in Nepal.* New Delhi: Abhinav Publications.

—— 1983. *Nepal's Politics of Referendum.* New Delhi: Vikas Publishing House.

—— (ed.). 1992. *South Asia: Democracy and the Road Ahead.* Kathmandu: Political Science Association of Nepal.

—— 1993. *Nepal: Problems of Governance.* New Delhi: Konark Publishers Pvt. Ltd.

—— 2000. *The Regional Paradox: Essays in Nepali and South Asian Affairs,* Delhi: Adroit Publishers.

—— (ed.). 2003. *Nepal: Political Parties and Parliament.* New Delhi: Adroit Publishers.

Baral, Lok Raj, Krishna Hachhethu and Hari Sharma. 2001. *Leadership in Nepal.* New Delhi: Adroit Publishers.

BDP. 1977. *Bhaktapur Development Project.* Bhaktapur: Bhaktapur Development Project.

Bernier, Ronal M. 1970.*The Temples of Nepal.* New Delhi: S Chand and Company Ltd.

Bhattachan, Krishna B. et al., (eds.). 2001. *NGO, Civil Society and Government in Nepal.*

Kathmandu: Central Department of Sociology and Anthropology/Tribhuvan University.

Bhattarai, Babu Ram. 1998. *The Political-Economic Rational of the People's War.* Kathmandu: Utprerak Prakshan.

Bista, Dor Bahadur. 1991. *Fatalism and Development: Nepal's Struggle for Modernization.* Calcutta: Orient Longman.

BM. 2000. *Budget of Bhaktapur Municipality, FY 2000/2001.*

—— 2001. *Bhaktapur: A Cultural City*. Kathmandu: Bhaktapur Municipality.

Borre, Ole, Sushil Raj Pandey and Chitra Krishna Tiwari. 1994. *Nepalese Political Behaviour*. New Delhi: Sterling.

Brass, Paul R. 1965. *Factional Politics in an Indian State: The Congress Party in Uttar Pradesh*. Berkeley: University of California Press.

Brown, T. Louise. 1996. *The Challenge to Democracy in Nepal: A Political History*. London: Routledge.

Chandhoke, Neera. 1995. *State and Society: Explorations in Political Theory*. New Delhi: Sage Publications.

Chauhan, R.S. 1971. *The Political Development in Nepal 1950-70: Conflict between Tradition and Modernity*. New Delhi: Associated Publishing House.

Chhibar, Pradeep K. 1999. *Democracy without Association: Transformation of the Party System and Social Cleavages in India*. New Delhi: Vistar Publications.

CNAS. 1996. *Democracy Watch-1*. Kathmandu: Centre for Nepal and Asian Studies/ Tribhuvan University.

Dangol, Sanu Bhai. 1999. *The Palace in Nepalese Politics*: Kathmandu: Ratna Pustak Bhandar.

Dahal, Dev Raj. 2001. *Civil Society in Nepal: Opening the Ground for Questions.* Kathmandu: Centre for Development and Governance.

Dixit, Kanak Mani and Shastri Ramachandaran (eds.). 2002. *State of Nepal.* Kathmandu: Himal Books.

Duverger, Maurice. 1964. *Political Parties: Their Origin and Activity in Modern State.* London: Methuen.

ECN. 1991. *Election Result: House of Representative 2048 (1991)*. Kathmandu: Election Commission of Nepal.

—— 1992. *Result of Local Elections, 1992.*Kathmandu: Election Commission of Nepal.

—— 1994. *Election Results: House of Representative 2051 (1994)*. Kathmandu: Election Commission of Nepal.

—— 1997. *Result of Local Elections, 1997*. Kathmandu: Election Commission of Nepal.

—— 1999. *Election Results: House of Representative 2056 (1999)*. Kathmandu: Election Commission of Nepal.

—— 1999. *The Election Code of Conduct, 1996* (first edition). Kathmandu: Election Commission of Nepal.

Elgie, Robert. 1995. *Political Leadership in Liberal Democracies*. London: Macmillan Press Ltd.

Gellner, David N., Jonna Pfaff-Czarnecka and John Whelpton (eds.). 1997. *Nationalism and Ethnicity in a Hindu Kingdom: the Politics of Culture in a Contemporary Nepal*. Amsterdam: Harwood Academic Publishers.

Gellner, David N. (ed.). 2002. *Resistance and the State: Nepalese Experiences*. New Delhi:

Social Science Press, 2002.

Goldstone, J.A. (ed.). 1986. *Revolution: Theoretical, Comparative and Historical Studies*. US: Harcourt B.J. Publishers.

Gupta, Anirudha. 1964. *Politics in Nepal: A Study of Post-Rana Political Development and Party Politics*. Bombay: Allied Publishers.

Gurung, D. B. (ed.). 2003. *Nepal Tomorrow: Voices and Visions*. Kathmandu: Koselee Prakashan.

Gutschow, Niels and Bernhard Kolver. 1975. *Ordered Space: Concepts and Functions in a Town of Nepal*. Germany: Kommissionsverlag Franz Steiner GMBH Wiesbaden.

Haaland, Ane.1982. *Bhaktapur: A Town Changing*. Kathmandu: Bhaktapur Development Project.

Hachhethu, Krishna. 2002. *Party Building in Nepal: Organization, Leadership and People, A Comparative Study of the Nepali Congress and the Communist Party of Nepal (Unified Marxist-Leninist)*. Kathmandu: Mandala Book Point.

—— 2004. *State of Democracy in Nepal: A Survey Report*. Kathmandu: SDSA/N and International IDEA.

Hachhethu, Krishna, Sanjay Kumar and Jivan Subedi. 2008. *Nepal in Transition: A Study on the State of Democracy*. Stockholm: International IDEA.

Hoftun, Martin, William Raeper and John Whelpton. 1999. *People, Politics and Ideology: Democracy and Social Change in Nepal*. Kathmandu: Mandala Book Point.

Hutt, Michael (ed.). 1994. *Nepal in the Nineties*. Delhi: Oxford University Press, 1994.

—— (ed.). 2004. *Himalayan People's War: Nepal's Maoist Rebellion*. London: Hurst and Co. Ltd.

ICG. April 2003. *Nepal Backgrounder: Ceasefire-Soft Landing Or Strategic Pause?*. Kathmandu: International Crisis Group.

—— September 2003. *Text of Babu Ram Bhattarai's letter to ICG, 26 September 2003*. Kathmandu: International Crisis Group.

—— February 2005. *Nepal: Responding to the Royal Coup*. Kathmandu: International Crisis Group.

IIDS. 1993. *The Second Parliamentary Election: A Study of Emerging Democratic Process in Nepal*. Kathmandu: Institute for Integrated Development Studies.

—— 1994. *The Third Parliamentary Election: A Study of the Evolving Democratic Process in Nepal*. Kathmandu: Institute for Integrated Development Studies.

INPR. 1995. *International Conference on Consolidating the Third Wave Democracies: Trends and Challenges*. Taipei: Institute for National Policy Research.

Joshi, Bhuwan Lal and Leo E. Rose. 1966. *Democratic Innovations in Nepal: A Case Study of Political Acculturation*. Berkley: University of California Press.

Karki, Arjun and David Seddon (eds.). 2003. *The People's War in Nepal: Left Perspectives*. New Delhi: Adroit Publishers.

Karki, Arjun and Binod Bhattarai (eds.). n.d. *Whose War? Economic and Social-Cultural Impacts of Nepal's Maoist-Government Conflict*. Kathmandu: NGO Federation of Nepal.

Katz, Richard S. and Peter Mair (eds.). 1994. *How Parties Organize: Change and Adaptation in Party Organizations in Western Democracies*. London: Sage Publications.

Kaviraj, Sudipta and Sunil Khilnani (eds.). 2002. *Civil Society: History and Possibilities*.

New Delhi: Foundation Books.

K.C., Surendra. 1999. *Nepal ko Communist Party KoItihas* (History of the Communist Movement in Nepal). Kathmandu: Vidyarthi Pustak Sadan.

Khanal, Krishna et al. 1996.*Nepal: People, Polity and Governance: A Survey Analysis of People's Response to the Democratic Experiment 1991-1995*. Kathmandu: Centre for Consolidation of Democracy.

Khanal, Krishna and Krishna Hachhethu. 1999. *Am Nirbachan 2056: Sansadra Sarkar ko Chunauti* (General Elections 1999: Challenge to Parliament and Government). Kathmandu: Centre for Nepal and Asian Studies.

Khanal, Krishna P. 2005. *Nepal's Discourses on Constituent Assembly: An Analysis*. Kathmandu: Friends for Peace.

Kholi, Atul. 1992. *Democracy and Discontent: India's Growing Crisis of Governability*. Cambridge: Cambridge University Press.

Kochanek, Stanley A. 1968. *The Congress Party in India: The Dynamic of One-Party Democracy*. Princeton: Princeton University.

Koirala, B.P. 1979. *Democracy Indispensable for Development*. Varanasi: Tarun Publication.

—— 1990. *Rastra, Rastriyatara Prajatantra* (Nation, Nationalism and Democracy).

Kumar, Dhruba (ed.). 1995. *State, Leadership and Politics in Nepal*. Kathmandu: Centre for Nepal and Asian Studies.

—— (ed.). 2000. *Domestic Conflict and Crisis of Governability in Nepal*. Kathmandu: Centre for Nepal and Asian Studies.

Kumar, Dhruba and Hari Sharma.N.d., *Security Sector Reform in Nepal: Challenges and Opportunities*. Kathmandu: Friends for Peace.

La Palombara, Joseph and Myron Weiner (eds.). 1960. *Political Parties and Political Development*. Princeton: Princeton University Press.

Lawson, Kay (ed.). 1980. *Political Parties and Linkages: A Comparative Perspective*. New Haven: Yale University Press.

Lecomate-tilouine , Marie and Pascale dollfus (eds.). 2003. *Ethnic Revival and Religious Turmoil: Identities and Representations in the Himalayas*. New Delhi: Oxford University Press.

Levy, Robert Il. 1990. *Mesocosm: Hinduism and the Organization of a Traditional Newar City*. Delhi: Motilal Banarsidass Publishers Pvt. Ltd.

Mahajan, Gurpreet (ed.). 2000. *Democracy, Difference and Social Justice*. New Delhi: Oxford University Press,

Maharjan, Pancha Narayan. 1998. *Local Elections in Nepal, 1997*. Kathmandu: Centre for Nepal and Asia Studies.

Malla, Kamal P. (ed.). 1989. *Nepal: Perspectives on Continuity and Change*. Kathmandu: Centre for Nepal and Asian Studies/ Tribhuvan University.

Maner, James (ed.). 1994. *Nehru to Nineties*. New Delhi: Viking.

MF. 1990. *The State of Present Economy*. Kathmandu: Ministry of Finance/HMG.

—— 1992. *Budget Speech of the Fiscal Year 1992/93*. Kathmandu: Ministry of Finance/ HMG.

—— 1996. *Economic Survey: Fiscal Year 1995-96*. Kathmandu: Ministry of Finance/ HMG.

Michel, Robert. 1968. *Political Parties: A Sociological Study of the Oligarchical Tendencies of Modern Democracy*. New York: The Free Press.

Mishra, Bal Chandra. 2001. *UML: Jhapa Andolan dekhi Bivajan Sama* (UML: From Jhapa Movement to Disintegration). Kathmandu: VidyarthiPustakBhandar.

MLD and UDLF. 2000. *Detailed Revenue and Expenditure Breakdown and Basic Financial Information of 58 Municipalities of Nepal, 1995/6-1998/99*. Kathmandu: Ministry of Local Development/His Majesty's Government and Urban Development through Local Efforts.

MLJ. 1990. *The Constitution of the Kingdom of Nepal, 1990*. Kathmandu: Ministry of Law and Justice/His Majesty's Government.

——2000. *Local Self-Governance Act, 1999*. Kathmandu: Ministry of Law/His Majesty's Government.

Morris-Jones, W.H. 1957. *Parliament in India*. Delhi: Longmans Green and Co. Ltd.

Muni, S.D. 2003. *The Maoist Insurgency in Nepal: The Challenge and The Response*. New Delhi: Rupa and Co.

NCCS. 2001. "Election and Governance" (unpublished report). Kathmandu: Nepal Centre for Contemporary Studies.

—— 2001. "Parties and Parliament" (unpublished report). Kathmandu: Centre for Nepal and Asian Studies.

NESAC. 1998. *Nepal: Human Development Report 1998*. Kathmandu: Nepal South Asian Centre.

NOSC. 1993. *Political Opinion Survey of Kathmandu Valley 1993*. Kathmandu: Nepal Opinion Survey Centre.

NPC. 1992. *Approach to the Eighth Five Year Plan, 1992- 1997*. Kathmandu: National Planning Commission.

—— 1998. *Approach to the Ninth Plan, 1997-2002*. Kathmandu: National Planning Commission.

Panday, Devendra Raj. 1999. *Nepal's Failed Development: Reflections on the Mission and the Maladies*. Kathmandu: Nepal South Asia Study Centre.

Pandey, Sushil Raj. 1985. *The Political Economy of Nepalese Land Reform*. Kathmandu: Himalayan Pioneers for Public Service and Research.

Parish, Steven M. 1997. *Hierarchy and Discontents: Culture and Politics of Consciousness in Caste Society*. Delhi: Oxford University Press.

Panebianco, Angelo. 1988. *Political Parties: Organization and Power*. Cambridge: Cambridge University Press.

POLSAN. 1991. *Nepalese Voters: A Survey Report*. Kathmandu: Political Science Association of Nepal.

—— 1992. *Political Parties and the Parliamentary Process in Nepal: A Study of the Transitional Phase*. Kathmandu: Political Science Association of Nepal.

Prakash, A. Surya. 1995. *What Ails Indian Parliament: An Exhaustive Diagnosis*. Delhi: INDUS.

Putnam, Robert D. 1976. *The Comparative Study of Political Elite*. New Jersey: Prentic-Hall Inc.

Raiper, William and Marten Hoftun. 1992. *Spring Awaking*. New Delhi: Viking.

Randall, Vicky (ed.). 1988. *Political Parties in the Third World*. London: Sage.

Rawal, Bhim. 1988. *Nepal ma Samyabadi Andolan: Udbhab, Vikas and Bartaman Avastha* (Communist movement in Nepal: Origin, Evolution and Recent Development).

Kathmandu: Samana Prakashan.
Rose, Richard. 1980. *Politics in England* (Third Edition). Boston: Little, Brown and Company.
Rosenblum, Nancy L. and Robert C.Post (eds.). 2002. *Civil Society and Government*. Princeton: Princeton University Press
Rudebeck, Lars and Olle Tornquist (eds.). 1996. *Democratisation in the Third World*. Sweden: Uppsala University
SAP-Nepal (ed.). 2001. *Quest for Peace*. Kathmandu: South Asia Partnership-Nepal.
SEARCH. 1994. *The Three District Political Opinion Survey*. Kathmandu: SEARCH.
Shaha, Rishikesh. 1982. *Essays in the Practice of Government in Nepal*. New Delhi: Manohar Publishing House.
Shapiro, Ian and Casiano Hacker-Cordon (eds.). 1999. *Democracy's Value*. Cambridge: Cambridge University Press.
Sharma, Kedar (ed.). 2000. *Wrong Path* (in Nepali). Kathmandu: Himal Association.
Sharma, Sudhindra and Pawan Kumar Sen. 1990. *The 1999 General Election Opinion Poll: How Voters Assess Politics, Parties and Politicians*. Kathmandu: Himal Association.
Shrestha, Ananda. (ed.). 1998. *The Role of Civil Society and Democratization in Nepal*. Kathmandu: Nepal Foundation for Advanced Studies.
Slusser, Mary Shepherd. 1998. *Nepal Mandala: A Cultural Study of Kathmandu Valley* (Reprint). Kathmandu: Mandala Book Point.
SP. 1997. *Anti-Defection Act, 1997*. Kathmandu: Secretariat of Parliament.
Thapa, Deepak (ed.). 2003. *Understanding the Maoist Movement of Nepal*. Kathmandu: Martin Chautari.
Thapa, Deepak and Bandana Sijapati. 2003. *A Kingdom under Seize: Nepal's Maoist Insurgency, 1996 to 2003*. Kathmandu: The Print House.
Thapa, Ganga B. (ed.). 1996. *Democracy and Decentralization*. Kathmandu: Political Science Association of Nepal.
TIN. 1999. *Transparency International, Nepal Newsletter* (2).
UNDP/Nepal. 2002. *Human Development Report 2001*: Kathmandu: United Nations Development Programme/ Nepal.
Upreti, B.C. 1993. *The Nepali Congress: An Analysis of the Party's Performance in the General Elections and its Aftermath*. Jaipur: Nirala Publications.
Upreti, Prem R. 1992. *Political Awakening in Nepal*. New Delhi: Commonwealth Publishers.
VNSC. 1998. *Vidyarthi Niketan Secondary School: Golden Jubilee Souvenir 1998*. Kathmandu: Vidyarthi Niketan Secondary School.
Ware, Alane. 1987. *Citizens, Parties and the State*. Cambridge: Polity Press.
Webb, Paul. 2000. *Modern British Party System*. London: Sage.
Weiner, Myron. 1967. *Party Building in a New Nation: The Indian National Congress*. Chicago: University of Chicago Press.

Articles

Baral, Lok Raj. 1986. "Political Dissent and Political Development" (Paper presented at the seminar on *Political Development and Social Change in Nepal*, organized by

Centre for Nepal and Asian Studies/ Tribhuvan University).
—— 1987. "Nepal in 1986: Problem of Political Management". *Asian Survey* (27:2), pp.173-180.
—— 1995. "The 1994 Nepal Elections: Emerging Trends in Party Politics". *Asian Survey* (35: 5), pp. 426-440.
—— 1998. "Consensus, Parties and Governance". *Kathmandu Post* (12 October).
—— 2005 "Direction to Republic Politics". *Kantipur* (14 September).
Bhattarai, Babu Ram. 2002. ""Nepal: Triangular Balance of Forces". *Economic & Political Weekly* (37:46), pp. 4606-4610.
Bhattachan, Krishna Bahadur. 2000. "Possible Ethnic Revolution or Insurgency in a Predatory Unitary Hindu State". In Dhruba Kumar (ed.). *Domestic Conflict and Crisis of Governability in Nepal*. Kathmandu: Centre for Nepal and Asian Studies, pp.135-162.
—— 2001. "(I)NGOs and Disadvantaged Groups in Nepal". In Krishna B. Bhattachan et al. (eds.). *NGO, Civil Society and Government in Nepal*. Kathmandu: Central Department of Sociology and Anthropology/ Tribhuvan University, pp. 67-99.
—— 2003. "Civil Society and Protection of Diversity in Nepal". In D.B. Gurung (ed.). *Nepal Tomorrow: Voices and Visions*. Kathmandu: KoseleePrakashan, pp. 32-62.
Brown, Deredk. 24 March 1990. "Nepal Land of the Midnight Knock". *Guardian*.
Chand, Diwakar. 2001. "Peace Building Role of the Civil Society in Maoist Areas". In SAP-Nepal (ed.). *Quest for Peace*. Kathmandu: South Asia Partnership-Nepal, pp. 214-222.
Chhatterjee, Partha. 2002. "On Civil and Political Society in Post-Colonial Democracies". In Sudipta Kaviraj and Sunil Khilnani (eds.). *Civil Society: History and Possibilities*. New Delhi: Foundation Books, pp. 165-178.
Chhetri, Ram B. 2001. "Comments on Dipak Gyawali's Paper; NGOs in Nepal: Old Wine or New Bottle". In Krishna B. Bhattachan, et al (eds.). *NGO, Civil Society and Government in Nepal*. Kathmandu: Central Department of Sociology and Anthropology/Tribhuvan University, pp. 34-40.
Dahal, Dilli Ram. 2001. "Problems and Prospects of Relationship between Government Organizations and NGOs/INGOs in Nepal". In Krishna B. Bhattachan et al (eds.). *NGO, Civil Society and Government in Nepal*. Kathmandu: Central Department of Sociology and Anthropology/Tribhuvan University, pp. 105-128.
Dahal, Rajendra. 1999. "Failed to Generate Hope" (in Nepali). *Himal Fortnightly* (16-30 December).
Dahal, Ram Kumar. 1992. "Electoral Campaign: Candidate Selection Process of Political Parties". In POLSAN. *Political Parties and the Parliamentary Process in Nepal: A Study of the Transitional Phase*. Kathmandu: Political Science Association of Nepal, pp.104-113.
—— 2000. "Candidate Selection in the 1999 Parliamentary Elections". *NCCS Occasional Paper 1*. Kathmandu: Nepal Centre for Contemporary Studies.
Elgie, Robert. 1995. "Britain: Prime Ministerial Leadership". In Robert Elgie. *Political Leadership in Liberal Democracies*. London: Macmillan Press Ltd, pp. 25-50.
Gaige, Fred and John Scholz. 1991. "The 1991 Parliamentary Elections in Nepal: Political Freedom and Stability". *Asia Survey* (31: 11), pp.1040-1060.

Gibbon, Peter. 1996. "Some Reflections on Civil Society and Political Change". In Lars Rudebeck and Olle Tornquist (eds.). *Democratisation in the Third World*. Sweden: Uppsala University, pp. 21- 50.

Goldstone, J.A. 1986."Introduction". In J.A. Goldstone (ed.). *Revolution: Theoretical, Comparative and Historical Studies*. US: Harcourt B.J. Publishers, pp. 1-17.

Gurung, Harka. 1997. "State and Society in Nepal". In David N. Gellner, Jonna Pfaff-Czarnecka and John Whelpton (eds.). *Nationalism and Ethnicity in a Hindu Kingdom: The Politics of Culture in Contemporary Nepal*. Amsterdam: Harwood Academic Publisher, pp. 495-532.

—— 1998. "Democracy and Social Development in Nepal: Ethnicity and Regionalism in Nepal Elections". In Ananda Shrestha (ed.). *The Role of Civil Society and Democratization in Nepal*. Kathmandu: Nepal Foundation for Advanced Studies, pp.92-119.

—— 2003. "Nepal: Maoist Insurgency and Indigenous People". *Nepali Journal of Contemporary Studies* (3: 2), pp. 1-18.

Gyawali, Dipak. 2001. "Are NGOs in Nepal Old Wine or New Bottle? A Cultural Theory Perspective on Nepal's Contested Terrain". In Krishna B. Bhattachan et al. (eds.). *NGO, Civil Society and Government in Nepal*. Kathmandu: Central Department of Sociology and Anthropology/Tribhuvan University, pp. 13-33.

Gyimah-Boadi, Emmanuel. 1995. "Civil Society and Democratization". In INPR, *International Conference on Consolidating the Third Wave Democracies: Trends and Challenges*. Taipei: Institute for National Policy Research, pp. 59-69.

Hachhethu, Krishna. 1992. "Nepali Congress: Issues of Inner-Party Democracy". In Lok Raj Baral (ed.). *South Asia: Democracy and the Road Ahead*. Kathmandu: Political Science Association of Nepal, pp. 96-110.

—— 1995. "Executive and Authority Building in Nepal: A Study of Premiership of Girija P. Koirala". In Dhruba Kumar (ed.). *State, Leadership and Politics in Nepal*. Kathmandu: Centre for Nepal and Asian Studies, pp. 68-91.

—— 2004. "The Nepali State and Maoist Insurgency, 1996-2001". In Michael Hutt (ed.). *Himalayan People's War: Nepal's Maoist Rebellion*. London: Hurst and Company, pp. 58-78.

—— 2005. "What People's Feel". *Seminar* (No. 548), pp.62-68.

Hawthron, Geoffrey. 2002. "The Promise of Civil Society in the South". In Sudipta Kaviraj and Sunil Khilnani (eds.). *Civil Society: History and Possibilities*. New Delhi: Foundation Books, pp. 269-286.

Harmel, Robert and Lars Svasand. 1993. "Party Leadership and Party Institutionalization: Three Phases of Development". *West European Politics* (16: 2), pp. 67-88.

James, Wilmot G. 1995. "Civil Society and Democratization". In INPR, *International Conference on Consolidating the Third Wave Democracies: Trends and Challenges*. Taipei: Institute for National Policy Research, pp. 59-69.

Jayarajaan, C. K. 2001. "Local Self-Government Act and its Implications for Human Resource Development in Municipalities in Nepal". *Administration and Management Review* (13: 2), pp. 1-11.

Kattel, Mukunda. 2003. "Introduction to the People's War and its Implications". In Karki and Seddon (eds.). *The People's War in Nepal: Left Perspectives*. New Delhi:

Adroit Publishers, pp. 49-72.
—— 2004. "Negotiating the Maoist Conflict: Problems and Possibilities". *Nepali Journal of Contemporary Studies* (4: 2), pp. 29-44.

Khatri, Sridhar. 1992. "Political Parties and the Parliamentary Process in Nepal: A Study of the Transitional Phase". In POLSAN. *Political Parties and the Parliamentary Process in Nepal: A Study of the Transitional Phase*. Kathmandu: Political Science Association of Nepal.

Khilnani, Sunil. 2002. "The Development of Civil Society". In Sudipta Kaviraj and Sunil Khilnani (eds.). *Civil Society: History and Possibilities*. New Delhi: Foundation Books, pp. 11-32.

Kirchheimer, Otto. 1960. "The Transformation of the Western European Party System". In Joseph La Palombara and Myron Weiner (eds.). *Political Parties and Political Development*. Princeton: Princeton University Press, pp. 177-200.

Koirala, B.P. 1990. "Revolution in the Context of Nation Building" (Reprint). In *Nation, Nationalism and Democracy* (in Nepali).

Kumar, Dhruba. 1989. "Beyond Blockade: Some Long Term Policy Consideration for Nepal". *CNAS Forum 10*.

—— 1995. "State, Leadership and Politics in Nepal: A Preliminary Note on Transition". In Dhruba Kumar (ed.). *State, Leadership and Politics in Nepal*. Kathmandu: Centre for Nepal and Asian Studies, pp. 1-16.

—— 1999. "Is South Asia a Conglomeration of Failed States". *Ishiki* (1:3), pp. 16-19.

—— 2003. "Consequences of the Militarized Conflict and the Cost of Violence in Nepal". *Contributions to Nepalese Studies* (30: 2), pp. 167-216.

—— 2004. "Military Dimension of the Maoist Insurgency" (an unpublished paper).

Luintel, Guna Raj. 2000. "Politics of Consensus" (in Nepali). *Kantipur Daily* (19 February).

Maharjan, Pancha Narayan. 2000. "The Maoist Insurgency and Crisis of Governability in Nepal". In Dhruba Kumar (ed.) *Domestic Conflict and Crisis of Governability in Nepal*. Kathmandu: Centre for Nepal and Asian Studies, pp. 163-196.

Mainwaring, Scott. 1998. "Party Systems in the Third Wave". *Journal of Democracy* (9:3), pp. 67-81.

Mathema, Padma. 2001. "National Planning Commission and NGOs". In Krishna B. Bhattachan et al (eds.). *NGO, Civil Society and Government in Nepal*. Kathmandu: Central Department of Sociology and Anthropology/Tribhuvan University, pp. 172-177.

Millard, Colin. 2002. "Perceptions of Democracy and Dissent in the Valley of Dhorpatan". In David N. Gellner (ed.). *Resistance and the State: Nepalese Experiences*. New Delhi: Social Science Press, pp. 281-304.

Mishra, Chaitnya. 2001. "New Predicaments of Humanitarian Organizations". In Krishna B. Bhattachan et al (eds.). *NGO, Civil Society and Government in Nepal*. Kathmandu: Central Department of Sociology and Anthropology/Tribhuvan University, pp. 1-12.

Mitra, Subrata K. 2001. "Indigenisation, Locally Embedded Values and Parties as Instruments for State-Society Relations: An Agenda for Research" (paper presented at the international workshop on *Political Parties in South Asia*, in

Nottingham, UK, March 29- April 1, 2001).

Mouzelis, Nicos. 1996. "Modernity, Late Development and Civil Society". In Lars Rudebeck and OlleTornquist (eds.). *Democratisation in the Third World*. Sweden: Uppsala University, pp. 51-73.

Oakeshott, Michael. 2000. "On Civil Association". In Gurpreet Mahajan (ed.). *Democracy, Difference and Social Justice*. New Delhi: Oxford University Press, pp. 138-149.

Pandey, Devendra Raj. 1989. "The State of Political Economy". In Kamal P. Malla (ed.). *Nepal: Perspectives on Continuity and Change*. Kathmandu: Centre for Nepal and Asian Studies/ Tribhuvan University, pp. 275-289.

Parajuli, Ramesh. 2003. "Civil Society and Parliament". In Lok Raj Baral (ed.). *Nepal: Political Parties and Parliament*. New Delhi: Adroit Publishers, pp. 172-200.

Pettigres, Judith. 2002. "Guns, Kinship, and Fear: Between Ethnic Claims and Maoism". In David N. Gellner (ed.). *Resistance and the State: Nepalese Experiences*. New Delhi: Social Science Press, pp. 305-325.

Philipson, Liz. 2002. "Conflict in Nepal: Perspectives on the Maoist Movement" (an Unpublished Report).

Pokhrael, Gopal. 1996. "Civil Society and the Role of NGOs in Political Education". In Ganga B. Thapa (ed.). *Democracy and Decentralization*. Kathmandu: Political Science Association of Nepal, pp. 39-45.

Pokhrel, Tika. 2001. 'Social Welfare Council and (I)NGO". In Krishna B. Bhattachan et al (eds.). *NGO, Civil Society and Government in Nepal*. Kathmandu: Central Department of Sociology and Anthropology/Tribhuvan University, pp. 165-171.

Rosenblum, Nancy L. and Robert C. Post 2002. "Introduction". In Nancy L. Rosenblum and Robert C. Post (eds.). *Civil Society and Government*. Princeton: Princeton University Press, pp. 1-25.

Schmitter, Philippe C. 1995. "Civil Society and Democratization". In INPR, *International Conference on Consolidating the Third Wave Democracies: Trends and Challenges*. Taipei: Institute for National Policy Research, pp. 59-69.

Shah, Saubhagya. 2002. "From Evil State to Civil Society". In Kanak Mani Dixit and Shastri Ramachandaran (eds.). *State of Nepal*. Kathmandu: Himal Books, pp. 137-160.

Shah, Sukh Dev. 1988. "Nepal's Economic Development: Problems and Prospects". *Asian Survey* (28:9), pp. 945-957.

Sharma, Hari "Popular Mobilization and Emergence of Collective Identity in Nepal's Transition to Democracy – 1990". *Nepali Journal of Contemporary Studies* (1: 2), pp. 14-32.

Sharma, Prayag Raj. 1995. "Political Kaleidoscope". *Kathmandu Post* (1 December).

—— 1997. "Nation Building, Multi-Ethnicity and the Hindu State". In David N. Gellner, Jonna Pfaff-Czarnecka and John Whelpton (eds.). *Nationalism and Ethnicity in a Hindu Kingdom: The Politics of Culture in Contemporary Nepal*, Amsterdam: Harwood Academic Publisher, pp. 471-494.

Sharma, Sudheer. 2002. "The Ethnic Dimension of the Maoist Insurgency" (an Unpublished Report).

Sharma, Sudhindra. 2002. "The Hindu State and the State of Hinduism". In Kanak

Mani Dixit and Shastri Ramachandaran (eds.). *State of Nepal*. Kathmandu: Himal Books, pp. 22-38.

Shrestha, Bihari Krishani. 2001. "The Sociological Context of (I)NGO work in Nepal". In Krishna B. Bhattachan et al (eds.). *NGO, Civil Society and Government in Nepal*. Kathmandu: Central Department of Sociology and Anthropology/Tribhuvan University, pp. 41-62.

Sivakoti Chintan, Gopal. 2001. "Rastriya Sarokar Samaj and NGOs". In Krishna B. Bhattachan et al. (eds.). *NGO, Civil Society and Government in Nepal*. Kathmandu: Central Department of Sociology and Anthropology/Tribhuvan University, pp. 178-183.

Smolar, Aleskander. 1995. "Civil Society and Democratization". In INPR, *International Conference on Consolidating the Third Wave Democracies: Trends and Challenges*. Taipei: Institute for National Policy Research, pp. 59-69.

Tamang, Seira. 2003. "Civilising Civil Society: Donors and democratic space in Nepal". *Himal South Asia* (16:7), pp.14-24.

Wachi, Yasuko. 1980. "The Newar Peasants of Bhaktapur Nagar, Kathmandu Valley". *The Journal of Social Science* (199:1).

Whelpton, John. 1994. "The General Elections of May 1991". In Michal Huut (ed.). *Nepal in the Nineties*. Delhi: Oxford University Press, pp. 48-81.

Young, Iris Marion. 1999. "State, Civil Society, and Social Justice". In Ian Shapiro and Casiano Hacker-Cordon (eds.). *Democracy's Value*. Cambridge: Cambridge University Press, pp. 141-162.

Periodicals

Bhaktapur (monthly), Bhaktapur.
Daily Diary, Kathmandu.
Deshantar Weekly, Kathmandu.
Gorkhapatra (daily), Kathmandu.
Guardian (daily), London.
Himal Fortnightly (Kathmandu).
Himal Khabar Patrikla (weekly), Kathmandu.
Hindustan Times (daily), Delhi.
India Today (weekly), Delhi.
Janaastha Weekly, Kathmandu.
Kantipur (daily), Kathmandu.
Kathmandu Post (daily), Kathmandu.
Mulyankan (monthly), Kathmandu.
Nawaras Weekly, Kathmandu.
Naya Nepal (weekly), Kathmandu.
Nepal Fortnightly, Kathmandu.
Nepali Awaj (weekly), Kathmandu.
Nepal Press Digest (weekly), Kathmandu.
Newsweek (weekly), New York.
Pratipaksha (weekly), Kathmandu.
Punarjagaran (weekly), Kathmandu.

Samaj (daily), Kathmandu.
Samikchhya (weekly), Kathmandu.
Saptahik Bimarsa (weekly), Kathmandu.
South China Morning Post (daily), Hong Kong.
Space Time (daily), Kathmandu.
Telegraph (weekly), Kathmandu.
The Himalayan (daily), Kathmandu.
The Rising Nepal (daily), Kathmandu.

INDEX